Mother Goose for Mothers and Fathers and Others

Mother Goose for Mothers and Fathers and Others

*A Historical Look at Nursery Rhymes:
Their Words and Those Who Used Them*

JOHN OHST

RESOURCE *Publications* • Eugene, Oregon

MOTHER GOOSE FOR MOTHERS AND FATHERS AND OTHERS
A Historical Look at Nursery Rhymes: Their Words and Those Who Used Them

Copyright © 2025 John Ohst. All rights reserved. Except for brief quotations in critical publications or reviews, no part of this book may be reproduced in any manner without prior written permission from the publisher. Write: Permissions, Wipf and Stock Publishers, 199 W. 8th Ave., Suite 3, Eugene, OR 97401.

Resource Publications
An Imprint of Wipf and Stock Publishers
199 W. 8th Ave., Suite 3
Eugene, OR 97401

www.wipfandstock.com

PAPERBACK ISBN: 979-8-3852-5802-4
HARDCOVER ISBN: 979-8-3852-5803-1
EBOOK ISBN: 979-8-3852-5804-8

10/10/25

For my family
and
for Professor Thomas Donahue

Contents

Introduction: Nursery Rhymes as Oral Literature		ix
Lexical Abbreviations		xix
Chapter 1	Lullabies and Pacifiers	1
Chapter 2	Baby Games	5
Chapter 3	Toys	13
Chapter 4	Short Stories	17
Chapter 5	Riddles	36
Chapter 6	Song and Dance	42
Chapter 7	Taunts and Satire: Making Fun of Others	51
Chapter 8	Pedagogical Poems	68
Chapter 9	Models, Maxims, and Morals	77
Chapter 10	News Reports	86
Chapter 11	Seasons and Traditional Observations	91
Chapter 12	Animals	98
Chapter 13	Occupations	112
Chapter 14	Myth and Legend	141
Chapter 15	Food	147
Chapter 16	Love and/or Marriage	153
Chapter 17	Rhymes of Scotland and Northern England	186
Chapter 18	Gray Goose and Gander	200
Afterword: Our Changing American Language		207

Contents

Appendix 1: "Green Grow the Rashes"	209
Appendix 2: The Power of Poetry	211
Appendix 3: Oral Literature	213
Bibliography	215
Index of First Lines	221
Index of Words and Phrases	225

INTRODUCTION

Nursery Rhymes as Oral Literature

Even today children still usually learn a nursery rhyme by having it told to them. And there are two sources: their peers and their elders. Thus, there are two general types of rhymes. One kind the children learn and use among themselves; the other kind they learn from adults.

The first type of nursery rhyme includes, for example, taunts, counting-out rhymes (to decide who is going to be first or "it"), jump-rope jingles, and the words used to accompany many children's games or dances. This lore is communicated from children to children primarily by tradition. A rhyme may be passed down in this way for decades—sometimes for centuries—with few or no changes. Children are very conservative about this, and upon hearing any kids misquote a line, will immediately stop them and say, "That's not the way it goes!" In fact, if it were not for this oral tradition, such rhymes would probably die out; they are seldom spoken by adults or by teens who regard those rhymes as "kid stuff."

The second type of nursery rhyme is perpetuated by people who watch over children. This type includes lullabies, knee-bouncers, toe-ticklers, aphorisms, riddles, and brief stories told in poetic form. These too owe their long existence mainly to oral tradition, because adults recall them from their own childhood. As youngsters they learned them well, begging their elders to repeat the favorite ones over and over.

Nursery Rhymes as Oral Literature

THE PRESENT STATE OF NURSERY RHYMES

Since the second half of the 1900s, the reciting of nursery rhymes has become less common, and many ancient rhymes have dropped out of use. This is partly due to our ever-changing language, but partly due also to our changing lifestyle.

For one thing, the old rhymes and stories told by grandparents, aunts, and uncles have decrease as multi-generational families have decreased. A large percentage of the elderly now live in retirement communities or assisted-living homes.

For another thing, today's children can entertain themselves with many kinds of toys, movies, DVDs, TV shows, electronic games, and computers. So now, when a child begs for attention, the adults need not rack their brains to remember some short song or snatch of verse, they merely hand the child a picture book or (more often) just flick on the TV or computer or play an album of songs or stories. Sometimes these things are good and helpful. But sadly it also means there is less personal contact between humans. Kids love it when a grown-up spends some time with them, taking a walk, playing a game, reading a book, or reciting a nursery rhyme.

POETRY IN NURSERY RHYMES

One reason for writing my book was to help keep alive an ancient set of oral literature. The English nursery rhymes were created to be spoken, and they were passed along this way from one generation to the next. For many of these rhymes, it was hundreds of years before they were ever written down. Until books became more affordable after the invention of the printing press, nursery rhymes, folktales, news reports, historical facts, etc. were commonly transmitted by word of mouth.

To help people remember the spoken lines, the composers of folk literature used the *repetition* of some words and phrases. However, the most important methods used were the different kinds of *sounds*. [For more detailed information and examples of oral literature, consult Appendix 2, The Power of Poetry.]

NURSERY RHYMES AS RECORDED LITERATURE

Some of the old rhymes have been lost; however, many have been preserved in print. It makes up that body of literature found in Mother Goose books. The compilation of children's rhymes into special anthologies did not begin until the 18th century. The first noteworthy nursery rhyme book, *Tom Thumb's Pretty Song Book*, was printed in English in 1744. Before that, these poems were seen only in some adult songbooks or as chance references in literature.

Today's popular Mother Goose books contain many old rhymes just as they were first set down over two hundred years ago. However, beginning in the second half of the 20th century, there has been a gradual editing process going on. In the more recent anthologies, the editors have left out rhymes which they felt were too violent, or too sad, or—especially—too hard to read because they had too many old or unusual expressions. This is understandable. People don't like to read anything that offends them or that they can't understand. It means, however, that as time passes, more and more of these rhymes move out of the contemporary literature, go out of print, and become part of historical literature, sometimes found only in college reference rooms . . . or they just disappear altogether.

Yet, as historical literature, these old poems offer us important insights into our historical past: our former customs, daily practices, beliefs, the kinds of food people used to eat, the kinds of public figures who excited their curiosity, the kinds of places they visited, the dances they danced, the songs they sang. So, like proverbs, nursery rhymes make up a truly folk literature. They have been uttered down through the years by people from all walks of life and from many different regional and social backgrounds. Much of the poetry is not perfect. It often lacks the carefully structured versification of professional poets, such as Chaucer, William Shakespeare, Edgar Allen Poe, Robert Frost, or Emily Dickinson. But then, hundreds of years ago, many of the composers of the oral traditional literature—the folk songs, stories, and poems—did not read or write. They were just the next-door neighbors. Until the printing press was invented, books were very expensive, and usually owned only by the wealthy.

NURSERY RHYME RESEARCH

Lately, there has not been a great deal of research done on nursery rhymes. Most of today's historical information on these rhymes tends to focus primarily on negative references that people have perceived being hidden within some ancient nursery rhymes (such as slavery, smuggling, betrayal, political insurrection, tyranny, raids on villages, greed, murder, etc.)

In the latter half of the 19th century there were some scholarly books written on nursery rhymes, and a few in the 20th century. The person who was the "father" of nursery rhyme research was James Orchard Halliwell (probably better known in literary circles for his Shakespearian studies). He collected several rhymes from various parts of England, mostly from oral tradition, and wrote comments on many of them, discussing the background or history behind certain lines or the possible identities of certain characters. His work was first published in 1844 as *The Nursery Rhymes of England*.

"Together with his *Popular Rhymes and Nursery Tales*, published in 1849, it is the basis (whether acknowledged or not) of almost every nursery anthology, and it has been the principal English source, often the sole source (other than the fertile imagination of the 'happy guessers,') of every essay and paragraph on the origin of nursery rhymes which has been published since."

The paragraph above is from the preface of *The Oxford Dictionary of Nursery Rhymes*. This classic 1951 work, edited by Iona and Peter Opie, stands head and shoulders above any other contemporary book in the field, both in scope and in depth. A compilation of over 500 children's rhymes, with historical annotation, it records many rhymes in published sources which Opie (and the many people who helped them) were able to find. An impressive work, it's the result of a highly concentrated effort.

Another 20th century nursery rhyme reference book is *The Annotated Mother Goose*, by William and Ceil Baring-Gould, published in 1962. This work sought to provide the sources and backgrounds for the rhymes along with definitions for some of the words.

Due to their accurate reporting and careful scholarship, I will occasionally mention some of the important facts that Opie and Baring-Goulds have already learned.

Although I regard Halliwell, Opie, and Baring-Gold as the three major scholars of English nursery rhymes, more than half of the rhymes in my book were not mentioned by these three.

PURPOSE OF THIS BOOK

Although the original purpose of my book was to discover more about the out-of-date and unusual words found in nursery rhymes, I soon realized that the more I dug into the history of words, the more I was digging into the history of the people who used the words. To adequately explain their poems, I often had to do research into their beliefs, customs, and traditions, but also into the specific facts about their daily life: what tasks they had to perform in their homes, in their fields, in their special trades, and the implements they used in all these places. I also learned how they enjoyed their leisure time: singing, dancing, joking, playing with children, traveling, celebrating festivals and weddings.

I loved doing the research. It took over two years in the 70s to write the original copy, living in libraries, poring through countless books. Then recently, I spent another two years year to do the rewrite, using websites on the computer, a tool that almost none of us had 50 years ago. I made hundreds of changes and additions, but during all my readings—past and present—not a day went by when I didn't say to myself, "Wow! I never knew that." I have no idea how many literary streets and alleys my mind must have meandered down just to get a fuller understanding of one word.

A WONDER-FULL FACT ABOUT SOUNDS AND SPELLINGS

One interesting result I discovered was that many words, with which I thought I was familiar, were once used in ways unfamiliar to me. The package looked the same, but the contents tasted different. In fact, I came across more than 200 words or expressions that were used in old nursery rhymes differently from how we use them today.

So, through this historical word analysis, a unique linguistic phenomenon revealed itself: the efficient conservatism of language. This is evident not only in contemporary homonyms that are spelled the same yet have different meanings (like *bat, saw, park*), but also in words that changed their meaning over the years without changing the spelling (like *pretty, fine, gay*). Just as English now functions synchronically with a basic stock of less than fifty phonemes (separate speech *sounds*) whose positions change around to make different words, our language also functions diachronically over centuries with a basic stock of *words* whose meanings change around to make different words. Why invent new sounds or new words if the old ones just need to be refitted? [For example: in Old English the noun *fix*, meant *fish*. In Modern English it's a verb for *repair*.]

If this seems like an over-simplification, it is. Of course, there are some words that die away never to be heard again; and completely new words are being added to the language all the time. But there are a great many old words, that have been around for centuries, whose phonetic forms have changed very little, if at all, but whose points of reference have changed.

Usually, the changes are very gradual. At one point in time a single term could have multiple usages. New and old meanings may co-exist for generations. But then after a while, the sense of the word, as it is usually understood by those who speak it, undergoes a transformation, and the meaning that was once primary is now secondary, and later it may drop out of use entirely.

Most of the words and expressions in my book were chosen on the basis of their being *archaic* (not used much anymore), *obsolete* (not used at all anymore), or *dialectal*. Such words sometimes can provide enough evidence to give the rhyme an approximate time and/or place of origin. The diachronic phonology of a word was occasionally examined to find out how its pronunciation changed over the years.

A word's history (etymology) was also brought into play, usually to help us understand its meaning, but sometimes simply because of its fascinating formation, historical development, and it relationship with similar words in other languages.

The semantic shifts vary in degree. A word may acquire a slightly different nuance or a completely different meaning. And the reasons for change are many: new physical environments (natural or manmade), new customs, ideas, etc. But the fact remains that the same word can be used down through the years over and over again, like a piece of iron, cast and re-cast into many different tools.

WORDS AS TIME-MARKERS

Reading and writing skills were not emphasized until the 15th and 16th centuries when printed books became available. Spelling rules weren't emphasized until the 18th century. So how a word was commonly spelled could vary from place to place or from year to year.

Sometimes the unusual spelling or pronunciation of a word can be traced back to a specific time period when it was in common use. If, for example, it was spelled or pronounced this way by English speakers only from the 1500s to the early 1600s, then that must have been when this poem or verse was first composted.

PEOPLE IN NURSERY RHYMES

Once in a while, I made the attempt to identify the nursery rhyme characters with people in real like. This is a tricky business at best, and each such interpretation (in this book or in others) must be taken with a grain of salt. We should always assume, first, that most of the people mentioned in Mother Goose rhymes were fictional, and then, second, that most of them who were real were probably local townsfolk or the author's neighbors, no more important than you or I. Above all, it should be remembered that the principal reason for trying to find out who these people were is that it's fun to guess.

METHOD OF ARRANGEMENT

The rhymes are divided into eighteen chapters. They are arranged according to how they were used (such as lullabies), or according to their main theme (such as food). Nursery rhymes that strongly reflect the dialects of Scotland and northern England are in a separate chapter. The final poem, "Gray goose and gander," has its own chapter due to all of the extra information.

These chapter divisions are not intended to be hard and fast classifications. Many rhymes could fit into any of two or more chapters.

RESEARCH MATERIAL

Because this book deals with a kind of literature that covers many centuries, it was necessary to consult several works concerned with the history, sociology, and folklore of Great Britain and America.

Also, since nursery rhymes deal with all aspects of daily life as it was lived centuries ago, my research often took me far afield into such topics as cooking, gardening, hunting, and clothing. I learned so much about marriage and dating customs, plant, animals, buildings, and shipping that

I never knew before. Putting all the facts together was a very enjoyable experience for me.

Excerpt from works in various periods of English literature were given to show how certain words or expressions were once used or pronounced. Many of my main sources were word and phrase books and dictionaries, especially the *Oxford English Dictionary*.

RHYMES USED IN THIS BOOK

Many of the poems that I collected were copied from a well-worn nursery rhyme book, even older than I am, which I picked up for fifty cents in a dingy used book shop in West Los Angeles about 60 years ago. It's called *Mother Goose*, published in 1940, and it was compiled by Dorothea J. Snow (1909–2007) the author of many children's books. Some of her rhymes, or variations of them, are found in Opie or Baring-Gould, but many of them are not. In the 1970s I wrote to her, hoping to find out the sources of many of the nursery rhymes she used in her anthology, but there was no response.

Rather than using footnotes for the sources (which can become very distracting), I sometimes briefly mentioned their names under the rhymes. When different wordbooks give strikingly different definitions, I tried to include all possible interpretations.

FOUR MAJOR TIME PERIODS IN THE HISTORY OF THE ENGLISH LANGUAGE:

Old English	450–1100
Middle English	1100–1450
Early Modern English	1450–1750
Modern English	1750–present

A WORD OF CAUTION

It sometimes happens, in studies of this nature, that in trying to do "a good job," a person is apt to research a poem *too* thoroughly: to read too much between the lines, to see or hear things that aren't really there, to give more importance to a word or line than was originally intended, to see double-entendres or hidden meanings where none exist.

If we guard ourselves against these extremes, we may then go ahead with a detailed inquiry. If not, then we deserve the sarcastic opinion pronounced on us in this nursery rhyme:

> Little dog, little dog, what do you there?
> Rest me, my lady, under the chair.
>
> Little dog, little dog, hear you what's said?
> Often and often, my dear little maid.
>
> Little dog, little dog, think you men wise?
> In closing their ears and shutting their eyes.

(And yes, "said" rhymed with "maid" since it came from "say" + "-ed")

> Lots of nursery rhymes here to put under your hat.
> Read a few each day, and you may hear yourself say,
> "I didn't know that."

J. W. O.
West Pierrepont, NY,
2025

Lexical Abbreviations

I abbreviated my commonly used dictionaries as follows:

AERS	An English-Reader's Dictionary
AH	American Heritage Dictionary
CD	Century Dictionary
DNB	Dictionary of National Biography
DWO	Dictionary of Word Origins
EDD	English Dialect Dictionary
F&W	Funk and Wagnalls New Standard Dictionary
ODECN	Oxford Dictionary of English Christian Names
OED	Oxford English Dictionary
UWRE	Universal World Reference Encyclopedia
Web NC	Webster's New Collegiate Dictionary
Web NW	Webster's New World Dictionary
Web III	Webster's Third New International Dictionary

CHAPTER 1

Lullabies and Pacifiers

Poems and songs have long been used to comfort troubled infants.

> Where was a jewel and pretty?
> Where was a sugar and **spicey**?
> Hush-a-bye, baby, in the cradle,
> And we'll go **abroad in a tricey**.
>
> Did his papa torment it?
> And **vex** his own baby, will he?
> Give me a hand and I'll beat him
> With your **red coral** and whistle.

spicey baby talk for "spice."

abroad not out of the country (as it's used now), but just out of the house, outdoors.

tricey baby talk for "trice," and "in a trice" literally meant at a single pull (or) at a pluck, hence: instantly, immediately (or, in more modern slang: in a jiffy). The noun "trice" comes from a 14th century verb meaning 'to haul up and fasten with a rope,' as a flag or a sail.

vex to tease; to cause one to fret.

red coral a teething toy made of polished coral. The name was later extended to refer to toys made of glass, bone, etc. used for teething

> **Bossy**-cow, bossy-cow, where do you lie?
> In the green meadows, under the sky.
>
> **Billy-horse**, billy-horse, where do you lie?
> Out in the stable, with nobody **nigh**.
>
> Birdies bright, birdies sweet, where do you lie?
> Up in the tree-tops,—oh, ever so high!
>
> Baby dear, baby love, where do you lie?
> In my warm crib, with Mama close by.

bossy a cow or other bovine animal, a term used by children or in calling cattle. There is a dialect term in England for a calf, "buss" or "boss," but "bossy" is more popular as an American expression (in fact, the word is not found in the OED). Its origin is uncertain. In Iceland, there's an exclamation used in driving cows into their stalls, "bas, bas," which may have come from the Icelandic word "bass," a 'boose' or 'stall.' One source (CD) conjectures that it may once have been a humorous use of the Latin word for cow: "bos," (which gives us "bovine"), but if so, it would probably date back to the days of the Roman occupation of Britain. One linguist noted that "bossy" is used as a call to cows in pasture in New York, New Jersey, northern Pennsylvania, eastern Ohio. (Kurath, *Word Geography of the Eastern United States*, 63).

I was raised in a country town in northern New York in the 1940s and 50s, and I remember the phrase "Mmmm, boss! Mmmm, boss!" that dairy farmers used to call in the cows.

billy-horse a male horse (as in "billy-goat"). So, "billy" is being used here as a male adjective (as "jack" is used in jackdaw or jackass.)

nigh near, nearby (archaic and dialectal). The term comes originally from the Old English words "neah," 'near.' Modern English "near" meant "nearer" in Old English.

> You shall have an apple,
> You shall have a plum,
> You shall have a **rattle-basket**
> When your dad comes home.

rattle-basket It's a baby's rattle, shaped like a small wicker sphere with a wooden handle. The rattle was woven with rushes, pine roots, or sweet grass with seeds or pebbles inside. These objects have been made by people in several different parts of the world.

> We're all **in the dumps**,
> For diamonds are **trumps**,
> The kittens are gone to **St. Paul's!**
>
> The babies are **bit**,
> **The moon's in a fit,**
> And **the houses are built without walls.**

A good poem to say when *everything* seems to be going wrong. This rhyme is about 200 years old (or more). Apparently, the earliest printed version was published in 1825. I wasn't sure how to classify this poem. Maybe it's just a silly rhyme to cheer up unhappy children by turning their thoughts. My daughter liked it when she was young. And I've been known to use it when losing at cards.

in the dumps (or, as my parents used to say in the mid-1900s, "down in the dumps"): sad, dejected, melancholy, in low spirits or heaviness of mind. The term probably comes from the Dutch word "dump," for 'haze, dullness.'

Apparently, (according to the OED) this was the sense that it had in the 16th century when Britain's poet laureate, John Skelton, wrote:

> "I am not laden of idleness [laziness] with lumpes [dull people]
> As dazed dotards that dreame in their dumpes."

trumps In a game of cards, when a suit is designated as "trump(s)" it out-ranks all other suits. Sad is the player with no trump cards.

St. Paul's probably St. Paul's Cathedral in London, a favorite hangout for pigeons and other city birds—and woe to them when the cats and kittens arrive.

    The original cathedral was built in the year 604, but it had to be rebuilt several times through the centuries due to fires. The present cathedral was designed by Christopher Wren in 1666.

bit bitten. This is the archaic past participle of "bite," but it is still used colloquially. In this poem it probably means "stung" as by a mosquito, flea, or other insect.

the moon's in a fit. An anthropomorphism. The moon looks dark and angry, probably covered with clouds,

the houses are built without walls Even the houses being put up are only partly finished.

CHAPTER 2

Baby Games

Body games have often been used to amuse young children. Two of the old favorites include: "Head-acher, eye-winker" and "This little piggy went to market." Babies readily respond to movement and touch, and each of these rhymes depends on these for its effect.

> Pit, pat, **well-a-day!**
> Little Robin flew away.
> Where can little Robin be?
> Gone into the cherry tree.

This may have been a hand-clapping game, similar to the old favorite "pat-a-cake, pat-a-cake, baker's man." This is only a conjecture, but maybe it went something like this:

> The baby's hands were held and clapped during line 1,
> flapped like bird's wings on line 2,
> put over the baby's eyes at line 3,
> and pulled away from the eyes on line 4, as in "Peek-a-boo."

well-a-day This was an archaic and dialectal exclamation of sorrow and meant "Alas!" It's an altered form of "well-a-way" (also spelled "wellaway") and comes from the Old English "weilawei," literally, "woe, lo, woe."

> Ride a **cock-horse** to **Banbury Cross**
> To see **a fine lady** upon a white **horse**,
> Rings on her fingers and **bells on her toes**,
> She shall have music wherever she goes.
>
> Ride a cock-horse to Banbury Cross
> To see what Tommy can buy,
> A penny white loaf, a penny white cake,
> And a **two-penny** apple pie.

cock-horse a toy horse, hobby-horse. The origin of the word is obscure. Different dictionaries give different theories, but the most logical one is that it might have been a position on the knee which was similar to that of being up on a horse. So, a "cock-horse" could be anything, especially a rocking horse, that a child rides astride, that is with legs "cocked" or pulled up, (just as when you "cock" a gun, you pull up the hammer). "Ride a cock-horse" is also still very popular as a knee-bouncing rhyme. In America, north of Oxford, Michigan, there is a therapeutic equestrian center called Banbury Cross.

horse This word makes a strong end-rhyme with "Cross." It's even stronger if spoken with a silent /r/ as in some British dialects and in some American dialects where it is spoken and sometimes written as "hoss." This absence of the post-vocalic /r/ occurred in the Western "cowboy" dialect, which was why, in the TV series *Ponderosa*, Michael Langdon's big strong sidekick was called Hoss Cartwright.

Banbury Cross For centuries, the market town of **Banbury** (north of Oxford) has had several large stone crosses. Around 1600, one was destroyed by Puritans, who disapproved of any man-made holy replications, be they crosses, statues, pictures, or stained-glass windows (believing them to be violations of the Second Commandment: "You shall make no idols").

Then in 1859 a new cross was erected to celebrate the wedding of Queen Victoria's eldest daughter. In 2005, a statue of a "fine lady on a horse" was placed near the cross.

a fine lady There are many other well-established versions of this nursery rhyme that call her "an old lady."

bells on her toes This may refer to the 15th century fashion of wearing bells at the toe-end of long, tapered shoes.

two-penny Since the 1400s, spelled as "twopence" or "tuppence," as in the song "Feed the birds. Tuppence a bag." from *Mary Poppins*. (In the U.S. the "two-" or "tu-" always rhymes with "you.")

> Here goes my lord:
> A trit, a trit, a trot, a trot.
>
> Here goes my lady:
> A **canter**, a canter, a canter, a canter.
>
> Here goes my young **master**:
> **Jockety-hitch**, jockety-hitch, jockety-hitch.
>
> Here goes my young miss:
> An amble, an amble, an amble, an amble.
>
> The **footman** lags behind to **tipple** ale and wine,
> And goes a gallop, a gallop, a gallop to make up his time.

canter This word, which refers to a 3-beat gait that's faster than a trot but slower than a gallop, has an interesting etymology. The term first appeared in print in 1706. Apparently, it referred to the easy gait used when riders made a pilgrimage to *Canterbury*, England.

master a boy too young to be called a mister. It was also used as a title. I remember when I was a youngster, back in the 1940s, my mom would send my birthday cards addressed to Master John Ohst.

jockety-hitch At first, I couldn't find this word. But then I noticed that this poem was first written down in 1849 by John Orchard Halliwell-Phillipps in his book *Popular Rhymes and Nursery Tales*.

He collected most of his rhymes from oral tradition, writing them just as he heard them, and no doubt had to improvise the spelling of unrecorded words. So, we might assume that "jockety-hitch" was his spelling of some word like "joggity-hitch" (which dictionaries tell us is a 'frequentative,' formed from "jog" + "hitch," to move jerkily, hobble.) These are common in children's jingles, for example "jiggity-jog" or "hippity-hop," as are the reduplications that change a vowel: trit/trot, clip/clop, flip/flop. Word play is fun. Try one! Make up your own.

footman so-called because, originally, he ran beside his master's horse or rode standing behind a carriage. Later, "footman" came to have a wider meaning: a male servant who waited on table, opened doors, or accompanied his employer on outings (as in this rhyme).

tipple to drink intoxicating liquor; in earlier times, to drink freely or hard, to booze; now used in a weaker sense: to drink habitually or constantly in small quantities. The word's origin is uncertain. It appears *earlier* than "tip," ('tilt'), so it's not a frequentative thereof.

>**Margery** Mutton-pie and Johnny **Bo-peep**
>They met together in **Gracechurch Street**
>In and out, in and out, over the way,
>"Oh!" said Johnny, "'tis **chop-nose** day."

I haven't seen nor read how this one is acted out, but the motions probably go something like this: the baby's feet or hands are held together, moved in to the body and out from the body, and lifted up in the air (perhaps over the baby's head), then her/his nose is tweaked.

Margery This name was a popular form of the French "Marguerite" (in English, "Margaret"). Apparently brought to England by the Normans in the 11th century, it has been registered as a separate name since the 13th century. During the 18th and 19th centuries, the name "Margery" almost disappeared, except among poor country people. (ODECN)

Bo-peep Not "Little Bo-peep" of lost sheep fame (1805). Here it's just used as a name, but originally it was a nursery game, otherwise known as "peek-a-boo" (still very popular, of course) which was first seen in print in 1599, but very likely was part of oral tradition for many years before that. The first part of the expression, "Bo," was used for hundreds of years as an exclamation of surprise, like "Oh!"

Gracechurch Street The north end of London Bridge used to open onto Grace church Street, a major thoroughfare for centuries in London, with many shops and inns. The street was mentioned in Jane Austin's *Pride and Prejudice*. The London Bridge was taken apart and then reconstructed in Havasu City, Arizona in 1968.

chop-nose a baby game. The baby's nose was held between someone's finger and thumb and then "chopped" off quickly with the other hand.

> Baby and I were baked in a pie.
> The gravy was **wonderful** hot.
> We had nothing to **pay** to the baker that day,
> And so, we crept out of the pot.

This sounds like it might be a game in which both baby and an older person are covered with a blanket, until the last line when they uncover their heads.

Henry Bett, in his *Nursery Rhymes and Tales*, tells us that in the 16th century it was a favorite trick to hide all kinds of surprises inside a pie. Other nursery rhymes speak of unusual ingredients. In "Sind a Song of Sixpence," there were four-and-twenty blackbirds baked in a pie presented to the king. The "plum" that Jack Horner pulled out of his pie has an interesting legend attached to it. According to a Smithsonian tradition, John Horner (or Thomas Horner) was the steward of the Abbot of Glastonbury. The abbot sent him to Henry VIII with a pie containing deeds to a dozen manors in Somerset County. On the way, he "put in his thumb and pulled out a plum," the deed to the fine manor of Mells, where his descendants live to this day. (Bett, 74).

wonderful This adjective is used here as an intensive adverb and means "amazingly, exceedingly."

pay It's hard to understand why anyone would pay a baker for being cooked inside a hot pie . . . unless "pay" meant something else. In Early Modern English (1450 to 1750) one meaning of "pay" was to whip or beat with a stick a person who did something wrong (in this case, the baker). Today we use the revengeful expression "pay back" in a similar way, to get restitution.

(For example: "At Halloween we soaped his windows to *pay* him back for soaping ours.")

> This crow says, "**What think you**, birds, I saw this **morn**?"
> This crow says, "I know, my dear. It must be corn."
> This crow says, "How many birds will go with me?"
> This crow says, "**Be patient**, friend. A man I see."
> This crow says, "Caw, caw! Caw, caw! He's got a gun!"
> Now let's be off! Fly, every one.

This is probably a finger game. The fingers are "crows" and are wiggled one by one. On the last line, they all flap away.

What think you Instead of Modern English: "What do you think?" This word order (syntax) is a direct carry-over from Middle English (1100–1450): "What thinkest thou?" English belongs to the Germanic family of languages (which includes Swedish, Norwegian, Dutch, and others), and they share many linguistic traits. The Modern German for "What think you?" is "Was denkst du?"

In the early 17th century, Shakespeare occasionally still used this type of construction: "What say'st thou? Ha?" *Henry VIII*. Act 5. Scene 1. Line 67. (Also written as 5.1.67.}

morn Now mostly poetic, this word was once used interchangeably with "morning," which itself was once a verb (*morn* + *-ing*) and meant "the coming of morn." Originally, "evening" was also a verb, formed the same way (from *even* + *-ing*)

Be patient This expression is being used here in an older way with a slightly different meaning, as a cautionary warning: "Wait and be still" or "Wait, watch, and be wary—something is not quite right."

> Two little **dickie-birds** sat upon a hill,
> One named Jack and the other named Jill.
> Fly away, Jack. Fly away, Jill.
> Come back, Jack. Come back Jill.

This little finger game has delighted children for over 200 years. Wrap the tip of each index finger with something brightly colored, like a piece of cloth or paper (use adhesive tape if needed). Extend these fingers and rest your hands on a "hill," (like your knees or the baby's tummy). At the first mention of "Jack," wiggle one index finger; then at the word "Jill," wiggle the other one. At "Fly away, Jack," the first finger quickly flaps away and is hidden behind a shoulder. Then the same is done with Jill. At the words "Come back, Jack," the first birdie quickly reappears on the hill. Then Jill returns the same way. The old rhyme "Jack and Jill went up the hill" may also have been used as a finger game.

dickie-birds This term was used to refer to any small birds, but it was also the dialectal word for the hedge-sparrows.

> **Peas-porridge** hot. Peas-porridge cold.
> Peas-porridge in the pot, nine days old.
> Somer like it hot. Some like it cold.
> Some like it in the pot, nine days old.

This popular rhyme is still used as a clapping game with babies, but older kids use it for a more complicated game, with a pair of youngsters using a pattern to quickly clap each other's hands. It's also for skipping rope. It is not known if there is any significance to the "nine days," but it was not uncommon to serve some soups cold. In an old cookbook (by Della Lutes, *Modern Priscilla Cook Book*, published in 1924) which belonged to my wife's grandmother, there were some half-dozen recipes for cold soup, two of which had vegetables as the main ingredient: beet soup and iced-tomato bouillon. Cold soups are now popular again, and today Google will give you several recipes for cold pea soup.

Peas In early Middle English "peas" was the *singular* form for the pea plant, and the plural form had an "-en" ending (as in "oxen" or "children.") So, it was one "pea" but two "peasen." Sometime in the 1500s, however, the final /n/ sound dropped out of use, so "peasen" became "pease." Now people had a new problem: the plural for "pease" and singular form "peas" sounded almost the same. Around 1600 people started to use "peas" as the plural form (since by then the plural of most English nouns ended in /s/) and a new singular arose: "pea." Conclusion: this nursery rhyme—which used "peas" as the old singular form—must be about 400 years old.

porridge a thick soup or a thin pudding. The word became common in the 1600s. Porridge was made by boiling the meal of grains or legumes in water or milk. Vegetables and/or meat could be added.

CHAPTER 3

Toys

When children become older, they outgrow baby games. As they learn to use their minds and muscles, they learn how to amuse themselves. And with the help of toys, the real world is made small enough for them to better imitate the actions of their elders.

> There was a little **nobby** colt.
> His name was Nobby Gray.
> His head was made of **pouce straw**.
> His tail was made of hay.
> He could ramble, he could trot,
> He could **carry a mustard**-pot
> Round the town of **Woodstock**.
> **Hey, Jenny,** hey!

nobby a hobby horse (a toy horse's head on a stick) or a rocking horse. One source (EDD) gives "nobby" as "a pet name for a young colt." The ultimate origin of "nobby" is a mystery, but exploring the possibilities is when the fun of research begins. Here are a few conjectures:

- a) "nobby" is a British slang word meaning: stylish, first-rate, excellent (from "nob," a wealthy person). Okay, but it doesn't quite seem to fit for a toy horse.
- b) "nob" as a slang or dialect term for "head." The only way this could fit would be as a reference to the nobby colt's straw-filled head.

c) "nobble" is a British slang variant of "hobble," to disable a horse by drugging or making it lame to keep it from winning a race. That meaning doesn't quite seem to fit here for nobby colt. However, in a different context, it's interesting to see that the word "hobble" comes from the Middle English word "hobelen," (to move along unsteadily) is related to the Dutch word "hobbelen," which means "to toss, to rock from side to side, or to *ride a hobbyhorse.*" Wow! How about that? When I read this information, I jumped to the conclusion that the "hobby" in "hobbyhorse" came from the Dutch "hobbelen, but I was wrong. The "hobby" in "hobbyhorse" actually comes from the Old French "hobi" or "hobin," the pet-name for a horse. According to the Web NW, "hobby" is still an English dialect term for a medium-sized, vigorous horse.

d) Now we're really getting someplace, because "nobby" could be a variant of "hobby." The /h/ sound may have been changed to an /n/ sound, and this is how it could have happened: In many dialects in central and south-eastern England when a word begins with /h/ the /h/ is silent. Phonologists call this "H-dropping," as in the expression '*ere come 'andsome 'arry with the auburn 'air.* This is not just the Cockney English of East End London. It occurs in several dialect regions. (American: "an **h**onest man, an **h**erb garden, an **h**istorical fact.")

How could the 16th century word "hobbyhorse" change to "nobbyhors?" Public schooling did not begin until the 19th century. For hundreds of years many people did not read or write, or if they did write, they sometimes just guessed where the letters went. That's how we got "a nickname" which came from Middle English "an ekename" (literally, "an added name").

So just maybe "a nobby colt" used to be "an (h)obby colt.

pouce straw a dialect form of "pulse straw," the stalks of leguminous plants, such as peas, beans, etc. (This word is *not* related to the "pulse" of a beating heart.)

Montgomerie, in *A Book of Scottish Nursery Rhymes,* had this version:

> I had a little hobby-horse.
> His name was dapple grey.

> His head was made of pease straw.
> His tail was made of hay.

As noted above (page 13) "pease" was the old singular form of "pea."

This poem brings back a fond memory for me. When I was a young child, my favorite stuffed animal and constant companion was a scraggly, one-eyed horse by the name of Dapple Grey.

carry a mustard pot For a horse to carry crockery on its back without breaking it would certainly testify to its smooth, even gait.

Woodstock a small town located about five miles from Oxford, England. (Not to be confused with the famous Woodstock Music and Arts Fair of 1969, located in Bethel, New York, a small town in the Catskills.)

Hey, Jenny "Hey" was a common call to dogs, in Elizabethan times. But here, the name "Jenny" appears to refer to the horse. "Jenny" is a common name for a female donkey. It's also a nickname for "Jane." It is, according to the ODECN, "properly pronounced 'Jinny,' though a *spelling pronunciation* is now heard." That is, some people say words the way they're spelled, like the /t/ in "often."

> I had a little doll,
> Its name was Alice **Gray**,
> And while I went **to call**,
> She did the **work** each day.
> Sometimes I would be sick
> And wish to stay at home
> I went for Alice Gray
> And she was sure to come
> And then we laughed and talked
> Or went awhile and walked
> Beside the running brook
> Or in the leafy grove
> And I would say, my dear
> And she would say, my love
> But **ah! mischance** befell

> My darling Alice Gray!
> She dropped from sister's arms,
> And broke her neck one day.

Tragic endings were more common in early children's literature. Let's hope someone someday could fix her Alice Gray.

Gray This might be an American poem, since the British spelling would usually be "Grey." However, both spellings are found in both dialects.

to call to visit with someone. The term is still used, but is followed now with a preposition, such as "to call on," or "to call upon" + a noun.

work We can probably assume this referred to the housework.

ah! Putting an exclamation mark in the middle of a sentence was commonly done in the 18th century and earlier, especially after certain expressions, such as "oh! ah! oh, no! oh, my!" etc.

mischance This term is somewhat archaic. The word "misfortune" is more common now. Both words carry the connotation of bad luck or an unlucky accident, but in former times "mischance" had a stronger sense of disaster or calamity. In fact, the obsolete meaning of "mischance" referred specifically to an accidental *injury*, which is exactly what we have in this rhyme.

CHAPTER 4

Short Stories

When parents were busy or pressed for time, they must have relied on little poetic tales such as these to silence the plea, "Tell us a story!" Many nursery rhymes even begin like a story: "There was an old women (or old man) who . . ." and some of them also proceeded like stories, having a beginning, a middle, and an end. They introduced the main character(s), set the scene, described what happened, and gave the result—all in a few terse lines.

> There was an old woman who lived by the sea,
> And she was as merry as merry could be.
> She did nothing but **carol** from morning **till** night,
> And sometimes she caroled by candlelight.
> She caroled **in time** and she caroled **in tune**,
> But **none** cared to hear, **save** the man in the moon.

carol (archaic) to sing lively or joyously. Now used only at Christmas time as a verb, "Christmas caroling," or as a noun, "a Christmas carol."

till This word means "to" or "until," but should not be confused with "'til" which is a shortened from of "until." In fact, the word "till" is a very old word in itself, and has been around since Old English times, whereas "until" is from Middle English.

in time using the correct musical time, beat, or rhythm.

in tune having the correct pitch.

none (archaic) no one, nobody.

save except

> There was an old woman who lived in a hat
> Her only companion was **Grom-skin**, the cat.
> And where she got **victuals** and where she got drink
> Has puzzled the neighbors to say or to think.

Grom-skin This name (formed from "groom" + "skin") no doubt refers to the cat's frequent habit of grooming its coat. (The first syllable probably rhymes with "prom.")

victuals food, provisions. This is pronounced like "viddles" and rhymes with "fiddles." It comes from Middle English and Old French "vittaille," hence often spelled as "vittles." The spelling "victuals," used in this rhyme, reflects the influence of the 18th century prescriptive grammarians who insisted it should conform to the original Latin: "victualis."

> There was an old man in a **velvet coat**
> Who kissed a **maid** and gave her a **groat**.
> The groat it was cracked and would not **go**.
> "Ah, old man, do you **serve me so**?"

velvet coat Many stories used dramatic contrast to get across their points. And here the stinginess of the old man's action is emphasized by his wearing a coat of very expensive fabric, usually possessed only by the wealthy or nobility. During the Renaissance, velvet was a symbol of class, as shown by Shakespeare: "... and leave 'in sooth' / And such protest of pepper gingerbread / To velvet guards and Sunday citizens." (*Henry IV*, Part 1, 3.1.2 57–259)

maid (archaic) a girl or young woman, especially an unmarried one. Today, the term almost always refers to a female servant.

groat fourpence. Last issued for circulation in 1662. (A fourpence piece minted in the 19th century was occasionally called a groat, but the name was neither officially recognized nor commonly used.) So, it is very likely that this poem is from the 17th century, or older.

go to circulate, to be accepted as currency. (For example: "This half-crown will never go; 'tis brass.")

serve me so treat me in such a way (with such a cheap coin!).

> There was an old woman, as I've heard tell,
> She went to market her eggs **for to** sell.
> She went to market **all** on a market day,
> And she fell asleep on the **king's highway**.
>
> There came a pedlar whose name was Stout
> He cut her **petticoats** round about.
> He cut her petticoats up to the knees,
> Which **made** the old woman **to** shiver and sneeze.
>
> When this little woman first did wake,
> She began to shiver, and she began to shake.
> She began to **wonder**, and she began to cry,
> "Oh! Deary, deary me! **This is none of I**!
>
> "But if it be I, as I do hope it be,
> I've a little dog at home, and he'll know me.
> And if it be I, he'll wag his tail.
> And if it be not I, he'll loudly bark and wail.
>
> Home went the little woman, all in the dark.
> Up got the little dog, and he began to bark.
> He began to bark, so she began to cry,
> "**Lack-a-mercy on me**. This is none of I!"

This old story has a number of 18th and 19th century versions, as well as several European equivalents. There were various theories as to why the old woman fell asleep. According to a Scottish version, she simply had a little too much to drink. In Grimm's *Fairy Tales*, the woman fell asleep while cutting corn. However, as the Norwegians tell it, it wasn't corn but hemp.

Newly cut hemp has strong narcotic properties and could easily make a person drowsy.

for to in order to. This expression was used for hundreds of years and still survives in some dialects after "would like" or "mean," as in "I'd like for you to help me." or "She meant for him to go with you."

all This seems to be a shortened form of "It all happened." It's an archaic use of the word now, but is still heard in ballad poetry. For example, there is a nursery rhyme/folksong/game called "Here We Go Loopty Loo" (which has been popular in America, England, Ireland, and France since the late 1800s). One version goes: "Here we go loppty loo. Here we go loopty lie. Here we go loopty loo. *All* on a Saturday night."

king's highway The two phrases "king's highway" and "king's peace" are intimately connected. They come from a time when the king ruled only what he could control. So, the king's peace was not for all people and for all time, but only where he could provide protection.

And in the countryside, such protection would be available only on a major waterway or a main road. But apparently this didn't stop the pedlar from perpetrating his mischief. Where are the king's men when you need them? I suppose all the king's horses and all the king's men were busy putting Humpty Dumpty together again.

petticoats At one time, these were outer skirts that hung from the waist to the feet. So, to cut them up to her knees was a naughty deed indeed. Today, petticoats are only underskirts, not in common use now, and they are shorter since most modern dresses are shorter.

made . . . to Using the word "made" followed by "to" + a verb is archaic now, except occasionally in the passive form, for example: "Those people can't be made to agree."

This is none of I (archaic) This used to be a way of saying "This is *not at all* who I really am!" Used this way since before the 12th century, the word "none" is occasionally heard today in such expressions as "That's none of your business."

Lack-a-mercy on me! Woe is me! Possibly an alternate form of "Lord, have mercy on me!" However, the word *lack* also used to mean an unfortunate failure or fault and was heard in a number of archaic exclamations, such as "Alack!" (from *ah* + *lack*) or "Alas and alack!" or "Lack-a-day!" (Woe is the day!) This is the basis of our word "lackadaisical."

> There was an old woman of **Gloucester**
> Whose parrot two **guineas** it cost her,
> But its tongue never ceasing
> Was **vastly** displeasing
> To the talkative woman of Gloucester.

Gloucester the county seat of Gloucestershire in the southwestern region of central England, not far from Wales. (Not to be confused with Gloucester, Massachusetts or with The City of Gloucester, New Jersey, a.k.a. Gloucester City, or simply Gloucester where my wife Victoria grew up.) It's the site of an imposing cathedral, founded in the 7th century and originally named "The Cathedral Church of Saint Peter and the Holy and Indivisible Trinity." (Seriously?) For some reason, the name was later changed to "The Gloucester Cathedral." The "Gloucester/cost her" end-rhymes share the "aw" sound. [See Appendix 4]

guineas A "guinea" was an English gold coin. First used for Britain's trade with the country of Guinea, West Africa, it was issued from 1663 until 1813. So, this nursery rhyme cannot be older than the late 1600s. The guinea was actually the very first of England's "milled" coins. That is, it was stamped out by machinery instead of being hammered out by hand. At first it was worth 20 shillings (or one pound), but its value fluctuated greatly until 1717 when it was fixed at 21 shillings. Britain switched to decimal currency in 1971. Neither guineas nor shillings are legal currency anymore, but the term "guinea" is still occasionally used—especially in buying and selling horses—to indicate a value of one pound and five pence.

vastly very. Originally it meant "to a vast extent," but the weakened meaning came into use and was very popular by the mid-18th century. In 1754 the Earl of Chesterfield complained of language abuse:

> "They take a word and change it, like a guinea into shillings for pocket-money, to be employed in the several occasional purposes

of the day. For instance . . . 'vast' and 'vastly' mean anything, and are the fashionable words of the most fashionable people, not knowing in truth where to place them properly, they are *vastly* obliged, or *vastly* sorry. Large object are *vastly* great. A fine woman pronounced a small snuff-box . . . to be *vastly* pretty, because it was *vastly* little." (Bough, *A History of the English Language*, 306)

In recent years, the overuse of a tern has happened to the word "awesome," which can now describe anything: "This fudge brownie is *awesome*." or "That joke was *awesome*. But when I was young, "awesome" was used only for things that truly filled us with awe, like our first sight of the Grand Canyon or witnessing a huge tornado.

You probably recognized that the form of this rhyme is a *limerick* (named after County Limerick in Ireland). It always has five lines. The 1st, 2nd, and 5th lines rhyme and each has 3 stressed syllables. The 3rd and 4th lines rhyme, but each has only 2 stressed syllables. This is one of my favorite limericks (sometimes ascribed to President Woodrow Wilson):

> "I sat next to the Duchess at tea.
> It was just as I thought it would be.
> > Her rumblings abdominal
> > Were simply phenomenal,
> And everyone though it was me."

This next nursery rhyme is another narrative limerick:

> There was an old man of **Tobago**
> Who lived on ride-**gruel** and **sago**,
> > Till, much to his bliss,
> > His physician said this,
> "To a leg, sir, of **mutton** you may go."

One source tells us that this fine limerick, published in 1822, was written by R. S. Sharpe, a grocer, amateur poet, and author of many children's books. (Opie, *Nursery Rhymes*, 407.)

Limerick poetry goes back hundreds of years, but it became very popular after the English writer and artist Edward Lear discovered the limerick form. In his own words, this is how it came about: "Long years ago, in days when much of my time was passed in a country home, where children and mirth abounded, the lines beginning, 'There was an old man of Tobago' were suggested to me by a valued friend, as a form of verse lending itself to limitless variety for rhymes and pictures. . . ." So, in 1846, Lear began writing his *Nonsense Books*. (Lear, xiv.)

Tobago An island in the West Indies, it is the smaller of two islands that make up the Caribbean country of Trinidad and Tobago, which is just off the northeast coast of Venezuela, between the Caribbean Sea and the Atlantic Ocean.

gruel a light, liquid food made by boiling grain in water or milk. (Here the grain used was rice.) Gruel was a thin, easily digested broth, chiefly used as a food for invalids.

sago (obsolete) a prepared food made by boiling sago in water or milk. Sago is a starch obtained from the pith of the trunks of several different palm trees.

mutton the meat from mature sheep. It was frequently eaten in the United States in the early 1900s, but not so much anymore. However, in the western and northern uplands of Britain, mutton is still often consumed. The slang term "muttonchops," (long, bushy sideburns, widely round at the top and narrow below) is also becoming archaic.

> There was a little guinea pig,
> Who, being little, was not big.
> He always walked upon his **feet**,
> And never fasted when he **eat.**
> When from a place he ran away.
> He never at that place did stay,
> And when he ran, as I am told,
> He **ne'er** stood still for young or old.
>
> He often squeaked, was sometimes **vi'lent**,
> And when he squealed, he ne'er was silent.

Though ne'er instructed by a cat,
He knew a mouse was not a rat.

One day, **as I am certified**,
He **took a whim** and **fairly** died,
And, as I'm told by men of sense,
He never has been living since.

    This rhyme and the next one ("In a cottage in Fife") both get their humor across in the same way: by making the common appear uncommon; the ordinary, extraordinary; and the obvious, bizarre.
    Little kids love to giggle at this kind of silly stuff. It reminds me of those lines in the old folksong *Oh, Susanna*: "It rained all night the day I left, / The weather it was dry. / The sun so hot I froze to death. / Susanna, don't you cry."

eat This is the archaic and dialectal *past* tense of "eat" and was often pronounced as "et" (which rhymed with "get"). In fact, my dad (born in 1900) used to jokingly say: "Have you *et* yet?" Moreover, to have "et" rhyme with "feet" in this poem was not too hard, since "feet" was pronounced like "fit" in Early Modern English (1450–1750).

ne'er This contraction for "never" was common since the 13th century, but not so common anymore. (Although a lazy person is still called a "ne'er-do-well.") The author of this poem sometimes used the one-syllable word "ne'er" and sometimes the two-syllable word "never," whichever one was needed to keep the iambic meter moving along smoothly.

vi'lent a contraction for "violent. (Similar to "vi'let," an obsolete form of "violet,") It makes a strong end-rhyme with "silent."

as I am certified as I am assured (or) as I am informed. A tag line similar to "as I am told." Perhaps this was phrased as a hyper-formal expression on purpose.

took a whim took a notion, got an (odd) idea.

fairly (obsolete) quietly, in a gentle manner.

In a cottage in **Fife**
Lived a man and his wife,
Who, believe me, were comical folk,
For to people's surprise,
They both saw with their eyes.
And their tongues moved whenever they spoke!

When quite fast asleep,
I've been told that to keep
Their eyes open, they **scarce** could **contrive**.
They walked on their **feet**,
And 'twas thought what they **eat**
Helped, with drinking, to keep them alive.

Fife A peninsula by the North Sea in eastern Scotland, just north of Edinburgh. (This area is known as the Home of Golf.)

scarce scarcely. Sometimes in Middle English, the adjective and adverb forms of a word would be spelled exactly the same, so people would have to tell by context what was meant. (For example, "He was a *rich* man, and his pantry was *rich* supplied.").

"Scarce" was used poetically as an adverb even in the 20th century, as in the third verse of the popular hymn *How Great Thou Art* (1949): "And when I think that God, His Son not sparing, sent Him to die, I *scarce* can take it in."

Moreover, in everyday casual English, the practice of dropping the -ly ending of adverbs is very common (much to the chagrin of many English teachers). A few examples: "Come *quick*." "Go *slow*." "You should go *easy* on him." or "Work *steady* at it."

contrive manage.

feet and **eat** Once again, they may have been pronounced as "fit" and "et," making them a near rhyme. (Yes, I know, I know. They rhyme better in Modern English as "feet" and "eat.")

Here's a long narrative poem (sixteen verses) which may date back 600 years! Ah, the power of *oral* tradition, back when people thought nothing of memorizing many lines of poetry.

A gentleman of **good account**
In **Norfolk** dwelt of late,
Whose wealth and riches did surmount
Most men of his **estate**

Sore sick he was, and **like to** die,
No help his life could save.
His wife by him as sick did lie.
And both were near the grave.

No love between these two **was lost**
Each to the other kind.
In love they lived, in love they died,
And left two babes behind.

Now if the children chanced to die
Ere they to age should come,
Their uncle should possess their wealth,
For so the will did run.

"Now, brother," said the dying man,
"**Look to** my children dear.
Be good unto my boy and girl.
No friends else have they here."

Their parents being dead and gone,
The children home he takes,
And brings them **unto** his house,
Where **much of them he makes**.

He had not kept those **pretty babes**
A twelvemonth and a day,
When for their wealth, he did **devise**
To **make** them both **away**.

He bargained with two ruffians,
Who were of savage **mood**,
That they should take the children **twain**
And slay them in a wood.

They **prate** and **prattle** pleasantly,
While riding on the way,
To those their wicked uncle hired
These lovely babes to slay.

So that the **pretty speech** they had
Made the ruffians' hearts relent,
And they that took the deed to do
Full sorely did repent.

Yet one of them, more hard of heart,
Did vow to do his **charge**,
Because the **wretch** that hired him
Had paid him very large.

The other would not agree thereto
So here they **fell at** strife.
With one another they did fight
About the children's life.

And he that was of milder mood
Did slay the other there
Within an unfrequented wood.
The babes did quake with fear.

These pretty babes, with hand in hand,
Went wandering **up and down**,
But never more they saw the man
Approaching from the town.

Thus wandered these two pretty dears
Till death did end their grief.

In one another's arms they died,
Poor babes! **Past all relief.**

No burial these innocents
Of any man received,
But **Robin Redbreast lovingly
Did cover them with leaves.**

Again, we see the tragic ending in another dramatic tale. In 1765, the English poet and antiquarian Thomas Percy, in his famous work *Reliques of Ancient English Poetry,* noted that this poem was one version of an old ballad "based on a play written in 1601 by Robert Yarrington concerning 'a young child murthered in a wood by two ruffians, with the consent of his uncle.'" The origin of the tale may be even earlier. According to another source (Henderson, *Christmas Holiday Book,* 63), the tale "is based on a true story of two English children who were abducted and abandoned in Norfolk in the 15th century. One of the kidnappers confessed, and the incident was so gruesome that it left an impression even on that tough age and was handed down in song and story."

The world's folklore is replete with stories of wicked step-parents who abandoned children. Part of this rhyme (verses 8–10) brings to mind the tale of "Snow White and the Seven Dwarfs" in which the wicked queen tells a hunter to take Snow White into the forest and kill her, but in the forest, he lets her go free.

good account high worth, importance. (Compare this to the expression used in the southeaster United States: "no 'count hound" which refers to a worthless dog.)

Norfolk a county in eastern England, bordering on the North Sea.

estate social class. This expression originated in feudal times when it referred to any of three classes of people, each of which had specific political power. The first estate was the Lords Spiritual (the clergy), the second was the Lords Temporal (the nobility), and the third was the Commons (the bourgeoisie). The first two came to form Parliament's House of Lords and the third, the House of Commons.

sore (archaic and dialectal) severely, dangerously, seriously—either physically (sore ill) or emotionally (sore afraid).

like to (dialectal) likely to, about to.

No love . . . was lost That is, their love didn't die away. This expression is still heard today, but now only in a sarcastic sense.

look to look after, take care of.

unto to. (see "till," above, page 195)

makes much of makes a fuss over, plays with. By the 18th century, this phrase shortened in many English dialects, and the word "much" was used as a verb. To "much" a child or an animal meant to pet it or soothe it with caresses.

pretty babes charming, delightful, or attractive children. This adjective was used to describe not just appearance, but more especially, the character of a person or situation.

devise plan, contrive.

make away to put (a person) out of the way, to put to death. (In Modern English, we'd say: "to do away with.") The expression "to make away" is obsolete now, but was common in the 16th and 17th centuries, which helps us date this version of the poem.

mood mind-set, a fixed state of mind, a permanent attitude. Today this word describes an emotional state, often a temporary one.

twain two. Old English was an inflected language (like modern German) with masculine, feminine, and neuter nouns and adjectives. So, it had three words for *two*: twegen (masc.), twa (fem.) and tu (neut.) In non-inflected Middle English, the masculine word became "twain" and the feminine and neuter forms became "two." "Twain" was common up to the late 19th century. Kids love to hear the story of how Samuel Clemens picked Mark Twain as his pen name.

prate to chatter, talk away, usually to speak a lot about trifling things without much purpose.

prattle another form of "prate." Note: Both these verbs are in the present tense form but are being used to describe an event in the past. This is the so-called "historical present" and is still very common in informal speech. For example: "Yesterday this guy walks up to me and says hello, and I don't even know who he is."

pretty speech a pleasing or nice manner of speaking. Now "speech" is used mostly in such expressions as "colloquial speech" or "Southern speech" or "a political speech."

full sorely with much grief, distress.

charge duty.

wretch a mean, despicable, contemptible person. (In Old English this word was even stronger and referred to an exile or outcast, a person driven out of town for being so bad.)

fell at (obsolete) were quickly drawn into or suddenly got into.
A frequent phrase in the late 17th century was "to fall at square," to quarrel. Since the 19th century, people have "squared off" when taking a fighting stance or getting ready for a fight.

up and down here and there.

past all relief beyond all help.

Robin . . . did cover them with leaves. According to the 19th century scholar Halliwell (p. 162), "the superstitious reverence with which these birds (the robin and the wren) are almost universally regarded takes its origin from a pretty belief that they undertake the delicate office of covering the dead bodies of any of the human race with moss or leaves, if by any means left exposed to the heavens. This opinion is alluded to by Shakespeare and many writers of his time, as by Drayton, for example: 'Cov'ring with moss the dead's unclosed eye, / the little red-breast teacheth charity.'"

The Shakespearian example Halliwell is talking about is found in *Cymbeline*: "The raddock (ruddock, the European robin, as opposed to the American robin, a different species altogether) would / With charitable bill . . . bring thee all this; / Yea, and furr'd moss besides, when flowers are none. / To winter-ground thy corse" (4.2.224–229).

And about 1611, John Webster (in *The White Devil*, 5.4) wrote these lines:

> Calls for the robin redbreast and the wren,
> Since o'er shady grove they hover
> And with leaves and flow'rs do cover
> The friendless bodies of unburied men.

Halliwell continues, ". . . the ancient belief attached to these birds is perpetuated chiefly by the simple ballad of the 'Babes in the Wood.'"

This poem—sort of a condensed version of the above nursery rhyme "A gentleman of good account"—was apparently known in the early 17th century:

> My dear, do you know
> How a long time ago
>   Two poor little children,
> Whose names I don't know,
> Were stolen away
> On a fine summer's day
>   And left in a wood,
> As I've heard people say.
>   And when it was night,
> So sad was their plight,
>   The sun it went down,
> And the moon gave no light!
> They sobb'd and they sigh'd
> And they bitterly cried,
>   And the poor little things,
>
> They lay down and died.
> And when they were dead,

> The robins so red
> > Brought strawberry leaves
> And over them spread;
> And all the day long,
> They sang them this song—
> Poor babes in the wood!
> Poor babes in the wood!
> > And don't you remember
> The babes in the wood?

This next old poem, according to Baring-Gould (*Mother Goose*, 309), dates back to 1807. Notice that the first letter of each animal's name is capitalized. This probably was done to show the importance of each participant at the feast. However, in the 17th and 18th centuries capitalizing common nouns was often done (as in the United States Constitution of 1787), and some writers, like Emily Dickinson, continued to do so into the late 19th century. We can see how this rhyme might have been composed as a ballad-play to be acted out in pantomime. The animals are called together in the first verse.

> Come take up your hats, and away let us haste,
> To the Butterfly's Ball and the Grasshopper's Feast.
> The trumpeter, **Gad-fly**, has summoned the crew,
> And the **revels** are now only waiting for **you**.
>
> On the smooth-**shaven** grass, by the side of the wood,
> Beneath a broad oak which for ages has stood,
> See the children of earth, and the tenants of air,
> To the evening's amusement together they **repair**.
>
> And there came the Beetle, so blind and so black,
> Who carried the **Emmet**, his friend, on his back.
> And there came the Gnat and the Dragon-fly too,
> With all their relatives, green, orange, and blue.
>
> And there came the Moth, with her plumage of down,
> And the Hornet with jacket of yellow and brown,
> And with him the Wasp, his companion, did bring,
> But they promised that evening to **lay by** their sting.

Then the **sly Dormouse** peeped out of his hole,
And led to the feast his blind cousin the Mole.
And the Snail, with her horns peeping out of her shell,
Came, fatigued with the distance, the length of an **ell**.

A mushroom, the table, and on it was spread
A **water-dock** leaf, which their table-cloth made.
The **viands** were various, to each of their taste.
And the Bee brought honey to sweeten the feast.

With steps most majestic the Snail did advance,
And he promised the **gazers** a **minuet** to dance.
But they all laughed so loud that he drew in his head,
And went in his own little chamber to bed.

Then, as **evening** gave way to the shadows of night,
Their watchman, the **Glow-worm**, came out with his light.
So, home let us hasten while yet we can see,
For no watchman is waiting for **you** or for me.

Gad-fly (a.k.a. horsefly or bot-fly) Any of various flies that bite and bother animals, including people. The English word "gadfly" has been in use since the early 1600s and has also been used to refer to people who motivate or annoy others with pointed comments or questions. In the 4th century B.C., Plato referred to his mentor Socrates as the "gadfly of Athens" because he kept "bugging" the rulers to do the right things. In this rhyme the job of the Gad-fly was to activate and to assemble the others by blowing the trumpet.

revels Wild parties and celebrations. In 1740, one lexicon (Dyche and Pardon, *A New English Dictionary*) defined *revels* as "sports, masks, balls, dancings, acting of farces or comedies, &c. in noblemen's or gentlemen's houses, colleges, inns or courts, &c." A "mask" (now usually spelled "masque") was a form of dramatic entertainment popular among the aristocracy in England during the 16th and 17th centuries, usually based on a mythical or allegorical theme, and with the dialog less important than the lavish costumes, scenery, music, dancing, etc. In fact, originally, a masque had no dialog at all.

shaven trimmed or mowed closely. So, a "shaven" meadow or lawn would be one that was cut close to the ground.

repair (ME) to go or to make one's way to a place, often as a group. (as in this rhyme). For example, "Let us repair to the dining room."

Emmet ant. (archaic, but still used in some dialects in England.) Both "ant" and "emmet" come from the same Old English word "aemete." The original Germanic word meant "the biter" or "the cutter off." I'm not sure why the **m** changed to **n**, but it's not an isolated case; "renown" was "renoume" in Early Modern English.

lay by lay aside.

sly Dormouse a small European rodent, intermediate in size and behavior between mice and squirrels. The term is known to have been used since 1475, but its origin is unclear. (The French word "dormeuse" (sleeper) is sometimes suggested as the source because the dormouse hibernates in winter for six months or more. However, that word is not known before the 17th century.) Before the 20th century, *sly* didn't mean sneaky or devious, just clever and cunning.

ell a former measure of length, used mainly on measuring cloth.
This word comes from the Old English *eln*, "arm" (related to the Latin "ulna" and the English "elbow," literally, "arm-bend"). The length of the English ell was 45 inches, but the Scottish ell was closer to a yard (37.2 inches). The Flemish and Dutch ell was even shorter: 27 inches.

We are *not* to conclude from this that the English people had longest arms! I think these variations in length come from the fact that the ell was used primarily for measuring cloth. And to measure cloth with the arms, the length obtained depended on how the cloth was *held*.

Using my wife as an example, I discovered that cloth held at arm's length (that is, from the fingertips of her outstretched left hand to the left armpit) equaled 27 inches: the Flemish and Dutch ell.

The distance from her fingertips of her left hand to her nose (as her head is turned to the right) was 36 inches, which is about the same as the Scottish ell. (By the way, the German word for "yard" or "yardstick" is "Elle"). My wife, a good seamstress, still used this method to measure material, having learned it from her Scotch-Irish grandmother. And finally, the distance from her left fingertips to the tip of her right elbow was 45 inches, the exact length of the English ell. Even today, if you go into a fabric store, you'll notice that material is sometimes sold in widths of 36 inches, but more commonly in widths of 45 inches, as well as 54 inches (palm to palm), and 60 inches (fingertip to fingertip). Europe and Canada use metrics now, but in the 1990s, venetian blinds in Ottawa were still sold in inches.

water-dock a broad-leafed plant that grows on the banks of European waterways.

viands food items, especially tasty dishes. [rhymes with "lions"] The word originated in popular Latin "vivanda (from Latin "vivere," to live). It may have been a slang word in the Roman army. At any rate, the Gauls picked it up, and by the 12th century it had passed into Anglo-French as "viande."

gazers onlookers, especially those who stare intently with curiosity.
The word has since been replaced by "spectators," though both words are equally old, dating back to the 16th century.

minuet This slow, stately dance was derived from France in the 1600s and was fashionable throughout the 1700s. (From an obsolete French word "menuet," tiny, fine, delicate, as in the English adjective "minute," very small.)

evening twilight. We now use this word more loosely to refer to the early part, or to the first half, of the night—even long after it's dark. An 18th century dictionary defines evening as "the close of day, or that part of it that is light after sun-set." (Dyche and Pardon)

Glow-worm This "watchman" is not only not a male, it's not a worm either. The glowworm of literature is actually a wingless lampyrid beetle—and only the female glows. Glow, girl, glow!

you In the last two lines of the poem, the narrator, as in the first verse, is again speaking directlyto the children listening to the story, telling them that it's getting dark and time to hurry home.
A similar list of party-goers is in "Mister Frog," (see below, page 180).

CHAPTER 5

Riddles

There are several different kinds of riddles. Some take a lot of work, while others have deceptively simple answers. Many riddles rely on puns for their effect. These riddles usually have the shortest life-span because they depend on the ability of the listener to understand the multiple meanings of certain expressions. And often these meanings are unique to a particular locality, occupation, and/or time.

> As high as a castle,
> As weak as a **wastle**.
> All the king's horses
> Cannot pull it down.   (smoke)

One source believes this may have been part of a group of riddle-rhymes from the 16th and 17th centuries (Halliwell-Phillips, *Archaic & Provincial Words*, 141). There are many popular riddles concerning things over which strong forces have no power. "Humpty Dumpty" is probably the most famous one.

wastle There are two possible definitions for this word:
It could be an obsolete form of "wastel," a bread that was made from very fine white flour. The word was used that way by Chaucer in the 14th century. "Wastel" is indirectly related to the French word "gateau," a cake or tart.

The other possibility is that "wastle" is an archaic dialectal word used in the northern part of Britain, at least until the mid-19th century, which referred to a "twig" or a "thin pliable branch." (My money's on this one.)

> Thomas **A'Tattlamus** took two **T's**
> To tie two **tups** to two tall trees.
> To frighten the terrible Thomas A"Tattamus,
> Tell me how many T's there are in that. (two, in "that")

This reminds me of a riddle-rhyme my mom used to say every time we drove over a railroad track:

> Railroad crossing! Look out for the cars.
> Can you spell it without any R's? (I-T)

The Thomas A'Tattamus poem is a tongue-twister as well as a riddle. Tongue-twisters are not only fun, but also help young children develop their pronunciation of different consonants.

I don't know if Thomas A'Tattamus was a real person, but if so, he may have come from Tatum in Lancaster. This British town is the source of other English surnames, for example: *Tatam* and *Tatum*. Tattamus may be one such name, with a **-us** Latinized ending. The **A** is an obsolete form of **of** or **from**, to indicate a person's *family* of origin or geographical *place* of origin. For example, the 12th century Archbishop of Canterbury, Thomas **a** Becket, was of the family of Becket. The famous medieval author Thomas **a** Kempis was from the town of Kempis. Also, Shakespeare speaks of "The name of John **a** Gaunt" (in *Richard II* 1.3.76)

T's T-shaped clasps, iron buckles suspended from a collar

tups male sheep, rams. The linguistic origin of this word is unknown, but it's a word found in Scotland and the northern counties of England—of which Lancashire is one! Referring again to Shakespeare, he uses "tup" a few times in *Othello* as a verb. For example, Iago says to Brabantio: "an old black ram / Is tupping your white ewe" (1.1.88).

> What if the rhyme for **porringer**?
> What is the rhyme for porringer?

> The King he had a daughter fair,
> And gave the Prince of Orange **her**.

   According to Opie (354): "This is a subdued part of a ranting Jacobite song threatening the life of William, Prince of Orange after he had 'ta'en the crown' from his father-in-law, James II." (in 1633)

porringer a small low bowl with a single handle, made of clay or wood, but usually of metal. It was used for soup, broth, porridge, or children's food. The earliest form of the word (16th century) was "pottanger" or "pottager," from a French word "potager," meaning *soup dish*. The spelling was later altered by association with the word "porridge."

her to her (pronounced with a silent /h/).

> To make your candles last for **aye**,
> You wives and maids give ear-o!
> To put 'em out's the only way,
> Says honest **John Bolero**.

aye forever (rhymes closely with "way"). This word is now archaic, except in Scots and north English dialects.

John Bolero I was unable to find out who, if anyone, he was. Perhaps, (according to Baring-Gould, 292) he was a relative of Edmund Bolero (d. 1679), a churchman who suffered much for the royalty cause in England and Scotland. In Bering-Gould's version of this rhyme, "Bolero" is spelled "Bolde'ro." So originally the name may well have been two separate words. "Bold hero" is a good possibility since it rhymes with "ear-o" in the second line.

> Little **Tom Tucker**
> Sings for his supper.
> What shall he eat?
> **White bread** and butter.
> How will he **cut it**
> Without **e'er** a knife?
> How can he **marry**
> Without e'er a wife?

The second stanza seems to have been a later addition, since the earliest known version (from about 1744) had only the first four lines. The second stanza could be an old sailors' riddle because of the double meaning of **cut it** and **marry**, both of which were nautical terms in the late 18th and early 19th centuries, and during that period, this popular rhyme was published at least a dozen times. (ODNR, 476

Tom Tucker According to Baring-Gould (30), "Tom Tucker is an exceedingly ancient English and Scottish phrase which meant a person who grasps all, or who stuffs himself at the expense of others."

white bread Dark bread used to be the cheapest bread because it was made of coarse flour. White bread was made from the more expensive finely ground flour, and it was considered a special treat.
Little did the wealthy know that it wasn't as healthy for them.

cut it This could be a pun on the nautical term meaning "to run away, to move off quickly," from the sailors' slang expression *to cut and run*, "to make off promptly, to hurry off." Originally it meant to escape danger by cutting the mooring lines and sailing away immediately, without even pulling up the anchor.

e'er an obsolete dialect form of *ever*, "even." In Early Modern English (1450–1750) the /v/ sound between vowels was often omitted. So, for example, the words *over*, *evil*, and *seven* became *o'er*, *e'il*, and *se'en*.

marry a nautical term meaning "to splice two ropes together."

> Pussy-cat sits by the **fire**.
> How can she be **fair**?
> In walks the little dog;
> Says, "Pussy, are you there?
> Mistress Pussy, **how d'ye do**?"
> "I thank ye kindly, little dog.
> I **fare** as well as you!"

The first two lines are the riddle. The final five lines are the answer, with the "clincher" in the last line: "I fare as well as you."

What I think we have working here is a three-way pun with the words *fire*, *fair*, and *fare*, based on the fact that in certain dialects the three words all sound the same. In the Northern dialect of Middle English, "fire" rhymed with "fair" and "fare." Parts of the American Midland dialect preserve this pronunciation, brought over by Scotch-Irish immigrants.

how d'ye do This contraction of "How do you do" became shortened even further in the American West cowboy slang to "Howdy."

> As I went over the water,
> And the water went over me,
> I saw two little **black birds**
> Sitting on a tree.
>
> The one **called** me a rascal.
> The other called me a thief.
> I took up my little black **stick**
> And knocked out all their **teeth**.
>
> As I went over the water,
> The water went over me.
> I heard an old woman cry,
> "Will you buy some **furmety**?"

The riddle-like phrase in lines 1 and 2 (repeated in lines 9 and 10) is difficult to decipher, but it might mean that the person was crossing a bridge when it began to rain. Or the person going over the bridge began to sweat upon seeing a sign of bad luck: the two black birds.

black birds perhaps crows or magpies, either of which could be bad omens. As Halliwell says (167), "in some counties, seeing two [magpie] is a sign of sorrow." And in his book *English Folk-Rhymes* (138), Northall tells us that "in English folk culture crows were generally regarded as birds of ill-omen. In the northern counties, peasants, across whose path they fly, exclaim: 'Crows, crows, get out of my sight / Or else I'll eat your liver and light.'" ("Light," usually found in the plural, was a dialectal term for the lungs of animals.)

According to Stefferud (*Birds in Our Lives*, 50):

"Indeed, the raven and all other members of the family Corvidae (jays and crows) were considered 'Devil's birds' in the folklore of northern Europe. The magpie, another of the Corvidae, was thought to have Devil's blood on its tongue. The European crow was said to visit the underworld each year in order to give the devil his due in the form of a tribute of feathers. This superstition may have been related to the bird's moult in mid-summer . . . At this season, it absents itself from its usual haunts and remains silent and mostly unseen until it has its new plumage."

called Various species of blackbirds have long been famous for their ability to imitate the sounds of the human voice. Ravens, for example, can say about 100 different words. They can also imitate the calls of other animals and even car alarms!

stick a walking stick.

teeth Knocking out birds' teeth isn't too difficult—since they don't have any. (My mother used to say of rare or nonexistent items: "They're scarcer than hens' teeth.")

furmety a dish made of hulled wheat boiled in milk and seasoned with cinnamon, sugar, plums or raisins, etc. (Also spelled as frumenty, furmenty, or fromenty) This comes from the Latin word for grain, "frumentum."
   I don't quite understand the significance of this last line, but maybe it's another pun. In provincial England, a person in a dilemma or nervous agitation was said to be in a "frumenty sweat."

CHAPTER 6

Song and Dance

The advantage of these nursery rhymes is that the children have a choice. They can just listen to descriptions of the actions, or they can join in and sing along and dance to them, either alone or with friends and family.

This poem was first published in Britain by Halliwell in the mid-1800s.

> Merry are the bells, and merry would they ring.
> Merry was myself, and merry could I sing.
> With a merry sing-song, happy, gay, and free.
> And a merry ding-dong, happy let us be!
>
> Waddle goes your gait, and **hollow** are your **hose**.
> **Noddle** goes your **pate**, and purple is your nose.
> Merry is you sing-song, happy, **gay**, and free,
> With a merry ding-dong, happy let us be!
>
> Merry have we met, and merry have we been,
> Merry let us part, and merry meet **again**.
> With a merry sing-song, happy, gay, and free,
> And a merry ding-dong, happy let us be!

hollow From the 14th to the 18th century, this word was used to describe something that was "full of holes." In this case, it referred to the person's tattered stockings.

hose tight-fitting stockings worn by men and boys from the mid-15th to the late 18th century, replaced by pants (trousers) in the early 19th century. The word "stockings" also has been used for hundreds of years to refer to cloth leg coverings for males and females, including the long knee socks that boys wore.

When I was a youngster and flopped down on my bed, too tired to finish getting undressed, my mother liked to recite this old nursery rhyme to me:

> Diddle diddle dumpling, my son John,
> Went to bed with his stockings on,
> One shoe off and one shoe on,
> Diddle diddle dumpling, my son John.

noddle to nod or shake the head, to beat time by nodding the head. (A nodding head and purple nose may well indicate that this rhyme originally was an old ale-house song.)

pate (archaic) head. This word was in common use from about 1300, but in recent times only in humorous use. The origin is unknown (although it's been suggested that it might be associated with the Latin "patina," *pan*.)

gay Since the 1300s, this word has meant "full of joy, carefree, merry." However, since the late 1900s it has come to mean "homosexual," and the older sense of the word is seldom used anymore, although occasionally an elderly person might say, "It was a wonderful party, and we all had a gay old time."

again This word probably rhymed with "rain" so it's a near-rhyme with "been" in the first line, which in Britain sounds like "bean."

> A **pye** sat on a pear tree.
> A pye sat on a pear tree.
> A pye sat on a pear tree.
> **Heigh ho**! Heigh ho! Heigh ho!

This, too, was originally an old drinking song. Apparently, this is how it went:

These lines are sung by a person at the table after dinner. His next neighbor then sings, "Once so merrily hopped she" three times, followed by three "heigh ho's, during which the first singer is obliged to drink a bumper [a glass or cup filled to the brim], and should he be unable to empty his glass before the next line is sung, he must begin again till he succeeds. The next line is "Twice so merrily hopped she," sung by the next person under a similar arrangement, and so on; beginning again after "Thrice so merrily hopped she, heigh ho! heigh ho! heigh ho!" till the ceremony has been repeated around the table. It is hoped so absurd a practice is not now in fashion. (Halliwell, 257)

(Sorry, Halliwell. The practice continues.)

However, the words "A pie sat in a pear tree, / Heigh ho! heigh ho!" may once have been a lament, a curse, or a charm. For one thing, the expression **heigh ho** was primarily used to voice *negative* feelings. It has been in use since the 1500s and is defined in Web NW as "an exclamation expressing dejection, uneasiness, weariness, etc." Sounds like a "Woe is me" phrase, doesn't it? It's certainly not the bouncy "Heigh-ho, heigh-ho! It's off to work we go!" that was merrily sung by the seven dwarves in Disney's movie *Sleeping Beauty*.

Moreover, in the mid-1800s, as Halliwell pointed out: "Widespread is the superstition that it is unlucky to see magpies under certain conditions . . ." As we noted above (page 50) in some counties it was considered bad luck to see two magpies; but in other places, "we are instructed that one magpie is a signal of misfortune, which can, however, be obviated by pulling off your hat, and making a very polite bow to the knowing bird. This operation I have more than once seen quite seriously performed." (Halliwell, 167–68)

pye This word for "magpie" is now obsolete, but it was the *original* term for the bird, from which "magpie" was formed. In the late 1500s, the feminine name "Mag" was added to the word "pye." (Both *Mag* and *Maggy* are nicknames for *Margaret*.) The English word "pye" (also spelled "pie") was formed from the Latin word for the bird: "pica." The origin of the other word "pie," meaning *a food-filled pastry*, is not known for sure.

It's probably just my personal opinion, but magpies and partridges appear to possess a peculiar penchant for picking pear trees for perching purposes. Since this particular practice is primarily performed in printed pieces, I'm prone to presume it's the product of poets who prefer to play on the alliterative possibilities.

> **Tom**, Tom, the piper's son,
> He learned to play when he was young.
> But all the tune that he could play
> Was "**Over the hills and far away**."
> Over the hills and a great way off,
> And the **wind** will blow my **top-knot** off.
>
> He saw a cross fellow was beating an ass,
> Heavy laden with pots, pans, dishes, and glass.
> He took out his **pipe** and played them a tune,
> And the **jackass's** load was lightened **full** soon.

These are the first and last stanzas of a longer poem in an 18th century chapbook, *Tom, The Piper's Son* (which includes the famous rhyme "Tom, Tom, the piper's son / Stole a pig and away he run."). Note that the second stanza's meter changes (due to a different composer?)

Chapbooks were tiny booklets containing songs, ballads, religious essays, etc. and were sold by street peddlers or "chapmen." Our word "chap" (fellow) is a shortened form of "chapman." The word "chap" comes from an Old English word for "sale," (a good sale would be a bargain, hence our word "cheap.") Chapbooks cost just a penny or so.

Tom For a long time this was a common name for pipers; a Tom Piper was mentioned by the 16th century poets Spenser and Drayton. (Opie, 409)

Over the hills and far away This was a very popular tune in the early 1700s. Perhaps the line was used here as a joke: "What shall I play?" "How about over the hills and far away," as in the 20th century witticism: "What shall I sing?" "Why don't you sing tenor . . . ten or twelve miles away." A further indication of Tom's annoying music comes in the last line of the rhyme. His playing the pipe even made a donkey so upset he jumped up and bucked off his load.

wind Apparently, the wind from Tom's lively blowing on his pipe.

top-knot At the end of the 1600s and into the 1700s, this referred to a knot or bow of ribbon worn on the top of ladies' heads.

pipe This could be any small flute made from tubes of reed or straw. Or, specifically, it could refer to the small, three-holed, end-blown whistle flute used in the one-man "pipe and tabor" band (the *tabor* being a small drum) that provided music for medieval court dances and was still know in Shakespeare's time: "You would never dance again after a tabor and pipe" (*The Winter's Tale* 4.4.183). On the other hand, perhaps the pipe Tom played was a bagpipe.

jackass The word "ass" is very old (OED "assa"). The word "jackass" did not appear in print until 1727 (the prefix "jack" indicating a male animal), so "ass" could no be a shortened form of "jackass." Since the word "donkey" was not used until 1785, this verse in the nursery rhyme may have been composed in the early 1700s.

full An archaic word for "very." This was once commonly used, especially in Middle English, but now it's rare, except in "full well," as my mom used to say, "You know full well what I mean, young man!"

> As I was going up the hill,
> I met Jack the piper,
> And all the tune that he could play
> Was, "Tie up your petticoats tighter."
>
> I tied them once, I tied them twice,
> I tied them three times over,
> And all the song that he could sing
> Was, "**Carry** me safe to Dover."

carry To escort, accompany; to "take" a person somewhere. The term is still occasionally used in this sense in certain dialects, for example in the southern United States (as in the old song: "Carry Me Back to Old Virginny.")

Song and Dance

> Hey ding a ding, what shall I sing?
> How many holes in a **skimmer**?
> > Four and twenty.
> > My stomach is empty.
> **Pray**, mama, give me some dinner.

skimmer a shallow perforated utensil for skimming liquids.

pray short for "I pray you," meaning "I beseech you." or "I ask you." or "Please."

> Sing, Sing, what shall I sing?
> The cat's run away with the **pudding-string**.
> Do, do, what shall I do?
> The cat has bitten it quite in two.

This nursery rhyme was "formerly a performer's appeal for what to sing next; more recently a child's rhyme in place of a song." (Opie, 114)

pudding-string a string used for tying off a "pudding" (now a term used only in certain English dialects and in Scotland), which was a kind of sausage made from the stomach or one of the entrails of a pig, sheep, or other animal, stuffed with a mixture of minced meat, suet, oatmeal, seasoning, etc., boiled and kept until needed.

> Come dance a jig
> **To my Granny's pig**,
> With a **rawdy, rowdy, dowdy**.
>
> Come dance a jig
> To my Granny's pig,
> And pussy-cat shall **crowdy**.

to my Granny's pig That is, to the rhythm of the pig's oinking.

rawdy just a nonsense word used as a segue to the next two words.

rowdy A fairly new word, first used in writing in 1819, it's still a common adjective to describe a *boisterous, rough* person.

dowdy (archaic) a term for a dowdy woman, one who dressed in shabby and/or old-fashioned clothes. (This noun had an even stronger meaning in Middle English "doude," a slut.)

crowdy fiddle (here used as a verb). This is an obsolete verb formed from the noun "crowd," an ancient Celtic instrument of the viol class. It is similar in shape to an Egyptian instrument used in 1700 B.C.

In 1906, Lina Eckenstein described it in *Comparative Studies in Nursery Rhymes* (32): "The crowd is the oldest kind of British fiddle, which has no neck and only three strings. It is mentioned as a British instrument already by the low Latin poet Fortunatus toward the close of the sixth century.... The instrument is well known to this day in Wales as the crwth." While in early times it had three strings; it later had six—four of which were played by a bow, two by fingers.

> My father he died, but **I can't tell you** how.
> He left me six horses to drive in my plow

Chorus
> With my **wing, wang, waddle** O, Jack **sing saddle** O,
> **Blowsey boys bubble** O, under the **broom**.

> I sold my six horses and bought me a cow.
> I'd **fain** have made a fortune, but I didn't know how.

> I sold my cow and bought me a calf
> I'd fain have made a fortune, but I lost the better half.

> I sold my calf and bought me a cat.
> A pretty thing she was, in my **chimney** sat.

> I sold me cat and bought me a mouse.
> He carried fire in his tail and burned down my house.

Halliwell (9) recorded this nursery rhyme in 1842 with almost the same wording, but the chorus was: "With a whim, wham, wabble ho! / Jack's lost his saddle oh! / Blossy boys, bubble oh! / Over the brow." He also quoted an 1820 version with the refrain: "With a wimmy lo! wommy lo! / Jack Straw blazey-boys! Wimmy lo! Wommy lo! wob, wob, wob!" On the basis of the reference to Jack Straw and his blazey-boys, Halliwell claimed this to be a relic of the past "in the form of a nursery rhyme, but in reality, part of a political song, referring to the rebellious times of Richard the Second."

Jack Straw was one of the leaders of the peasant revolt of 1381, a protest against the feudal system. Among other things, he led a raid against the Savoy on the Strand. Noted for its vastness and its richness, this medieval palace belonged to the Earls and Dukes of Lancaster for generations. It was reputed to be the most magnificent castle in England. Straw and his followers burned it down and destroyed its treasures. (Lindsay, *The Peasants' Revolt 1381*, 106–07.) So, the "blazey-boys" literally set the place ablaze.

Through the ages there have been many stories and folk songs of silly characters who happily make increasingly bad bargains. One is Hans Christian Anderson's "What Papa Does Is Always Right" (a delightful tale which I heartily recommend). A similar theme is used in an English story (based on an old German folktale) called "The Story of Mr. Vinegar."

I can't tell you due to lack of knowledge; a common British way of saying, "I don't know."

wing, wang, waddle This phrase might have referred to the provisions for a trip. "Wing" could have been the slang term for a quid of tobacco. "Wang" may be a variant of "whang," a lump, a large piece, or a slice, especially of bread or cheese. "Waddle" was a dialectal term meaning "a sloppy mess," perhaps bad tea or broth. "Wing, wang" may also have been a shortened form of "wingle-wangle," meaning weak or shaky. Then "wind, wand, waddle" would mean "weak broth."

sing saddle to give the cry, "Saddle up!" At the time of the peasant revolt in the late 1300s, the letter **a** in "w**a**ddle" and "s**a**ddle" probably had an "ah" sound, making an even stronger rhyme.

blowsey red-face, untidy, disheveled, slovenly.

bubble A Scottish and Northern dialect word for "weep, snivel, blubber."

broom These are the common European bushes with several yellow flowers and long, slender branches from which sweeping brooms can be made

fain gladly, willingly, with pleasure. This adverb is now archaic or poetic when used next to "would." Otherwise, it's obsolete.

chimney (obsolete, except in some dialects) As a British expression, it meant "a flat place *near* the fire, a hearth" (as opposed to the American usage: "a hollow structure *above* the fire").

The next chapter's poems are grouped under sub-titles:

CHAPTER 7

Taunts and Satire: Making Fun of Others

Tattle-tale Taunts:

I'll tell my own daddy, when he comes home
All the good work my **mammy** has done.
She has **earnt** a penny, and spent a **groat**,
And **burnt** a hole in the child's new coat.

Weary mothers, after listening to the tattle-tale refrain of "I'm gonna tell!" all day long, may have sarcastically spoken these lines.

mammy a variant of "mamma" or "mama." The OED shows no record of it before 1500. All three variants were chiefly British English. (Although by the 19th century, "mammy" came to be used in America as a southern dialect word referring to a black woman who was taking care of white children.)

earnt earned. During the English Renaissance (late 15th to the 17th century) the /d/ sound at the end of words often became /t/. So, "salad" became **salat** and "burned" became **burnt**. This happened to the past tense form of many irregular verbs and is still heard in some of the American dialects, but is more common in British English. Other examples are: dreamt, knit, knelt, learnt, leapt, leant, spelt, spilt, and spoilt. Interestingly, the verbs "spent," and "felt" have not yet returned to their 14th century regular verb forms of "spended" and "feeled." (If you are a prescriptive grammarian, beware, because the word "lended" is slipping back into some informal dialects!)

groat fourpence (see above, page 18 for more information). The phrase "earnt a penny and spent a groat" sounds as if it might have been a proverbial expression, much like "penny-wise and pound-foolish."

We now have enough time markers to give an approximate date for this nursery rhyme:

- The word "mammy" wasn't used before 1500.
- The words "earnt" and "burnt" weren't used until the late 1400s.
- The groat coin was not minted after 1662.

Therefore, the rhyme was probably composed sometime between the early 1500s and the late 1600s.

Tell-tale Tit
Your tongue shall be slit,
And all the dogs in the town
Shall have a **wee** bit.

Poems of such macabre nature are seldom found in contemporary nursery rhyme anthologies. But the threat to cut out the tongue was based on actual fact. In former times the tongues of liars and perjurers were removed. This form of punishment was part of the "lex talionis" (that is, the law of retaliation) in which the part of the body used to commit the crime was mutilated or removed. Thus, thieves would lose their hands and spies would lose their eyes.

This type of punishment was practiced for thousands of years. It goes back to Hammurabi's Code of Babylon (1750 B.C.) and was used in England until the early 1500s. Cutting off ears and hands continued until the 1700s.

tell-tale a tattle-tale.

tit (archaic) This was a slang word used since 1590 as a disrespectful term for a girl or woman, comparable to "hussy" (which originally was just a short form of the Old English word "huswif," that became our Modern English "housewife.")

wee little. Originally Scottish, this word wasn't used in England's dialects until the 18th century.

Name-calling:

> Charley **wag**.
> Charley, wag,
> Ate the **pudding**
> And left the **bag**.

wag a joker. Perhaps this is a shortened form of the obsolete word "waghalter," a rogue, joker (which is similar to the German "waghals," a dare-devil).

pudding a kind of sausage (see "pudding-stick," on page 93)

bag the animal gut into which the pudding ingredients were stuffed. The plural form, **bags**, is used in the Scots and northern British dialects for "entrails, stomach."

> Teeter, teeter, little Peter
> Took a wife and then he beat her
> Many times, in **common meter**.

This may have been a rhyme to chant while going up and down on a seesaw or "teeter-totter," but unless Peter is just tapping her gently, it isn't something we would want today's children to say, as we continually try to do away with physical abuse against women.

common meter In music, 4/4 time is common measure or common time; four "beats" to the measure.

Political Satire:

> **Doctor Sacheveral**
> Did very well,
> But **Jacky Dawn**
> Gave him a **warning**.

Doctor Sacheveral Dr. Henry Sacheverell (correct spelling) was an English clergyman of the Anglican church who advocated extreme Tory and high church views during the reign of Queen Anne. He was officially condemned in 1709 for "seditious libel," which brought about great popular indignation. According to one source, "His abilities, even to writers of his own side, were very slight." (*Encyclopedia Americana*) Yet his inflammatory sermons were so emotional, both in language and delivery, that in 1709 when the House of Commons impeached him, 40,000 copies of his "St. Paul's sermon" were circulated.

An iron stove door was invented in the 1700s which directed the air towards the fire. This was called a "blower," but also known as a "sacheverell," after he who blew the fires of discontent.

Jacky Dawbin This would be John Dolben, one of the parliamentarians who was instrumental in the impeachment of Sacheverell (whose "punishment" was that he should stop preaching for three years!). Dolben died in 1710 when the furor was at its peak, and one of Sacheverell's many followers wrote him this epitaph:

> Under this marble lies the dust
> Of John Dolben, the chaste and just.
> Readers, read softly, I beseech ye,
> For if he wakes, he'll straight impeach ye.

Ironically enough, Dolben's father, John Dolben Sr. (d. 1686), was the archbishop of York and was strongly opposed in his day for using high church practices, with a heavy emphasis on traditional liturgy, vestments, sacraments, and priestly authority similar to those used in the Roman Catholic church. Archbishop Dolben was also, by the way, a close friend of Dr. Fell, the subject of another nursery rhyme:

> I do not like thee, Doctor Fell,
> The reason why I cannot tell,
> But this I know, and know full well,
> I do not like thee, Doctor Fell.

Taunts and Satire: Making Fun of Others

These lines were written by Thomas Brown, the 17th century satirist. The story goes that John Fell, dean of Christ Church and bishop of Oxford, threatened to expel Brown from Oxford unless he could translate the lines from Martial: "Non amo te, Seabed, nec possum dicers quare; / Hoc tantum possum dicere. Non amo te."

Brown had plagiarized the Latin words to write his English poem.

warning pronounced as /warnin'/. In Elizabethan English, the final /ng/ in unstressed syllables was /n/ (as now, informally).

> **Hector** Proctor was dressed all in green.
> Hector Proctor was sent to the **Queen**.
> The Queen did not like him, no more did the King.
> Hector Proctor was sent back **again**.

This has been a very popular poem for a long time and has appeared in most of the children's nursery rhyme books that I've read. However, it's no known for sure who **Hector** was. At any rate, here are a few guesses:

In 1569, Thomas Percy, the Earl of Northumbria, revolted in the interest of Mary, Queen of Scots. When the rebellion failed, he took refuge in Aberdeen under the protection of Hector Armstrong (or Hector Graham, as the DNB calls him) of Harlaw, a robber-chieftain who plagued the area. The protection, however, turned out to be hollow. In the following year, Hector, for a sum of money, turned him over to the regent of Scotland, and two years later, Thomas Percy was beheaded in England.

But Hector himself didn't fare much better. After the betrayal, he prospered poorly and eventually died a beggar by the roadside. The story of his misdeed gave rise to a popular expression: "to wear Hector's cloak," which meant 'to receive the right reward for treachery.'

Semantic shifts are often interesting, and the etymology of "Hector" is no exception. Originally, the word had a good connotation, for it meant 'a valiant warrior' like Hector, the Trojan hero in *The Iliad*. Later it meant 'a swaggering fellow, a swash-buckler.' However, eventually it acquired a negative connotation and was used as a slang expression to refer to a 'blusterer' or 'bully.' It was frequently used this way in the second half of the 17th century and came to be applied specifically to a set of disorderly young men who roamed the streets of London.

Another supposition for who Hector was comes from Katherine Elwas Thomas who, in 1931, wrote *The Real Personages of Mother Goose*. She believed that **Hector** referred to Edward Seymour, Earl of Hereford and Lord Protector of England, who was sent by Henry VIII to invade Scotland. This he did in 1544, devastating many villages and towns. Thus, the queen regent of Scotland "did not like him," and (according to Katherine Thomas) "nor more did the king," because the Earl did not achieve the intended conquest.

This last theory seems possible, but there are certain problems. For one thing, the name "Hector" is not mentioned; rather, we are asked to accept "Hertford" as the earlier form of the name. For another thing, no conquest was actually intended. The invasion was conceived only as a punitive raid (because Scotland did not agree to the marriage of Henry's son to Mary, Queen of Scots) and as a "back-door" protection while England invaded France. (Lacey Smith, *Henry VIII*, 200–01)

Queen . . . again These two words sort of rhyme (poets call this a "near rhyme") but not exactly. "Again" rhymes with "men" or "in" for American English (OED lists it as an alternate pronunciation in the UK), but "again" rhymes with "main" in British English. In either case, there does not seem to be an exact rhyme here. In the history of the English language "again" had over 40 different spellings, including "agen," which was commonly used from the 13th to the 18th century (and from which the American pronunciation may have come). The Old English word "cwen" for "woman" or "queen" would have rhymed well with the British pronunciation of "again," but in this poem, we probably should just be satisfied with the strong rhyme between "green" and "Queen" in lines 1 and 2.

Poking Fun at Pomposity:

Good people all, of every sort,
    Give ear unto my song.
And if you find it **wondrous** short,
    It cannot hold you long.

In **Islington** there was a man,
    Of whom the world might say,
That still a **godly race** he ran,

Taunts and Satire: Making Fun of Others

>
> Whene'er he went to pray.
>
> A kind and gentle heart he had
>   To comfort friends and foes.
> **The naked every day he clad**
>   When he put on his clothes.
>
> And in that town a dog was found.
>   As many dogs there **be** —
> Both mongrel, puppy, **whelp**, and hound,
>   And curs of low degree.
>
> This dog and man at first were friends,
>   But, when a **pique** began,
> The dog, to gain some **private ends**,
>   Went mad and bit the man.
>
> Around from all the neighboring streets
>   The **wondering** neighbors ran
> And swore the dog had lost his wits
>   To bite so good a man.
>
> The wound **it** seemed both sore and sad
>   To every Christian eye.
> And while they swore the dog was mad,
>   They swore the man would die.
>
> But soon a wonder came to light
>   That showed the rogues they lied —
> The man recovered of the bite.
>   The dog it was that died.

    According to Baring-Gould (48–50), this poem was written by the prominent Anglo-Irish writer Oliver Goldsmith, who may have helped edit one of the first "Mother Goose" books, *Mother Goose's Melody: or Sonnets for the Cradle* (London: John Newberry, c. 1765). Goldsmith had written many of the jesting notes and maxims therein.

wondrous astoundingly. (see above, "wonderful hot," page 10)

Islington a posh and respectable borough in London. Charles Lamb, the English critic and essayist, lived there for a while. (Pronounced as /**iz** ling tn/)

godly race a pun on the metaphorical "race" that Christians run in striving after holiness (as St. Paul said in Heb 12.1 and 1 Cor. 9.24).

The naked . . . he clad a satirical reference to the passage in Matthew: "I was naked, and you clothed me" (Matt 26.35–36).

whelp (archaic) young dog. Now we use *pup* or *puppy*.

pique a personal quarrel, with resentment caused by wounded pride. This word comes from the French "piquer, 'to sting, prick.' (similar to the archaic use of the English word "piquant," 'piercing' or 'stinging.')

private ends a pun referring to the seat of the man's pants.

wondering amazed, surprised, bewildered. As in: "When what to my wondering eyes should appear / But a miniature sleigh and eight tiny reindeer," in Clement Moore's *A Visit from St. Nicholas* (1822).

it Such a word seems unnecessary now, but *pleonastic pronouns* were once very common. For example: My son *he* likes your boat. (from Gk. "pleo," more)

>If many men knew what many men know,
>If many men went where many men go,
>If many men did what many men do,
>The world would be better—I think so, don't you?

>If muffins and **crumpets** grew already toasted.
>And **sucking** pigs ran about already roasted,
>And bushes were covered with jackets all new.
>It would be convenient—I think so, don't you?

crumpets soft cakes. The term was not known until late in the 17th century. For you baking buffs, here's a 300-year-old recipe which I found in the OED:

Beat two eggs very well. Add a quart of warm milk and water (half and half?). Mix in a large spoonful (apparently any old spoon will do) of barm. (If you're out of barm—a leavening made from the head of a beer—use yeast.) Then beat in as much fine flour as will make it rather thicker than common batter. Bake on an iron plate.

The result, I discovered, is something like a thick, floury pancake—not bad, with a little melted butter and marmalade!

sucking suckling, unweaned.

> The late **Madam Fry**
> Wore **heels an ell high**,
> And when she walked by me,
> I thought I **should** die.

Madam Fry "Madam" was a title of courtesy once applied to women of the highest rank. I'm not sure who this Madam Fry was, but perhaps it was Anna Fry, wife of Joseph Fry of Bristol, a prominent English businessman and type founder. He established a chocolate factory which, after he died in 1787, his wife carried on under the name of Anna Fry & Son. She didn't become "late" until 1803 when she died in London at the age of 83. High heels were out of fashion by then, but that doesn't mean that she didn't still wear them; eccentric habits of the rich and elderly have long been favorite targets of ridicule.

heels an ell high Long heels did not come into fashion until 1670.
But by then "shoes had become truly French, with slender pointed toes and high, slim, curving heels, set well forward." (Payne, *History of Costume*, 384). The style remained popular until the mid-18th century.

The "ell" (as we have seen above, page 34) was a measure of length varying in different countries from about two to four feet. In England, "ell" became an obsolete word after the early 19th century. The German adjective "ellenlang" (an ell long) is a colloquial term for "extremely long." In this rhyme "ell" fits very nicely as a sarcastic exaggeration.

should Today, this word is usually replaced by "would" (or, more frequently, simply contracted to "I'd"), except in a cultured dialect. In formal speech, the distinction between "should" and "would" (I should say so) is the same as between "shall" and "will." (I shall be there).

In most American dialects today, "would" is much more common than "should," which now is primarily used as a substitute for "ought to."

Trade Satire:

The nursery rhymes in this section are jibes against members of various occupations.

> Four-and-twenty **tailors** went to kill a **snail**,
> The best man among them **durst** not touch her tail.
> She put out her **horns** like a **Kyloe** cow.
> Run, tailors, run, or she'll kill you **e'en** now.

tailors This rhyme, first recorded in the late 18th century, made fun of those in the tailoring trade, which had been regarded as an "unmanly" profession since medieval times, apparently just because tailors did the same kind of work as seamstresses.

snail In Elizabethan times this word referred not only to the snail with a shell, but also to its less attractive cousin, the slug.

durst This is the archaic and dialectal past tense of "dare." It was formed from the Old English "dorst." (Our word "dare" comes from OE "dearr,"). Notice that "durst" is used here in a negative expression and is followed by "not." In the 20th century, the OE /s/ sound survived in the present tense of "dare" when used negatively. In the mid-1950s, I heard—mostly from elderly folks—"daresn't," "darsn't," and "dasn't" as contractions of "dare not." As a youngster, I often heard my Uncle Dave (born in 1882 in northern New York) use the word "dasn't" in the same sense that we use "shouldn't," as in "I dasn't have any more coffee, or I'll be up all night."

horns The heads of most large snails have two sets of soft, harmless, horn-like tentacles, upper and lower. The upper ones are longer, and the tips are used for seeing, smelling, and tasting.

Taunts and Satire: Making Fun of Others

Kyloe (a Scots term) A hardy breed of small, shaggy cattle with long horns. Kyle cows were reared in the Highlands and Western Islands of Scotland.

e'en even. The /v/ sound between vowels was sometimes dropped in Early Modern English (1450–1750) and occasionally is still heard, e'en now in Modern English (1750-present), for example in ("ne'ertheless") or in poetry ("o'er the hills and far away").

> **Millery**, millery, **dustipole**,
> How many sacks have you stole?
> Four-and-twenty and a **peck**,
> **Hang** the miller up by his neck!

After the harvest was in, it was a time of high activity at the mills, for all the farmers would be converging on them at the same time to have their grain ground into flour. With so many rapid transactions taking place amidst the bustling confusion, it probably wasn't too difficult for a greedy miller to shortchange someone a few bags. But even if a mix-up were not his fault, the harried miller would be the easiest to blame. At any rate, suspicion of foul play occurred often enough to give rise to the old English proverb, "Many a miller, many a thief."

millery This word really dates this ancient poem. It's a Middle English form of the word "miller" (also spelled *millere, mellere,* or *myllare*) and was used in Middle English between 1100 and 1450.

dustipole dusty-head. This old nickname for a miller comes from Middle English "dusti" (that is, covered with flour dust) + "pole," an obsolete form of "poll," *head*. Today the "polls" are the places where the "heads" are counted in a vote. My mother used to call a moth a "moth-miller" or, less often, just a "miller." The name comes from the dusty appearance of its wings.

peck one-fourth of a bushel.

hang Even into the 18th century, people could be hanged for minor crimes: stealing a handkerchief, cutting down a tree, or stealing food, including grain.

This is the death of little Jenny Wren,
And what the doctors all said then.
Jenny Wren was sick again, and Jenny Wren did die.
The doctors **vowed** they'd cure her, or know the reason why.

Doctor Hawk felt her pulse, and, shaking his head,
Said, "I fear I can't save her, because she's quite dead."
Doctor Hawk's a clever **fellow**,
He pinched her wrist enough to kill her.

"She'll do very well yet," then said Doctor Fox,
"If she'll take but one pill from out of this box."
Ah! Doctor Fox, you are very **cunning**,
For if she's dead, you will not get one in.

With **hartshorn** in hand, came Doctor **Tom-Tit**.
Saying, "Really, good sirs, it's only a fit."
You're right, Doctor Tit, you need make no doubt on,
But death is a fit folks seldom get out on,

Doctor Cat says, "I don't think she's dead.
I believe if I try, she might yet be **bled**."
You need not a **lancet**, Miss Pussy, indeed,
Your claws are enough a poor wren to bleed.

"I think, Puss, you're foolish, "then says Doctor Goose,
For to bleed a dead wren can be of no use."
Why, Doctor Goose, you're very wise.
Your wisdom profound might ganders surprise.

Doctor Jack Ass then said, "See this **balsam**, I make it.
She still may survive if you get her to take it."
What you say, Doctor Ass, perhaps may be true.
I ne'er saw the dead drink though; pray, doctor, did you?

Doctor Owl then declared that the cause of her death,
He really believed, was—the want of more breath.
Indeed, Doctor Owl, you are much in the right.

Taunts and Satire: Making Fun of Others

> You as well might have said that day was not night.
> Says **Robin**, "Get out, you're a **parcel** of **quacks**,
> Or I'll lay this good whip on each of your backs."

Before the advent of modern medicine, there were many self-styled physicians who pretended to be adept at medical skills. This satirical poem makes a burlesque of their ineptitude. (Admittedly, it was harder, many years ago, to detect weak signs of life.)

vowed Once quite common, this use of the word has now been replaced with "promised."

fellow This word was pronounced "feller" and rhymes with "kill her" at the end of the next line. "Feller" is still common in dialects in southern Britain and in some parts of the U.S. (see *holler*, on page 181 below)

cunning This was pronounced "cunnin" and rhymes with "one in" at the end of the next line. The /g/ sound in words ending in -ing was often omitted in the 16th and 17th century England (as with "warning," see above, page 55).

hartshorn carbonate of ammonia, commonly known as smelling salts. Hart's horns (deer antlers) were once the chief source of ammonia, which was obtained by rasping, slicing, or burning the horns.

tom-tit a common name for the titmouse, a small songbird about the size of its cousin the chickadee. The Blue Titmouse is often seen in Britain. The name "titmouse" is sometimes misapplied to other small birds, such as the wren and the tree creeper. The most common titmouse in North America is the Tufted Titmouse.

bled Blood-letting (phlebotomy) was a common practice from medieval times up to the mid-19th century, used for many medical conditions to relieve the body of "impure fluids."

lancet a surgical tool, dating at least from the 1400s, usually having two edges and a lance-like point; used for bleeding, or opening abscesses, etc.

balsam an oily or resinous, aromatic medical preparation, usually for external application for healing wounds or soothing pain. It was obtained from various plants and trees, especially the balsam fir. The word "balm" originally meant the same thing, and both words were ultimately derived from the ancient Greek "balsamon."

Robin In English folk tradition, the robin was considered the mate of the wren: "The robin and the wren are God's cock and hen."

For other Robin & Wren poems, see "It was on a merry time" (page 165) and "Little Jenny Wren" (page 175).

parcel a bunch, a group (used in a deprecatory or contemptuous sense). Sometime in the 15th century, the /r/ in the middle of many words was dropped. For this word, it led to the spelling of "passel" or "passell." This spelling and pronunciation continued thereafter in dialectal use. The change was part of a general phonetic development which started in Late Middle English. Thus *curse*, *burst*, and *horse*, for example, became *cuss*, *bust*, and *hoss*. (ODNR, 164) This also explains why we have dasn't as a form of daresn't (see page 60).

quacks individuals who pretend to have medical knowledge, charlatans. First recorded in the mid-1600s, this word is an abbreviation of "quacksalve," and the OED defines it as "one who 'quacks' or boasts about the virtues of his salves." It has also been suggested that, as a verb, "quack" may mean 'to work in a feeble, bungling way.' The Modern Dutch word "kwak" may have similar connotations: *flop* or *thud*.

> Rub-a-**dub**-dub,
> Three men in a **tub**.
> And who do you think they be?
> The butcher, the **baker**,
> The **candlestick-maker**,
> **Turn** 'em **out, knaves** all three.

dub This word comes from the Old English verb "dubbian," to strike, hit. One meaning of the term is "to dress leather by rubbing; to work grease or neat's oil into leather." Perhaps this rhyme was spoken by leather workers to make fun of the "lesser" trades. Maybe it was a working song or chant;

the rhythm seems to be similar to that made by the hand-arm movement while rubbing hard.

tub Also known as the "sweating-tub," it was mentioned frequently in the 17th century literature (for example, in Shakespeare's *Measure for Measure* 3.2.60), and was considered to be a cure for venereal disease. One 19th century slang lexicon (by Farmer & Henley) described the process this way: "The patient was disciplined by long and severe sweating in a heated tub, combined with strict abstinence." (ODNR, 164)

Apparently, there had been some "hanky-panky" going on, as indicated by verses in two other versions of the rhyme (Opie, 376):

> Hey! rub-a-dub, ho! rub-a-dub, three maids in a tub,
> And who do you think were there?
> The butcher, the baker, the candlestick-maker,
> And all of them gone to the fair.

And again:

> Rub-a-dub, three men in a tub.
> And how do you think they got there?
> The butcher, the baker, the candlestick-maker,
> They all jumped out of a rotten **potato**.
> 'Twas enough to make a man stare.

potato was probably pronounced "potater" and had the same end-rhyme as "baker" and "-maker." (See above *fellow* and *feller*, page 62) As used here, "potato" could be a nickname for a provocative woman. (Similar to "tomato," U.S. slang for a woman or girl.) Both the OED and the EDD record that "potato" was used of persons in a pejorative or humorous sense. Here a "rotten potato" could refer to a female with VD. In Elizabethan times, the potato (which in those days referred to the Spanish potato or sweet potato) was believed to stimulate sexual desire, as indicated by Robert Nares' 1822 glossary:

> It is curious enough to see that excellent root...
> spoken of continually as having some powerful
> effect upon the human frame, in exciting the
> desires and passions. Yet this is the case in all the
> writings contemporary with Shakespeare.

baker This worker in flour, like the miller, was often the butt of ridicule. As Farmer & Henley say, "Bakers, against whom severe penalties for impurity of bread and shortness of weight were enacted from very early times, have been the subject of much colloquial sarcasm." They give a number of examples, including the proverbial expression: "'Tis not the smallness of the bread, but the knavery of the baker" and "Pull, devil, pull the baker."

candlestick-maker In Elizabethan English this was very commonly *pronounced* "canstick-maker." In fact, "candlestick" was frequently *written* as "canstick."

turn . . . out This phrase as it is used here could mean either 'to drive out' or 'to dismiss from employment.'

knaves rogues, unprincipled men.

Satire of Humans in General:

> How do you do, neighbor?
> Neighbor, how do you do?
> I am pretty well,
> And how does **cousin** Sue do?
>
> She's pretty well
> And sends her **duty** to you.
> So does **bonnie** Nell —
> **Good lack**, how does she do?

This rhyme is just poking a little fun at one of the "games" people play: the greeting ritual. (For an analysis of this ritual, see Eric Berne's *Games People Play*, 37–40.]

cousin This word used to refer to kinfolk in general or to any near relative other than the immediate family. It was frequently used of nieces and nephews, as well as of cousins in the modern sense. Thus, in Shakespeare's *Hamlet* (1.2.64), the king speaks of his nephew Hamlet as his "cousin."

duty respect, regard. (Modern English would pluralize this, as in "She sends you her regards.") The CD has a quotation from the *Wentworth Papers* of 1730: "... give my duty to Lord Bathirst."

bonnie also spelled "bonny," a common Scots adjective for "attractive, good-looking" or "excellent, fine." It's been in use since the 15th century.

good lack Similar expressions are "alas and alack" or "lackaday." But here it's more in the sense of "Good Lord! or "Good heavens!"

> Two monkeys came from **native wood**,
> To view the **haunts** and ways of **men**.
> Two mortal hours they silent stood,
> And then, content, went back again.

This sardonic nursery rhyme is one of my favorites!

native wood This could be a local or nearby woods, but more likely a virgin woods or forest, unchanged by human hands.

haunts This doesn't refer to places frequented by spirits or ghosts. The word simply means places where people habitually go

men not just males, but humans in general.

CHAPTER 8

Pedagogical Poems

The nursery rhymes in this chapter were used to help or encourage young children to learn their school lessons. We need to remember that before the 19th century *public* education, almost all children were taught by *home* schooling.

With a **tingle, tangle, titmouse**!
Robin knows **great A**.
And B, and C, and D, and E,
F, G, H, I, J, K.

Come hither, pretty cockatoo.
Come and learn your letters,
And you shall have a knife and fork
to eat with, like your betters.

"No, no!" the cockatoo replied,
"My beak will do as well.
I'd rather eat my **victuals** thus
than go and learn to spell."

Come hither, little pussy cat.
If you'll your grammar study,
I'll give you silver **clogs** to wear,
Whenever the gutter's muddy.

"No, **whilst** I grammar learn," says puss,
    Your house will **in a thrice**
Be overrun from top to bottom
    With flocks of rats and mice."

Come hither, then, good little boy,
    And learn your alphabet,
And you a pair of boots and spurs,
    Like your papa's shall get.

"Oh, yes! I'll learn my alphabet.
    And when I well can read,
Perhaps Papa will give me, too,
    A pretty long-tailed steed."

With a tingle, tangle, titmouse!
    Robin knows great A,
And B, and C, and D, and E,
    F, G, H, I, J, K.

tingle, tangle In the 1800s "tingle-tangle" was an onomatopoeic phrase for the ringing of bells (like "jingle-jangle).

titmouse There are several species of this songbird in Britain. (See above, "tom-tit," page 62.) They are long-tailed and usually of dull-colored plumage. Despite the way it's spelled, the name "titmouse" has nothing to do with a mouse.

Historically, here is how the name evolved: In Middle English, it was formed from two words: *tit* and *mose*.

The word *tit* has had two separate meanings for hundreds of years. One definition is "breast," which (with its alternate form "teat") goes back to Old English; in the plural form it's now used in slang English.

However, *tit* was also used as a term for a small animal or object, but actually it occurred in words like "titling" (sparrow) and "titmouse" much earlier than the 1300s, when it began to be used by itself.

The other word, *mose* (or *mase*) was a rare Old English word for titmouse (akin to the Modern German for titmouse, "Meise"). By the 16th century, *mose* had become obsolete as an independent word and had been replace by the longer word for the little bird: *titmose.* As people began to interpret the second part of the word as "mouse," it led to the plural form *titmice.*

This mistaken impression was quite probably aided by the bird's tiny size, dull color, and quick mouse-like movements.

Robin This could refer to a bird, but more likely it refers to the little boy mentioned at the end of this poem. Today, it's a popular name for males or females, but originally it was a nickname for Robert, as are Rob, Robbie, Bob, Bobby, and—in some dialects—Dob or Dobbin.

(In the mid-1900s, Dobbin was a common name for a horse.)

great A British for capital A.

victuals Before the spelling was changed in the 18th century (by the "Let's-make-strict-writing-rules" grammarians, during the new Age of Enlightenment), this had been written as "vittles" based on the actual pronunciation of the word. (See also "victuals," page 18.) Apparently, in France prescriptive grammarians were active as well because there "vitaille" was changed to "victuaille," with the /c/ pronounced.

whilst while (chiefly British). Actually, *while* is the original form of the word from Old English; *whilst* developed from it in the 1300s.

in a thrice A variant of "in a trice," meaning "in an instant" or "right away." The noun *trice* comes from the verb *trice* meaning 'to haul up' (to raise a sail, flag, etc,) and secure it with a small line.' Therefore, "in a trice" originally meant "in one pull." (See "in a tricey," page 1.)

A Curious Discourse About an Apple-pie:

Says A, Give me A good large slice.
Says B, A little Bit, But nice.

Says C, Cut me a piece of Crust.
Says D, It is as Dry as Dust.

Says E, I'll Eat now, fast who will.
Says F, I vow I'll have my Fill.

Says G, Give it to me Good and Great.
Says H, A little bit I Hate.

Says I and J, I love the Juice the best.
And **K** the very same **confessed**.

Says L, There's nothing more I Love.
Says M, It Makes your teeth to Move.

N Noticed what the others **said**.
O, Others' plates with grief surveyed.

P, Praised the cook **up to the life**.
Q, Quarreled, **'cause** he'd a bad knife.

Says R, It Runs short, I'm afraid
S, Silent Sat and nothing **Said**.

T, Thought that Talking might lose Time.
U, Understood it at meals a crime.

V, Watched it Vanish.

W, Wished there had been a **quince** in.
Says X, Those **cooks**, there's no **convincing**.

Says Y, **I'll** eat, let others wish
Z sat **as** mute **as** any fish.
While **ampersand**, he **licks the dish**.

According to Halliwell (138), this poem was written down about 1800 "by Marshall in Aldermary Churchyard." Opie stated (47–52) that 18th and 19th century ABC rhymes were very popular. In fact, there were hundreds of them published, and the favorites (such as "A was an Apple-pie" or "A was an archer") were reprinted time and time again, (ODNR, 138).

More recently, in 1972, several of these old poems were collected by Ruth Baldwin and chronicled in a large, beautifully illustrated book called *One Hundred Nineteenth-century Rhyming Alphabets*.

K . . . confessed To teach not only how the letters *looked*, but also how they *sounded*, the writer was using phonology. The sound of the letter **K** is heard in the first letter of "**confessed**."

said This word rhymed here with "surveyed" and, a few lines later, with "afraid." In fact, it was often spelled as "sayed" in the 15th and 16th centuries.

up to the life exceedingly, to the extreme. Ironically, we now used the phrase "to death" in the same sense, as in "She pestered me to death for another story."

'cause The letter **c** in this word has the same *sound* as the letter **Q**.

Watched it vanish An interesting bit of poetry here: The end-rhymed couplet "vanishes." The *trimetric* lines "vanish" too. Instead of *three* stressed syllables, this short single line is *dimetric*, having only *two* stressed syllables.

quince Note the **w** sound in "quince." This dark yellow, apple-shaped fruit is still on some grocery shelves today. Quinces are very tart, but at one time they were commonly used in making pies, jams, jellies, and marmalades. My mom had a broad, six-foot high quince bush right next to her flower garden. We kids didn't eat them raw, but we did play catch with them. (Go to Google to find recipes for apple quince pies. Yum!)

X . . . cooks This is further evidence that the poem was used as a phonics lesson, since **X** is pronounced like the **ks** in "cooks."

convincing This is pronounced as **convincin'** and rhymes with "quince in." As we have seen above (page 55, *warning*), the -ng at the end of words became /n/ in Early Modern English and is still very common in informal speech. An old song my dad liked to sing was "Paddlin' Madeline Home." (Published in 1924)

Y, I'll The semivowel /y/ sound is heard in the middle of "I'll."

Z . . . as The /z/ sound is heard at the end of "as."

ampersand This is the name of the symbol for *and* which, on most keyboards, looks like this: **&**. The word *ampersand* is relatively new, first appearing in print in 1835. Actually, it comes from the words "and per se and," literally: [the sign] & by itself [is] *and*.

The "&" character represents the letter **e** of the Latin word **et** (and).

lick the dish probably a reference to the tongue-like appendage on the right side of the ampersand.

Here is another nursery rhyme where the action took place at Banbury Cross, apparently one of the popular towns in southern England. (For more information on it, see page 6)

> Have you seen the old woman of **Banbury Cross**,
> Who rode to the fair on the top of her **horse**?
> And since her return she still tells, **up and down**,
> Of the **wonderful** lady that she saw in town.
>
> She had a **small mirror** in each of her eyes,
> And her nose is a **bellows** of **minikin** size.
> There's a neat **little drum** fixed in each of her ears,
> Which beats a **tattoo** to whatever she hears.
>
> She has in each jaw a fine **ivory** mill.
> And day after day, she keeps **grinding** it still.
> Both an **organ and flute** in her small throat are placed,
> And they are played by a **steam engine** worked in her breast.
>
> But the wonder of all, in her mouth it is said,
> She keeps a loud **bell** that might wake up the dead;
> And so frightened the woman, and startled the horse,
> That they **galloped** full speed back to Banbury Cross.

This poem was a neat little lesson in anatomy for older children. The poem briefly describes the organs of sight, respiration, hearing, eating, and

speech. It's also a riddle for older children to come up with the real names of the body parts.

horse pronounced "hoss" and rhymes with "Cross" in the first and last lines. This is another case of the /r/ sound being dropped before /s/ (as in "parcel," on page 64).

up and down here and there, up and down the streets.

wonderful Here the word is used in the literal sense: 'full of wonder, marvelous, amazing' (as in the German word "wundervoll").

small mirror the pupil. This part of the eye, being smooth, black, and shiny, reflects images by acting as a tiny convex mirror.

bellows This refers to the contracting and flaring of the sides of the **minikin** (tiny) nostrils that take place with the inhaling and exhaling of air during rapid or forceful nasal respiration.

little drum The eardrum is the tympanic membrane that vibrates when struck by sound waves. The vibration is then transferred ("tattooed") to the small bones of the inner ear.

tattoo any continuous drumming or rapping. The earlier form of the word was "taptoo," which comes from the 17th c. Dutch phrase "tap toe," (Shut the tap!) a signal to close the taproom or barroom. So the playing of "taps" also became a signal on a bugle, drum, trumpet, etc. summoning soldiers to their quarters at night.

ivory mill the teeth, of course. But this is more than a figure of speech because most of the tooth, under the enamel, is composed of ivory (also known as dentine), a hard, dense, calcareous tissue.

grinding Unlike other primates with interlocking canine teeth, humans are capable of rotating ("grinding") as well as up-and-down chewing.

organ and flute probably the windpipe and voice box. However, the vocal cords correspond more to violin strings than to a flute.

steam engine the lungs. Since steam engines were not in practical use until the 18th century, we can suppose that the poem did not originate before then.

said rhymes perfectly with "head," so the poem may be Modern English.

bell This probably refers to the uvula, which hangs like a bell from the back of the soft palate above the tongue. It also sways like a bell, which you can see for yourself if you try the following exercise:

To help kids find their *bell* at the top of their throat, tell them: "Go into the bathroom, look into the mirror, open your mouth wide so the *bell* (uvula) is visible, and let loose with a Tarzan yell." When the voice is pitched low, the uvula hangs down vertically; when it's pitched high, velar muscles swing it back to the top of the throat.

For younger children, some of the baby-game nursery rhymes were also pedagogical poems. For example, the infants could learn the names of the different parts of the face and what each part did.

My parent loved to use this one with me: "Head-acher, Eye-winker, Nose-smeller, Mouth-eater, Chin-chopper, Bread-basket (the throat), Giddy, giddy, giddy, giddy, goo!" They'd gently touch each part of my head, until they got to the "giddy" words, then they'd vigorously tickle my chest. My response? I'd giggle like crazy, and then I'd say, "Do it again!"

galloped If you're dandling a small child on your knee, this would be a good time to bounce your leg up and down as you "gallop full speed."

Johnny's **clocked stockings**
Ran off with his shoes.
His necktie ran off with his **collar**,
The culprit was "found,"
Says the next morning's news,
And each one was "fined" a **dollar**.

This was an American poem (judging from the use of **dollar** in the last line) and it was a grammar lesson to teach children the correct past tense forms of the verbs "find" and "fine."

clocked stockings long knee socks embroidered with "clocks," bell-shaped patterns in silk thread sewn on the sides of stockings. They have been in fashion since the 1500s, and were first worn by men. Since the 1900s, as dresses became shorter, women's clocked stockings have become popular as well. (The origin for this word comes from "klok," a Dutch word for *bell*)

collar Detachable collars, completely separate from the shirts, were once quite common. They were invented in 1827 by Hannah Montague in Troy, New York, after she snipped off the collar from one of her husband's shirts to wash it, and then sewed it back on. The popularity of removable collars faded in the 1920s and 30s, but they are still worn by Roman Catholic and some Protestant clergy.

(So, the date for this poem could be early 1800s to early 1900s.)

> Little Bob Snooks was fond of his books,
> And loved by his **usher** and master
> But naughty Jack Spry, he got a black eye,
> And carried his nose in a **plaster**.

usher an assistant to a head teacher or school-master; a teacher's aide. This was once a common term in Great Britain, but now it is obsolete.

plaster A bandage made of muslin or some similar material, infused with honey or pitch, and applied to the skin. It was adhesive at the temperature of the body and was used for external injuries. A "plaster" is now the British word for a Band-Aid.

CHAPTER 9

Models, Maxims, and Morals

These poems were designed to set good examples, to teach proper manners and good behavior, or to point out the wisdom of right actions and the folly of bad ones.

> As I was going up **Primrose Hill**,
> Primrose Hill was dirty.
> There I met a pretty Miss,
> And she **dropped me a curtsy**.
>
> Little Miss, pretty Miss,
> Blessings **light** upon you.
> If I had **half-a-crown** a day,
> I'd spend it all upon you.

This rhyme was doubtless used as a model for good manners. The idea of using poems or stories to teach proper behavior is an old one. *Beowulf* was, in many respects, a "courtesy" book. That is, through stories of brave, noble, and respectful deeds, it taught young princes and thanes (elite warriors) how to act in a courtly manner.

Primrose The yellow Evening Primrose (so called because its blooms close up at sunset) is still a popular garden flower. Believe me: this perennial can spread quickly and cover a *wide* area.

Primrose Hill is now a posh area in the London Borough of Camden, with green spaces and beautiful views.

dropped me a courtesy made a curtsy for me. (This older spelling of "curtsy" was often used from the 16th to the 18th century.) The description of the hill was used to emphasize the extreme politeness of the girl's action. That is, she bent down for a curtsy, even though her dress might get soiled with dust or mud because the hill was dirty.

light to land, fall, or descend upon; as might a piece of good fortune.

half-a-crown a coin worth two-and-a-half shillings. (In the mid-1900s it was worth about 60 pence.) The coin was minted from 1526 to 1969.

> Come when you're called.
> Do as you're **bid**.
> Shut the door after you.
> Never be **chid**.

    During the 17th and 18th centuries, the duties mentioned in the first three lives were expected of house-servants. Apparently, the formula was not directed at children until the 19th century.
    I wonder why. Were parents more tolerant in times past?

bid told, commanded.

chid scolded, chided.

> **Hickle** them, **pickle** them,
> Catch them and **tickle** them.
> I'll teach the villains
> To eat my fine pears!
> **Gobble** them, **hobble** them,
> Till all of them **fancy**
> They have fallen downstairs.

Hickle to chastise, rebuke, scorn. It was a dialectal form of "heckle" used in the early 1800s. Occasionally it had a harsher meaning: to beat, or to "rake over the coals."

pickle This was used in a figurative sense. There are a couple of different possibilities.

One meaning was to rub salt (or salt and vinegar) on the back after flogging. This was a nautical term referring to a form of punishment used on sailors—primarily during the 18th century.

From the 16th to the 18th century, "a rod in pickle" was a common threat of impending punishment, based on the practice of pickling rods in brine or urine to make them tougher. So "pickle" in this poem could have meant to spank or whip with a "pickled" switch. Quite a stiff punishment for eating pears.

tickle to beat. A 19th century expression was "tickle them with the birch."

Gobble (obsolete) U.S. slang: to grasp, seize, "collar."

hobble early 19th century slang: to take into custody, to "nab."

The vocabulary of this next nursery rhyme points to an American origin in the first half of the 19th century:

> A little **cockerel**, pert and vain,
> Grown fat and fierce by eating grain,
> The only pet of mother dear,
> Would **brook** no other cockerel near.
> And e'en when other cockerels crowed,
> You'd think with rage he'd soon explode.
>
> One day a pond he chanced to pass
> And glancing in, as in a **glass**,
> He saw himself reflected there.
> He paused an instant just to stare.
> Believing that a foe he'd found,
> Straight in he dashed and so was drowned.

This rhyme reminds me of two pieces of traditional literature:

The first is the Greek myth of Narcissus, the beautiful young man who saw the reflection of himself in a pool. He fell so much in love with himself that he couldn't stop staring at his own image, and he continued to stare day after day until he died. A plant grew where he had been, and it turned into a flower so beautiful that it was named Narcissus. Today his name is also found in the English word "narcissistic," being in love with oneself, egocentric.

The other traditional story is one of Aesop's fables about a dog that was carrying a bone in his mouth and saw a reflection of himself in a stream. He thought it was another dog with a bone. Greedy that he was, he dropped his bone into the water so he could get the other one. He ended up, of course, with nothing.

cockerel (archaic and dialectal) a young rooster or cock (from OE "cocc," a male bird). Roosters are infamous for being very bold and brash, hence the term "cocky." Apparently, the term "cockerel" is a diminutive form of "cock," just as the freshwater fish "pickerel," means a small pike.

The word "cockerel" was used by Shakespeare in *The Tempest* (2.1.28–31). A bet was wagered on which of two talkative men would "crow" first. Sebastian said the elderly Gonzalo, "the old cock," would be the first to start gabbling; but Antonio bet on young Adrian, "the cockerel," and won.

brook to put up with, tolerate, (from Old English, "brucan," to use, to possess.)

For example: The stern teacher would brook no opposition in class.

glass a mirror, a looking-glass.

> Old **Toby** Sizer is such a miser,
> No cloak he'll buy to keep him **dry, sir**.
> He'll not permit his neighbor, Randal
> To light his pipe by his short candle,
> For fear, he says, he might **convey**
> A little bit of light away.

This old poem aptly illustrates the stupidity of stinginess.

Toby a name used a good deal in the 17th century (a diminutive of "Tobias" or "Tobiah.")

dry, sir pronounced /dryzer/ and rhymed with "miser." In Renaissance English, the /s/ sound in the middle of words was pronounced as /z/. So "listen" was pronounced as /lizen/.

convey This word was used here in the obsolete sense of "to carry off clandestinely, to make away with'" or, euphemistically, "to steal."

> **Crossparch, draw** the latch.
> Sit by the fire and **spin**.
> Take a cup and drink it up.
> Then call your neighbors in.

Some good advice here: if you're grumpy and can't get along with people, go off by yourself for a while and do a quiet activity until you're in a better mood.

crosspatch (archaic, dialectal) a grouch, a bad-tempered or irritable person. It comes from "cross," (ill-tempered) + "patch," (a fool, dolt, or clown). Schmidt (*Shakespeare Lexicon,* 843) said that many fools in the 16th century had the nickname of "Patch." For example, this was the name of Cardinal Wolsey's famous jester in the early 1500s.

draw pull, close. Now used mostly in "drawing the curtains shut."

spin use a spinning wheel. Mahatma Gandhi found peace of mind while using his portable spinning wheel. He was fond of saying, "The music of the wheel will be as balm to your soul. I believe that the yarn we spin is capable of mending the broken warp and weft of our life . . ."

"Early to bed and early to rise makes a man healthy, wealthy, and wise." Even back in the 1400s this was called an "olde english proverbe," and it seems to be the keynote of the rest of the nursery rhymes in this chapter.

> Kitten, **kitten**, in my lap.
> Now be good and eat your **pap**.

> We'll have a nightcap for your head,
> And put you in the **trundle bed**.

kitten here, probably just an affectionate name for the baby.

pap a semi-liquid baby food made of bread, meal, etc. and moistened with water or milk. The word had been used since the 1400s. It may once have been a term for breast milk, since "pap" is also an archaic word for "nipple" or "teat."

trundle bed a low bed on casters (trundles), rolled under a higher bed when not in use. The word "trundle" comes from the same root as the verb "trend," to turn. And yes, trundle beds are still popular.

> "Come, let's to bed,"
> Says Sleepy-head.
> "Tarry a while," says Slow.
> "Put on the pan," says **greedy Nan**,
> "Let's **sup** before we go.

greedy Here the word has a specialized sense of "wanting to eat and drink too much, gluttonous." The word "greedy" comes from an Old English word meaning "hungry."

sup This was the verb form of "supper" used since the Middle Ages.

Nan a familiar form of "Ann." The OED claims it was used in the early 18th century as a nickname for a serving-maid, but in 1896 Farmer & Henley (*Slang and Its Analogues*) found a 1598 manuscript that used "Nan" for *maid*.

From the late 17th to the mid-19th century, "Nan" was also a nickname for a prostitute. (This usage may have been influenced by the fact that in Elizabethan times the word "nun" was sometimes employed sarcastically to refer to a prostitute. In the late 1500s, the poet Christopher Marlowe used the word that way.)

Probably because of its association with women of low status, the name was not used among "respectable" folk, who replaced it with "Nancy" in the 18th century. In the 1900s "Nan" came into popular use again, its former negative connotations forgotten.

> **Robin and Richard** were two **pretty** men.
> They lay in bed till the clock struck ten.
> Then up starts Robin and looks at the sky.
> "Oh, brother Richard, the sun's very high!
> You go **before**, with the **bottle and bag**,
> And I will come after on little **Jack Nag**."

Robin and Richard In 1906, Lina Eckenstein said that in England the names Robin and Richard (among others) were used to represent huntsmen. (*Comparative Studies in Nursery Rhymes*, 182.)

pretty fine, capable (here, used sarcastically).

before first, in front.

bottle and bag For the sake of making an end-rhyme with "Nag," this expression is an inversion of "bag and bottle." Used since the 1600s, it was once a common phrase for the provisions of food and drink.

Jack Nag Here this is used as a proper name, but originally it may have been a common name, "jack nag" (similar to "jack ass," but here signifying a male horse).

Beginning in the 15th century, the term "nag" was also used to refer to a young horse, a small horse, or a pony (similar to the Dutch "negge," small horse). Since the late 1800s, "nag" simply means 'horse' (often used affectionately), but especially one that's old or broken-down.

> **Elsie Marley is grown** so **fine**
> She won't get up to feed the swine,
> But lies in bed till eight or nine,
> And, surely, she does take her time.
>
> Do you **ken** Elsie Marley, honey,
> The **wife** who sells the **barley**, honey?
> She won't get up to feed her swine,
> And do you ken Elsie Marley, honey?

This is part of a much longer ale-house song of the mid-1700s.

Elsie Marley Alice Marley (known to her friends as Elsie or Ailcie) was a real person, born about 1715. She was the attractive owner of a pub in Picktree called The Swan. (Picktree was a village in northern England in the count of Durham, south of Northumberland.) According to Opie (160), "Judging from further verses about her . . . it is evident that the way she served her ale was not the entire cause of her fame, and a contemporary writer confirms that she enjoyed a certain reputation."

is grown has grown, has become. This archaic use of the verb-to-be was carried over from Old English. So, the helping verbs (*am, is, are, was, were*) were used next to some other verbs (such as *come, gone, set, fallen, arrived, departed*, and *risen*) to indicate that a change of place or condition had been completed. For example, "He is risen." (1611 *King James Bible*, Matt. 28.6) or "I am returned." (This verb form was used in the late 1600s in *Paradise Lost*, by John Milton.) In fact, Jane Austen used these verbs the same way in the early 1800s.

fine refined, dainty, delicate, fastidious.

ken know (akin to the German "kennen," to know, to be acquainted with) This word is found chiefly in the Scots dialect, but also in northern England, where Picktree was located.

wife archaic for "woman." It comes from the Old English word for woman, "wif." As used in this rhyme, it's probably short for "alewife." Many languages have a word that can mean either "woman" *or* "wife," as in Greek "gyne," Latin "mulier," French "femme," German "Weib." However, in English the second use of the word has overcome the first, (except in certain combinations such as "midwife," "fishwife," or "housewife," and in certain phrases, such as "old wives' tales").

Apparently, however, "wife" was still used for "woman" in the mid-1900s in some provincial dialects; Trench's *Dictionary of Obsolete English* states: "In the rural districts of central Yorkshire a grown woman is a young wife, though she's not married."

barley Elsie wasn't growing it for barley soup! It's the principal ingredient in malt liquor; and a nickname for strong ale or whiskey.

> Under the **furze** is hunger and cold.
> Under the **broom** is silver and gold.

I can well imagine this proverb done in needlepoint and hanging prominently on a parlor wall.

furze the popular name, since Old English times, of a spiny evergreen shrub with yellow flowers, growing abundantly on wastelands throughout Europe. The bushes have long served as shelter for many a vagabond. Nicholas Breton, writing in 1626, said that after sunrise on a typical Elizabethan day, when most working people are already up and about, ". . . now the beggars rouse them out of the hedges, and begin their morning craft." (Wilson, ed., *Life in Shakespeare's England*, 348)

broom Here we have a word-play on "broom." Like furze, it is also a shrub, but it's the bush from which sweeping brooms were made. Thus, this rhyming proverb warns against laziness and extols industriousness. Slothfulness brings misery, but riches come only through hard work. So, push that broom!

CHAPTER 10

News Reports

Before the advent of mass media, news was carried mostly by word of mouth. The town crier was the official reporter. But news of the latest happenings could travel just as fast—or faster—by way of the proverbial grapevine: in the fields, in the marketplace, across the fence, and in the taverns. No doubt fleet-footed children delighted in being the first to spread the word, be it good news or bad. There would be announcements of new arrivals in town, news of local disasters, or just items of general human interest. The nursery rhymes in this chapter are poetic parodies of such news reports.

>   Hark! Hark! The **dogs do bark**.
>   **Beggars** are come to town.
>   Some in **jags**, some in rags,
>   And some in **velvet gowns**.

dogs do bark Due to their acute sense of hearing, dogs are usually some of the first to notice the approach of strangers. In my hometown, late on a quiet summer's night, we could tell the approach of someone walking up the street from blocks away—not by their footsteps, but by the barking of dogs. If the pedestrian came towards my house, the barking grew louder as our neighbors' dogs took up the call, then would fade away as the person passed down the street, until other dogs took up the call.

Beggars According to Opie (179), "Popular tradition has it that 'the Beggars coming to town' were the Dutchmen in the train of William III."

(Hence, the *velvet gowns*?) After 1688 "Beggars was a common epithet for the Dutch." Another fact to consider: "beggar's velvet" was an old name for "dust bunnies."

jags shreds of cloth, tattered rags. ("Jag" has also been an American dialect word for inebriation. My parents said that if you got too close to a drunken person, you could get a "second-hand jag.")

> Some **up and** some **down**,
> There's **players** in the town
> You **wot** well who they be.
> The sun **doth arise**
> To three **companies**,
> One, two, three, four make we!
>
> **Besides** we that travel,
> With **pumps** full of gravel,
> Made all of such **running leather**,
> That once in a week,
> New masters we seek,
> And never can hold together.

According to Baring-Gould (154): "This rhyme reflects the low opinion held of traveling players by townspeople, who regarded the mummers as being little more than companies of beggars." Or, on the other hand, this rhyme may have been a song sung by the players themselves as they walked from town to town.

up and . . . down here and there, in several places at once within the town. For example, in Shakespeare: "She says up and down the town that her eldest son is like you" (*Henyt IV Part II*, 2.1.113). Today "up and down the street" is still a common expression.

players people who acted in plays. (or an obsolete term for 'acrobats.')

wot know (archaic variant of "wit"). The word was used frequently by Shakespeare, for example, "You wot well my hazards still have been your solace" (*Coriolanus* 1.4.127). The word *wot* rhymes with *not*.

doth does. This was replaced by the northern England form "does," which was in general use by the 16th or 17th century, but "doth" was used poetically even after that time.

companies theatrical groups. Dobson (*English Pronunciation 1500–1700*, 845) states that in the 17th century, the word "companies" rhymed with "arise."

besides moreover.

pumps These were light shoes, originally of a delicate material and color, having no fastening, and kept on the feet by their close fit.

In the 17th and 18th centuries, the term was applied to more substantial low-heeled shoes of this type worn where freedom of movement was required, as by dancers, acrobats, etc.

running leather "To have shoes of running leather" was once a very common phrase and meant 'to be given to rambling about.'

> Tommy **Tonsey's** come from France
> Where he learned the latest dance.
> He has brought a scarlet dog,
> And now the town is all **agog**.

Tonsey (?) perhaps from "tonser," an Early Modern English word for "barber."

agog excited with curiosity, great interest. The word is akin to the French "gogue," "fun, diversion." The French expression "a gogo" is found in such phrases as "vivre a gogo," "to live like a lord, in abundance" and "avoir l'argent a gogo" "to have lots of money," which is similar to the English phrase "money a-plenty" or "money galore." In fact, the French word "gogo" means "galore" and is the source of "go-go clubs" and "go-go dancers." Apparently, that all started in 1947 at a cafe and discotheque in Paris called "Le Whisky a Gogo."

> "Fire! Fire!" said the town crier.
> Where? Where?" said **Goody** Blair.
> "Down the town," said Goody Brown.
> "I'll go **see't**," said Goody Fleet.
> "So will I," said Goody Fry.

Goody This is short for "Goodwife," (just as "hussy" was, originally, short for "housewife.") "Goodwife" was a word that referred to a woman, especially an older woman or a housewife, who was of lowly social status. It was formerly used in New England as a title before the surname, so apparently this rhyme dates back to colonial times.

As Baring-Gould explains it (154), "In Puritan Boston, you were called 'Mister' only if you had the franchise" (owned property worth at least 40 pounds, about $80). "A person without such property, and therefor without the right to vote, was called 'Goodman' and his wife 'Goodwife' or 'Goody.'"

see't see it. This was an Early Modern English contraction. It sounds just like "seat" and rhymes perfectly with "fleet.

> "What's the news of the day,
> Good neighbor, I **pray**?"
>
> "They say a balloon
> **Is gone** up to the moon."

This short poem enjoyed a brief popularity in the summer of 1969 when humans first went to the moon. But long before that, the poem showed the fascination people had in the new science of hot-air ballooning that began in 1783.

pray A common word from about 1500 to 1800, this was used often at the end of a question to add a note of urgency, or courtesy, or curiosity. At first, it had a stronger sense: "to entreat, beseech, implore." It was also written as "I pray thee" or (in 1700s) "prithee." It's still used informally with ironic courtesy, as in "What, pray tell, do you think you're doing?"

is gone has gone. (For more information on this kind of verb usage, see above "is grown," on page 84.)

> **Brave** news **is come** to town.
> Brave news is **carried**.
> Brave news is come to town.
> **Jemmy** Dawson's married.

brave good, great, excellent, splendid (from the Italian word "bravo," meaning "brave, gallant, fine").

is come has come ("is" was commonly used as a helping verb).

carried sent from place to place, usually by word of mouth, but often by the town crier who would read the news regularly in the town square. For hundreds of years, most people were illiterate. But after the invention of the printing press in the 1430s, books, pamphlets, and newspapers became cheaper, so more people learned how to read.

Jemmy This was a nickname for "James." It's not known if Jemmy Dawson was a real person, although there was a Jacobite by the name of James Dawson who, upon being convicted of high treason, was hanged, drawn, and quartered in 1746. The DNB states that "had he been pardoned, the day of his enlargement (so runs the story) was to have been that of his marriage." His fiancee followed his execution and died of grief the same day. The incident was made the subject of a ballad by William Shenstone, recorded in 1875 in *Harland's Ballads and Songs of Lancashire* (which is still in print!).

At any rate, Opie (242) thought that the poem was from the 17th century, based on the fact that the following words were contained in a ballad of 1690, and the lines may be a parody of the above nursery rhyme:

> "Bad news is come to Town; bad news is carry'd;
> Bad news is come to Town, my love is marry'd."

CHAPTER 11

Seasons and Traditional Observations

> **Bounce, buckram**, velvet's **dear**,
> Christmas comes but once a year.

To this short rhyme, Opie (104) added two more lines:

> And when it comes, it brings good cheer,
> But when it's gone, it's never near.

Lines 2 and 3 were recorded together in 1573; limes 1 and 2, in 1639. And all four lines were written down in 1670. Opie (120) says they were used as opening lines for a mummers' Christmas play. Mummers are ones who go merrymaking in disguise during festivals. Every New Year's Day, 10,000 Philadelphians still march in their Mummers Parade!

bounce In Elizabethan times, one of the meanings of this word was "boast, bluster."

buckram a coarse linen cloth, stiffened with glue as a filler.

dear precious, valuable. This word is the usual British term for "expensive" and is still used by some Americans (such as my wife, who grew up in south Jersey in the mid-1900s).

The first two lines were a 17th century proverb and meant: we can boast all we want about mediocre goods, but true quality speaks for itself; and since "Christmas comes but once a year," we should not be reluctant to use, display, and give our best.

> On Christmas Eve I turned the spit.
> I burnt my fingers; I feel it yet.
> **The cock sparrow flew over the table.**
> The pot began to play with the ladle.
> The ladle stood up like an angry man,
> And vowed he'd fight the frying pan.
> The frying pan behind the door
> Said he never saw the like **before**.
> And the kitchen clock I was going to wind
> Said he never saw the like **behind**.

The first four lines were traditionally used in the 19th century versions of the mummers' Christmas play. (Opie, 124)

'**The cock sparrow flew over the table**. This line may be a relic of an Old English parable. It's found in Bede's *Ecclesiastical History of the English People* in the story of how Edward, king of Northumbria, (from 617 to 633) adopted Christianity. One of his wise men, speaking about the brief sweetness of life, compares it to a sparrow in winter who flies through the house—in one door and out another—while the king and his thanes are seated at the banquet table before a fire. "In the time that he is inside, he is not smitten with the storm of winter, but that is the twinkling of an eye . . . So that this life of men appears for a middling space of time; what might go before or what might come after, we do not know." (Dobson, 845)

before This gives us the pun for the poem's last line, because besides meaning "previously," the word **before** can also mean "in front."

behind referring to the frying pan behind the door.

> The **sow** came in with the saddle,
> The little pig rock'd the **cradle**,
> The dish jumped up on the table

Seasons and Traditional Observations

> To see the pot swallow the ladle.
> The spit that stood behind the door
> Threw the **pudding-stick** on the floor.
>
> "**Odsplut!**" said the gridiron,
> "Can't you agree?
> I'm the head **constable**,
> Bring them to me."

A funny exaggeration of what could happen if livestock got into the house.

sow a female pig. (OE "su") In American dialect "soowee," is a call to pigs.

cradle Before the Great Vowel Shift (from about 1400 to 1700), "cradle" rhymed with "saddle" (having the same vowel sound as "paddle). The OED gives an example from 1650: " . . . fair in the Cradle and Saddle too . . ." (Compare this with the Scottish saying: "Fair in the cradle may be foul in the saddle."). In fact, "cradle" kept this pronunciation until the early 1700s. In Modern English, "cradle" rhymes with "fable," or as my mom used to say in the 1950s—when she witnessed my sloppy eating habits—"Fair in the cradle, ugly at the table."

pudding-stick This may be similar to the wooden spoons used today to stir mixtures of dessert puddings. But in the 1700s when this poem was written down, it more likely referred to a slender wooden skewer with which the ends of a gut containing a sausage were fastened.
(For more information on this, see "pudding-string," page 47 above.)

odsplut an exclamation (rhymes with "shut"). It came from the words "ods blud," short for "God's blood!" which started to be used around 1600 to avoid profaning a sacred name. It was a common expression in the 17th and 18th centuries. (Similarly, Modern English has "Jeepers Creepers" for "Jesus Christ.")

constable a local peace officer. The constable of medieval times was the "count of the stable," a high office in a noble or royal household.
    A man of this importance could become the chief officer of the household, the army, or even the kingdom.

This rhyme, like the two before it, was also used as part of the mummers' folk play. The lines are very similar to those in the above poem on page 92. In fact, a version published in 1868 included verses from *both* poems.

Mumming (literally, "playing in masks") dates back to the time of the Crusades (11th to 13th century) with ultimate roots in the Roman Saturnalia festivities. The play itself was a community affair, prepared for and performed by the local people. It usually featured mock battles between St. George (a "Valiant Soldier of the Christian Army") and a Turkish knight (among others), whose wounds were attended to by a quack doctor. The drama was short, simple, and rustic.

In his 1878 book *The Return of the Native* (185–87, 211), Thomas Hardy described it in some detail:

> The lads who formed the company of players lived at different scattered point around . . . The mummers [had no contempt] for their art, though at the same time they were not enthusiastic . . . The agents seemed moved to say and do their allowed parts whether they will or no. This unwitting manner of performance is the true ring by which . . . a fossilized survival may be known from a spurious reproduction
>
> The piece was the well-known play of "St. George," and all who were behind the scenes assisted in the preparations, including the women of each household. Without the cooperation of sisters and sweethearts, the dresses were likely to be a failure. But . . . the girls could never be brought to respect tradition in designing and decorating the armour; they insisted on attaching loops and bows of silk and velvet in any situation pleasing to their taste . . . [Howeve] the Leech or Doctor preserves his character intact: his dark habiliments, peculiar hat, and the bottle of physic slung under his arm could never be mistaken. And the same might be said of the conventional figure of Father Christmas, with his gigantic club, an older man who accompanied the band as general protector in long night journeys from parish to parish, and was the bearer of the purse. The play ended: the Saracen's head was cut off, and St. George stood victor. Nobody commented, any more than they would have commented on the fact of mushrooms coming in autumn or snowdrops in spring. They took the piece as phlegmatically as the actors themselves. It was a phase of cheerfulness which was, as a matter of course, to be passed through every Christmas; and there was no more to be said.

Seasons and Traditional Observations

> **Trip** and go, heave and ho!
> **Up and down**, to and fro.
> **From the town to the grove**,
> Two and two, let us rove.
>
> **A-maying**, a-maying;
> Love hath no **gainsaying**!
> So merrily trip and go!
> So merrily trip and go!

Trip The *first* definition of this verb, according to Merriam Webster (MWCD), is "dance, skip, or caper with light quick steps." This is exactly what's going on here, as youngsters sing and dance around the May Pole. We still hear the old phrase "Trip the light fantastic," which is attributed to a part of John Milton's 1645 poem "L'Allegro,"

"Come and trip it as ye go / On the light fantastic toe."

up and down here and there.

From the town to the grove On May Day eve, in the last day of April, "the young people of the village [went] out overnight into the woods and fields to look for fresh green boughs and flowers, and (some say) to indulge in too free lovemaking." At dawn, "the young men, returning from the woods with branches of birch and larch, stuck them in the ground at the doors of their sweethearts." (Baring-Gould, 188). This practice is alluded to in another May Day carol:

> Rise up, fair maids, fie, for shame,
> For I've been four lang miles from hame,
> I've been gathering my garlands gay.
> Rise up, fair maids, and take in your May.

This, according to Halliwell (252), was an old Northumberland May Day song from Newcastle.

Elsewhere, similar customs were followed. Families in Derbyshire would hang garlands above their doors. And another tradition (still carried out in my own family) was for the children to get up early on May Day morning and fix a "surprise" bouquet of flowers for their mother. This was placed into a small wicker basket and hung outside on a doorknob.

a-maying formed from the obsolete verb "to may," to take part in the pleasures of the month of May (or) to gather flowers in May.

The **a-** prefix is a shortened form of **on**. So originally a sentence like "The boys were on playing" meant that they were in the process of playing (or) they were continuing to play. Today we still use **on** in the same sense when we encourage people to continue doing what they're doing: "Dance on! Sing on! Play on!"

At any rate, after the **on** + a verb with an -ing became shortened from "They were on walking" to "They were a-walking," this verb form continued into Modern English. In fact, it's still used in informal and dialectal English, as when people go "a-fishing" or "a-hunting."

The use of the **a-** prefix may also have been used as a mild *intensive*, to add a little additional emphasis to the sentence:

"He's a-cussin' and a-yellin' enough to wake up the dead!" or

"She was a-runnin' up the hill as fast as she could go."

In Old English the **ge-** prefix also worked as an *intensive*. The Old English verb "ascian" meant "to ask," but "geascian" meant "to ask in order to learn." Similarly, "niman" meant "to take," but "geniman" meant "to take by force."

gainsaying denying. So, the meaning of this line in the poem is: "Love won't take no for an answer."

> Maid Marian is **Queen of May**
> All good children **own** her **sway**.
> Her **waist** is white; her skirt is red.
> A crown of gold is on her head.

Queen of May (also "May Queen") a girl chosen queen of the merry-making on May Day and crowned with flowers.

own (archaic) acknowledge, admit. The term is almost obsolete, except in such phrases as "He won't own up to it," meaning: "He won't acknowledge the fact or admit that he did it."

sway sovereign power, authority.

waist blouse. (This definition has been used chiefly in the United States.)

> **St. Swithin's Day**, if thou dost rain,
> For forty days it will remain.
> St. Swithin's Day, if thou be fair,
> For forty days 'twill rain **na mair**.

St. Swithin's Day July 15. St. Swithin (or Swithun) was Bishop of Winchester (about 50 miles WSW of London) from 852 to 862. He was tutor to Egbert's son Ethelwulf, under whom he was made bishop. (King Ethelwulf was father to Alfred the Great.) A devoted builder of churches and a man of unusual piety and humility, he died in 862 and was buried in the church of Winchester, having asked to be laid where "passers-by might tread on my grave, and where the rain from the eaves might fall on it." A century later monks exhumed his body to be put into the cathedral (Old Minster, the predecessor of the larger imposing Winchester Cathedral). However, the monks were said to have been delayed by violent rains. Hence, the legend originated that if rain falls on July 15, it will continue to rain for forty days. (UWRE)

na mair no more. (Scotland and northern England dialect)

CHAPTER 12

Animals

Animals hold a special fascination for a child. Outside of humans, they are the only other creatures that move about so freely. Animals appeal to many of a child's senses: they run, jump, swim, wiggle, or fly; they make all kinds of different sounds; and many are soft or smooth and pleasant to touch. It's no wonder, then, that animals are frequently the subjects of children's prose and poetry.

In this chapter, the nursery rhymes are, in general, arranged according to the different kinds of animals mentioned in the poems.

> **Barnaby** Bright he was a sharp **cur**.
> He always would bark if a mouse did but stir.
> But now he's grown old, and can no longer bark.
> He's condemned by the **parson** to be hanged by the **clerk**.

Sounds like a pretty gruesome ending, doesn't it? However, according to Opie (68) this rhyme is described in a song, written in 1709, about a Parson's old dog called Barnet, and this version has two additional lines that went something like this:

> I pray good Sir therefore, weigh right well his case,
> And save us poor Barnet; hang the cleric in his place.

This sarcastic parody echoes the theme of the downfall of the righteous, as portrayed in "Good people all, of every sort" (see above, page 56).

Animals

Barnaby This is the English form of the Hebrew name "Barnabas." It was in common use until the early 1700s, but was revived in the mid-1900s.

cur dog. The term is now used only contemptuously for dogs that are vicious or cowardly.

However, at one time it was applied without deprecation, especially in referring to a watchdog (as here) or to a shepherd's dog. The OED states that the *Cheshire Glossary* (1884) defined "cur" as "a good sharp watchdog."

parson a minister in charge of a parish. The word is not related to "parish," but rather comes from Middle English "persone" (person). In many ME words with **e** followed by **r**, the **e** had an /eh/ sound. But gradually, by the 1700s, that vowel sound had often changed to /ah/. So "person" came to be pronounced "parson." Today in southern England, "clerk" and "derby" are still pronounced like "clark" and "darby."

Our colloquial word "varmint" comes from "vermin." This phonological development also explains why we pronoun "sergeant" the way we do.

clerk (rhymes with "bark") a cleric, clergyman. The clerk appears to have been a minor church official, subordinate to the parson. His status and function were probably analogous to those of the present-day deacon. The term "clerk" is defined in Schmidt's *Shakespeare Lexicon* as "a reader of responses in church service." In the 19th century, "clerk" came to refer to a layman in charge of minor ecclesiastical duties.

> A dog and a **cock**
> A journey once **took**.
> They traveled along till it was **late**.
> The dog he **made free**
> In the hollow of a tree,
> And the cock in the boughs of it **sate**.
>
> The cock, not knowing,
> In the morning **fell** a-crowing,
> Upon which comes a fox to the tree.
> Says he, "I declare

> Your voice is above
> All the creatures I ever did see.
>
> Oh, would you come **down**,
> I would hug you **my own**!"
> Said the cock, "There's a **porter beneath**.
> If you'll ask his advice,
> I'll come down **in a thrice**!"
> So he did, and was **worried** to **death**.

made free to clear a space of obstruction; in this case: to clear away debris in order to make a bed.

sate archaic form of "sat" since the 1300s. Rhymes with "late."

fell began.

my own as my own friend. In the 1500s, **down** and **own** had the same vowel sound: /uh-oo/.

porter a gate-keeper, one who's in charge of a door (from French and Latin "porte," door). As opposed to the other kind of "porter" who carries luggage, packages, etc. (from Latin "portare," to carry).

beneath ... death Before 1650 both words rhymed with "bath."

in a thrice immediately, at once. (See also page 70 and "in a tricey," page 1) This noun "thrice" should not be confused with the archaic adverb "thrice" which means 'three times,' as in "once, twice, and thrice."

worried past tense of the archaic verb "worry," 'to seize by the throat with the teeth and tear or lacerate, to kill by biting and shaking.' The word come from Old English "wyrgan," to kill. The "strangle" sense of the word became obsolete by 1600 and is now used only in a milder sense ("The dog worried my old slipper.") Otherwise, the word is usually used in a figurative sense of something worrying us by "gnawing" at our minds.

A look at this poem's rhyme scheme gives us a number of insights into the phonological developments that were taking place at the time of the poem's origin.

From the 1300s through the 1500s, the words "cock" and "took" had similar spellings: cok, tok (or) coke, toke. They also had a similar sound. The vowel **o** in both words sounded like /oh/. But in Early Modern English, after 1400, the letter **o** in cok(e) changed: at first to an /aw/ sound, and later to /ah/, which it still has today. However, the letter **o** in tok(e) followed a different phonetic path: so, at first, instead of rhyming with "poke," it began to rhyme with "duke" and later (between 1650 and 1700) it started to rhyme with "book"—and it still does.

In this poem, the words **cock** and **took** may have had only a consonant rhyme. But if the **o** in both words had an /oh/ sound (in the 1500s, or earlier), these words would've had a vowel rhyme too.

In the past 1000 years, from Old English to Modern English, there have been many changes in the vowel sounds of words, so it's often very hard to determine *why* this was so, or *which* words changed *when*. Sometimes, through the centuries, linguists have scratched down on paper some logical explanations. Sometimes, however, they have just scratched their heads.

At any rate, to over-simplify the history of "late" and "sat:"

In Old English both words rhymed with "pat."
In Middle English, both rhymed with "pot."
In Early Modern English, both rhymed with "plate."
In Modern English, "late" kept this sound, and still does.

But after 1750 or so, "sat" once again rhymed with "pat," and still does.

Judging from all the historical information on the words in this poem, the early 16th century seems to be a logical "guesstimate" for the origin of this nursery rhyme.

> Pussy-cat, wussy-cat, with a white **foot**,
> When is your wedding? for I'll come **to't**.
> The beer**'s to** brew, the bread's to bake,
> Pussy-cat, wussy-cat, don't be late.

foot In Early Modern English (1450–1750) this word commonly rhymed with "hoot" or "boot."

to't to it. A contraction like this was common in Early Modern English. It was pronounced like "toot" and rhymes with "foot" in the first line.

-'s to is to. The expanded forms (such as "The beer is to be brewed." or "The bread has to be baked.") came about since the 18th century.

Up to then, these forms were non-existent or uncommon. (Peters, *A Linguistic History of English*, 238)

> The mice with satin slippers on
> Came slowly dancing through the town,
> Whilst all the cats, turned **Grahamites**,
> Were out in **hoops** to see the sights.
> The ducks and geese in **army blue**,
> By companies came marching through,
> Whilst all the dogs, intent to please,
> Sang **Negro songs** and **German glees**.

Grahamites followers of Sylvester Graham (1794–1851). This Presbyterian minister from Connecticut was a crusader for temperance and dietary reform. From about 1830 to 1840, his lectures on diet attracted a large following, but also drew ridicule from the press. His proposed diet (which he claimed would cure alcoholism) included vegetables, fresh fruit, rough cereal, pure drinking water, and bread made from coarsely ground whole-wheat flour. Both graham crackers and graham flour are named after him.

He also advocated open bedroom windows, hard mattresses, cold showers, daily exercise, and light, loose clothing. There were Graham boarding houses which carefully followed his recommendations. These practices have never died out. In fact, many of his ideas got a fresh emphasis in the 1960s as Americans became increasingly concerned about health. Today we could all benefit if we consciously developed a world-wide effort to have better health for better living.

hoops hoop skirts. In the early 19th century, women's skirts gradually increased in fullness, so that by the 1840s there was a revival of the 18th century hoops. (Large skirts worn over basket-like frames had been the general fashion by 1730.) Only this time it was in a different form: the crinoline, "stiff fabric made of horsehair and linen thread. This was soon replaced by a series of flexible steel hoops, sometimes forming a separate structure and sometimes sewn into the petticoat." (EB & WBE) This remained a popular fashion until the 1870s when it was replaced by the bustle. During the decade after World War II, certain Victorian modes were revived and the crinoline skirt was worn on formal occasions. Should we look for it again around 2040?

army blue At the time when Graham's philosophy had its greatest following, from about 1830 to 1845, dark and/or pale blue uniforms were worn by American soldiers.

Negro songs The African-American rich tradition of spiritual songs and work songs is very extensive, for example "Swing Low Sweet Chariot" and "The Rock Island Line."

German glees The German-Americans brought many folk songs from their European homeland, including "Muss I Denn" and "Schnitzelbank." *Glees* were musical compositions for three or more voices, sung *a capella* (without instrumental accompaniment).

The noun "glee" is archaic as a synonym for 'song' (or 'happiness'). However, it is still common as an adjective when referring to some singing groups, such as a "glee clubs."

> As **Tittymouse** sat in the **witty** to spin
> Pussy came to her to bid her **good e'en**.
> "Oh, what are you doing, my little '**oman**?"
> A-spinning a **doublet** for my **gude** man."
> "Then shall I come to thee and wind up thy thread?"
> "Oh no, Mr. Puss, you will bite off my ear."

tittymouse a small bird." This is a childish or rustic adaption of "titmouse." (see above, page 69)

witty None of my sources had this noun, but apparently, it is an alternate spelling of "widdy," a Scots and northern dialect variant of "withy," which is an old word for "willow." The British willow trees are a common habitat for many songbirds.

good e'en good even(ing). As noted above (pages 39 and 61), in Early Modern English, the /v/ between vowels was often dropped. The word "evening" comes from "even," an Old English word which is archaic now, but began to drop out of use sometime in the mid-15th century and be replaced by "evening." Of course, "evening" and "morning" were originally verbs, indicating the coming of *even* and *morn*, just as "dawning" is still a verb.

'oman According to the OED, this was a 15th century form for "woman." So this poem may be 600 years old. However, later spellings also omitted the /w/ sound.

For example, it was not pronounced in the 17th c. Anglo-Welsh "o'man," the 17–19th c. "uman," and the 19th c. "ooman." Dropping the **w** at the beginning of "**woman**" is unique. This usually occurs only with contractions, such as in the word "zounds" ('God's wounds') or with "I'd" ('I would') and with "I'll" ('I will').

doublet a close-fitting, often elaborate, jacket worn by men of Western Europe in the Renaissance, primarily from the 14th to the 16th century.

gude a Scots and northern form of "good." Usually pronounced as "gwid" or "gweed."

> **Hickory, dickory, dock!**
> The mouse ran up the clock.
> The clock struck one,
> And down he **run**.
> Hickory, dickory, dock.

This well-known nursery rhyme may be one of the oldest limericks in English poetry. (This type of a five-line poem was not given the name "limerick" until the late 1800s when the poet Edward Lear wrote 212 of them.) The earliest version of this rhyme was written down about 1744 in Britain's first important nursery rhyme book: *Tom Thumb's Pretty Song Book*, published by Mary Cooper.

(A 20th century joke goes: "Hickory, dickory, dock. *Two* mice ran up the clock. The clock struck one. The other got away.")

hickory, dickory, dock This little three-word phrase is very difficult to decipher, and no one seems to know for sure where it originated. Here are a few possibilities—*all* of which may be wrong.

If the rhyme began in colonial America, **hickory** could refer to the well-known nut tree, and **dock** is the name of several plants in the buckwheat family, some of which have been used as salad greens.

Dickory is the most difficult word to figure out, but there are at least a few possibilities, each of which is best understood in context:

1. hickory **decorate** dock: This phrase could have been found in an old kitchen recipe. Nuts have long been used as a garnish for salads.
2. hickory, **chicory**, dock: The leaves of chicory were also used for salad greens.
3. hickory, **duckweed**, dock: These three names of common plants may have been chosen at random. Duckweed is a very small green plant that floats in profusion on top of fresh still water and is often eaten by ducks.
4. hickory **dicker** dock: This could have been a shipping dock, made of hickory wood, on which dickers were piled. A "dicker" was a term used by tanners to refer to a parcel of ten hides (from the Latin word for ten "decem"). A quantity of ten was the common European unit of barter, and from the noun "dicker" we get the verb "to dicker" which means to barter, especially on a small scale.

In 1923, in his book *Nursery Rhymes and Tales: Their Origin and History*, Henry Bett suggested that "hickory, dickery, dock" may have been a corrupt form of "hevera, deckera, dick," the ancient Celtic numerals for eight, nine, and ten, used by shepherds to count their sheep (Bett, 60–63). Hmmm. Could be, Henry.

In 1974, when I asked my seven-year-old daughter why the words "hickory, dickery, dock" were used in this poem, she said it's because they've got the "tick-tock" sound of a clock. Hmmm. I do believe she hit on a logical possibility.

run For many years "run" has been a dialectal form of "ran."

Mother Goose for Mothers and Fathers and Others

Pretty John Watts,
  We are troubled with rats—
Will you drive them out of the house?
  We have mice, too, in plenty,
  They feast in the **pantry**.
  But let them stay
  And nibble away—
What harm in a little brown mouse?

 Rats are less timid than mice and have been known to destroy poultry and game as well as stored grain. Their size and jumping ability give them access to many places denied to smaller rodents. People with pet rats know that they are intelligent, clean, inquisitive, inventive, and amiable. Moreover, if you've ever had "a little brown mouse" in your house, you know how much harm it can cause.

pretty One meaning of this word, as used in the 1400s and 1500s, was "clever, skillful." In 1516, the British poet John Skelton wrote, "He said that he was the prettier man than I was, in the opening of locks" (p. 234). And in *A Midsummer Night's Dream,* Shakespeare used it as an adverb: "Lysander riddles very prettily" (2.2.53)

John Watts a common British name, but perhaps this was an ironic reference to the Sir John Watts who fought against the Spanish Armada in 1588. If he could drive off the Spanish Armada, so much the better in driving out rats! **Watts** has a consonant rhyme here with *rats*.

pantry a room for bread and other provisions. In the late 20th century, there were not as many pantries in new-built American homes, but it was a standard feature in older houses, such as the one in which I grew up. In it my mother stored baking utensils, mops, brooms, and—in a large metal can (to keep out any mice)—popcorn, on the cob. But now, pantries are becoming popular again.

  Little **Poll Parrot**   A little brown mouse
  Sat in her **garret**,   Jumped into the house
  Eating toast and **tea**. And took it all away.

ANIMALS

Poll Parrot This nickname for a parrot goes way back to about 1630. I was very surprised to learn that the name "Poll" came from "Mary," but this is how it happened: "Poll" and "Polly" were variant forms of "Moll" and "Molly" which, in turn, were nicknames for "Mary." (Well, okay.) I do remember when my mom and dad would take me to visit a pet store that had a parrot, we would always ask it, "Polly want a cracker?" The nickname was applied to all parrots, regardless of their gender. In fact, in 1853, Halliwell had "Sat in *his* garret" for the second line of the rhyme. (Opie, 353)

garret This comes from the Old French word "garite" (from "garin," 'to preserve, defend'), 'a place of lookout atop a building.' In Middle English, "garrete" still meant 'watchtower,' but as the need for keeping such lookouts diminished, "garret" came to mean the room or part of the house just under the roof, where the lookout used to be.

tea pronounced like /tay/ and rhymed with "away." In 1712, Alexander Pope wrote:

> "Soft yielding minds to water glide away.
> And sip, with nymphs, their elemental tea."
> (*The Rape of the Lock*, 1.61.62)

It was the English pronunciation of "tea" from the early 17th century (when tea was first imported to England) until the mid-18th century. And /tay/ is still the pronunciation in other European languages. However, since other English words ending in -ea (such as *pea*, *sea*, and *plea*) had acquired an /ee/ sound, "tea" was eventually given the same vowel sound—a late comer in the Great Vowel Shift. The older /ay/ sound of -ea- is still heard in such words as "great" and "steak."

> Little Miss **Muffet**,
> She sat on a **tuffet**,
> **Eating of curs** and **whey**.
> There came a **great** spider,
> Who sat down beside her,
> And frightened Miss Muffet away.

This popular rhyme, in style and theme, is very similar to the above six-line poem: "Little Poll Parrot," on the previous page.

muffet Little Miss Muffet is usually pictured as a little girl. However, like Little Poll Parrot, she was probably a *bird*. The word "muffet" (also spelled as "muffit") comes from "muff," the British dialect name for the white-throated warbler. Perhaps so called because this warbler has a conspicuous ring of white feathers around its neck, which brings to mind the cylindrical hand-warming muff worn by ladies in the wintertime.

Opie mentions (with justifiable caution) the theory that Miss Muffet may have been the daughter of Dr. Thomas Muffet, a 16th century collector of spiders! (323) Although "Muffet" appears to be a proper name, the names of animals were frequently capitalized in nursery rhymes.

tuffet The OED defines this as 'a grassy hillock, a small knoll or mound,' and it regards the usual definition ('a hassock, footstool') as "doubtful: perhaps due to a misunderstanding of the nursery rime." The word "tuffet" may come from the Old French word "touffe," 'a bunch of small things: leaves, grass, hair, etc.' (similar to "tuft"). The final /t/ is evidently an English addition.

eating of This is an archaic use of the word "of" which used to come between the verb and object to show that only a part of something was intended. For example: The goats in the meadow were eating [some] of the grass.

curds curd (often used in the plural, as here) is the coagulated substance formed from sour milk and eaten by itself or made into cheese. Middle English used the words *curd*, *crud*, and *cruddle*, all of which came from Old English "crudan," 'to press' (which was also the root of our word "crowd").

It should be noted that the spelling *crud* goes back to the 14th century, but the spelling *curd* did not appear until the 15th century.

It's interesting that the older spelling still appeared around 1900 in certain American dialects which used the phrase "cruds and whey."

The late 19th century folk-speech of Yorkshire (which retained many Middle English and Old English elements) used "cruds" instead of "curds" as well as the verb "cruddle" instead of "curdle."

There is also an American slang term "crud" which means (among other things) 'coagulated dirt' or just 'dirt' in general.

whey the watery part of milk which remains after the thicker part (the curd) has separated by coagulation. The origin of the word doesn't make it sound very appetizing: from Old English "hwaeg," slime, mud.

great (British) big. So, for the Brits, their big toe is called "the great toe" and a very foolish person would be "a great fool."

However, in the U.S. "great" is seldom used in this sense, except when combined with "big" for a stronger emphasis, such as "a great big house," or in certain expressions of quantity, as in "a great deal of rain" or "a great many people." And by itself, "great" in the U.S. usually means 'fine' or 'good,' or even 'wonderful,' for example, "He did a great job." or "That was a great movie."

The next nursery rhyme probably originated in northern Britain.

>When I was a little girl.
>About seven years old,
>I **hadn't got** a **petticoat**
>To cover me from the cold.
>
>So, I went into **Darlington**
>That pretty little town,
>And there I bought a petticoat,
>A cloak, and a gown.
>
>I went into the woods
>And built me a **kirk**,
>And all the birds of the air
>They helped me to work.
>
>The hawk with his long claws
>Pulled down the **stone**.
>The dove with her rouge bill
>Brought me them **home**.
>
>The parrot was the clergyman.
>The peacock was the **clerk**.
>The **bullfinch** played the organ,
>And we made merry work.

hadn't got didn't have. (For information on **petticoat**, see page 20.)

Mother Goose for Mothers and Fathers and Others

Darlington a market town in northern England, locate on the Tees River in County Durham (formerly Durhamshire) about 70 miles southeast of Scotland, now a thriving city of about 50,000 people.

Most likely this nursery rhyme originated in this area, because it has linguistic features of the Northern Midland dialect:

kirk church (very similar to the word for "church" in several north European languages). For the authors in this region, as in Scotland, the /k/ consonant sound was used instead of the /ch/ sound; whereas the dialects in southern England used "church," from the Old English word "circe" (pronounced like /chirch-eh/).

So, why the difference? Well, it goes back to the Vikings. They controlled much of northern and eastern England, and the southern and far western parts of Scotland, for three centuries—from about 800 to 1100. The Norse people initially came as invaders from Denmark and Norway, but eventually stayed as inhabitants, sharing their land and their language with their Saxon neighbors. In fact, their languages were so similar that the Saxons gradually adopted almost a thousand every-day Norse words, such as "*get, hit, let, low, root, skin, same, want,* and *wrong*" (McCrum, *The Story of English*, 71), as well as the word *kirk* that we find in this rhyme.

stone rhymes with **home** here. This poet did not live far enough north to say "stane" (rhymes with "mane") or "hame" (rhymes with "fame").

According to Opie (189), this poem was first written down in 1853 by Halliwell. A later Scots version, recorded in 1870, did use "stane" and "hame."

(Note that the singular word "stone" was used here, even though the plural form "stones" was intended. This usage is still common when referring to building materials. For example, "Put all the tile here, and the brick should be stacked up over there.")

clerk Yet the author of this poem did live far enough north for "clerk" to rhyme with "work." Farther south, in most of England, "clerk" would rhyme with "bark."

The word "clerk" in this poem means 'a clerical assistant,' unlike in the poem above (on page 99) about Barnaby Bright where "clerk" rhymes with "bark" and refers to a minor church official.

bullfinch This could refer to a European songbird, related to the grosbeak, having red on its cheeks, breast, and throat; or it could be any of a number of small, variously colored songbirds, of Europe and Asia, with a short, thick, rounded beak.

CHAPTER 13

Occupations

As folk literature, nursery rhymes reflect life as we live it. And a great part of life is spent working. The joys, problems, procedures, and techniques of various kinds of work were often "brought home" to children by means of poems or songs.

The rhymes in this chapter are arranged under sub-titles. The first five sections of this chapter describe the activities of farmers, blacksmiths, sailors, hunters, and street vendors. Each rhyme in the last section is sort of a medley dealing with a variety of occupations.

Farming

This is the largest section of this chapter—and with good reason. Up until the 20th century, many civilizations in the world were primarily agricultural, so most of the people lived and worked on farms. For example, in 1900 sixty percent of the U.S. population was still rural. (Now it's only fifteen percent.) So, the children's poems of an agrarian society would, naturally enough, deal with growing crops and taking care of farm animals.

> **Ply** the spade and ply the hoe.
> Plant the seed and it will grow.

ply (a shortened form of the verb, "apply"): to use, do work with, handle, to wield vigorously or diligently.

Occupations

> When the sand doth **feed** the clay,
> England woe and **well-a-day**.
> But when the clay doth feed the sand,
> Then it is well with **Angle-land**.

Different plants prefer different kinds of soil. But in general, soil that has too much clay, with only some sand, has poor drainage and deprives roots from oxygen. Whereas light sandy soil, mixed with some clay, is good for growing many crops, like rye, wheat, and white clover. Plus, the soil is easier to work and warms faster in the Spring.

feed one meaning of this word was "to supplement."

well-a-day Also "well-a-way!" Similar to "woe is me." (See above, page 5)

Angle-land a very old name for England. There were two variations in Old English:

"Angle land" and "Engle land," both of which meant "land of the Angles" (as opposed to the Saxons). According to the OED, *Angle* (pronounced something like /on-gall/) was the district in Schleswig, near Denmark, from which the Angles migrated to Britain and was so called because it was shaped like an "angle" or "fish-hook" (from which we get the word "angling," the art of fishing with a hook and line). The language they spoke was *Angle-ish*, and now is *English*.

> **Cock-a-doodle-do,**
> Daddy's gone to **ploo**.
> **Mammy's** lost her **pudding-poke**
> And knows not what to do.

cock-a-doodle-do Only the roosters of English-speaking farmers go "cock-a-doodle-do." In other languages, the sound of his crow is written differently. For examples: in French: "coquerico" or "cocorico," in Italian: "chic-chi-ri-chi," in Spanish: "quiquirequi," in Poruguese: "cocoroco" or "quiquiricui," in German: "kikeriki," in Dutch: "kukeleku."

ploo This is a 15th century form of "plow" and rhymes with "do."

Mammy's short for "Mammy has." (For more on the word *mammy*, see above, page 51.)

pudding-poke the bag in which a pudding (that is, a sausage) was boiled. "Poke" is still used in Scottish and in some U.S. dialects to refer to a small sack or bag. There's an old saying: "Never buy a pig in a poke." (Good advice for not purchasing anything sight unseen.)

> Cock-a-doodle-do!
> My dame has lost her shoe,
> My master's lost his fiddle-stick
> And knows not what to do.
>
> Cock-a-doodle-do!
> What is my dame to do?
> Till master finds his fiddle-stick,
> She'll dance without her shoe.

Most people are familiar with the first verse of this nursery rhyme, but actually there were more verses that followed. (There are variations of this poem, but none before the early 1800s.)

> Little **Bo-peep** has lost her sheep
> And can't tell where to find them.
> Leave them alone and they'll come home,
> And bring their tails behind them.
>
> Little Bo-peep **fell fast asleep**,
> And dreamt she heard them bleating,
> But when she awoke, she found it a joke,
> For they were **still a-fleeting**.
>
> Then up she took her little crook,
> Determined for to find them.
> She found them indeed, but it made he heart bleed,
> For they'd **left their tails behind them**.

Occupations

It happened one day, as Bo-peep did stray
Over a meadow **hard by**,
That there she espied their tails, side by side,
All hung on a tree to dry.

She heaved a sigh, and gave, by and by,
Each careless sheep a **banging**.
And as for the rest, she thought it was best
Just to leave the tails a-hanging.

Bo-peep from the baby game "bo-peep," also known as "peek-a-boo," a nursery favorite for many centuries. (See also, page 8 above.)

fell fast asleep This reminds us of Little Boy Blue, who was "under the haystack fast asleep," when he should have been minding his livestock. It's hard for youngsters to stay alert for long hours. ("fast" has the OE meaning of "firmly." It didn't mean "rapid" till the 1550s.)

still constantly, continually. According to Charles T. Onions' 1911 book *Shakespeare Glossary*, this was "a very frequent meaning in Shakespeare and in Tudor and Stuart times." Even after 1700, it continued to be used in poetry.

a-fleeting disappearing, moving away quickly. The verb "fleet" (from Old English "fleotan") originally meant *float* (and still does in some British dialects). Over the centuries, its meaning gradually shifted from *float* to *drift*, *flow*, *fade away*, and finally to *vanish*. It still appears in such expressions as "a fleeting moment."

left their tails behind them This pun may be based on fact. It is the common practice of most sheep owners to dock the tails of young sheep in order to reduce the danger of flies and maggots and to facilitate the breeding of ewes, and it may make shearing easier.

hard by near, close by. This phrase was frequent in Shakespeare, for example: "How near is he, Mistress Page? Hard by, at street end." (*The Merry Wives of Windsor* 4.2.41).

banging a beating or a spanking.

> Dame, what makes your duck to die?
> **What the pize** ails 'em? What the pize ails 'em?
> They kick up their heels, **and there is that.**
> What the pieze ails 'em?
> **Heigh, ho!** heigh, ho!
> Dame, what makes you ducks to die?
> What the pize ails 'em? What the pize ails 'em?
> Heigh, ho! heigh, ho!
> Dame what makes your ducks to die?
> **Eating o'** pollywogs, eating o' **pollywogs.**
> Heigh, ho! heigh, ho!

What the pize This was an exclamation of an oath used in the same sense as "What in God's name!" or "What the blazes!" The word "pize" was also spelled "pyze" or "pies." The OED says that the origin of the word is uncertain, but perhaps "pies" was used as an arbitrary substitute for "pox," which was used in the same sense around 1600.

and there is that Today Americans usually say, "And that's that."

heigh, ho probably an expression of distress or worry (as on page 44), like "woe is me."

The problem stated here is enough to make any duck-keeper moan. The repetition of phrases makes this rhymes sound like a song, albeit a sad song of lament.

Of course, since 1937, when Disney made the film *Snow White and the Seven Dwarfs*, we think of "Heigh ho! Heigh ho!" as a happy song that the dwarfs sing merrily, whether they're going home from work or off to work.

eating o' eating of (used the same way as on page 108 above).

pollywogs Some people call them "tadpoles," but when we were kids, (in northern New York) we always called them pollywogs. It was a special joy for us every spring to hike down to the local woods, scoop the elusive creatures out of the creek by hand, and carry them home in old glass canning jars.

Occupations

Until pollywogs are about seven weeks old and their legs begin to form, they appear to be little more than heads with wiggly tails, hence their name: "pollywogs," literally *head-wigglers* (in Middle English "polwygles) from "poll" (head) + "wiggle."

Today, "*poll*-takers" count heads of those interviewed. Also, on election days, heads are counted at *polling* places.

So, why was it sad for ducks to eat pollywogs? Ducks could indeed become very sick from eating too many pollywogs. Like other domestic fowl, they are primarily grain eaters, and a sudden change of diet to "raw meat" would be a severe jolt to their digestive system.

> Ho ho ho! Ha ha ha!
> Never saw the like since I was born.
> Pigs in the **pound**,
> Ned's got the **hound**,
> **Four and twenty** cows are in the corn.
>
> Ho ho ho! Ha ha ha!
> Never saw the like since I was born.
> Saddle up the cat,
> Bridle up the rat,
> And hand me down my **dinner horn**.

pound a public enclosure for any stray livestock. Now used mostly for stray cats and dogs (though the term is also used as a holding place for property seized by the official authorities (a car pound). The origin of the word is not known, but it is not found before Late Middle English.

hound This probably refers to the farmer's working dog, which is not around to help gather the stray animals. Therefore, in the last verse, the suggestion is made to commandeer the services of any available animals—including cats and rats!

four and twenty We get the impression that this phrase was commonly used as an indefinite number, much as people nowadays say "a couple dozen." It was often used in nursery rhymes. For example, there are the four and twenty blackbirds in "Sing a song of sixpence." In "Millery, millery, dustipole" (above, page 60), the miller stole four and twenty sacks; and there is also the rhyme "Four and twenty tailors went to kill a snail" (page 61).

dinner horn According to the *Dictionary of American English*, this was an American term used on a farm or plantation (and usually made from an animal's horn) and "suitable for blowing as an announcement of dinner to those working in distant fields." However, it may also have been used to summon the farm hands in case of an emergency or urgent situation—such as we have here.

> **Cushy** cow, **bonny**, let down thy milk,
> And I will give thee a gown of silk;
> A gown of silk and a silver **tee**,
> If thou wilt let down thy milk to me.

This was a charm used by milkmaids to get milk from cows—be they nervous, stubborn, or bewitched.

cushy (dialectal) a call to cows. The 1949 *Word Geography of the Eastern United States* (Kurath, 297) stated that this word was still used in New Jersey as a call to cows during milking. "Cush, cush" is used to call cows in James Herriot's *All Creatures Great and Small*, an autobiography of his early veterinary practice in the farming region of Yorkshire (221, 285). Opie, however, refers to "cushy cow" as a "hornless cow" (137).

bonny bonny one, dear one. Obsolete as a noun, but as an adjective it can mean *good*, *fine*, or *pretty*. Perhaps "bonny" is related to Old French "bon(e)," good.

tee a dialect form of "tie," a buckle or a hair-rope with which to shackle cows during milking. (see **T's**, above, page 37)

> There was an old man who lived in a wood,
> As you may plainly see.
> He said he could do as much work in a day
> As his wife could do in three.

"With all my heart," the old woman said,
 "If that you will **allow**,
Tomorrow you'll stay at home in my **stead**,
 And I'll go drive the plow.
But you must milk the **tidy** cow,
 For fear that she go dry,
And you must feed the little pigs
 That are within the sty.

And you must mind the speckled hen,
 For fear she lay astray,
And you must reel the spool of yarn
 That I spun yesterday."

"**High**, Tidy! **Ho**, Tidy! High!
 Tidy, do stand still!
If ever I milk you, Tidy, again,
 'Twill be **sore** against my will."

He went to feed the little pigs
 That were within the sty.
He hit his head against the beam,
 And made the blood to fly.

He went to mind the speckled hen,
 For fear she'd lay astray,
And he forgot the spool of yarn
 His wife spun yesterday.

So, he swore by the sun, the moon, and the stars
 And the green leaves on the tree,
If his wife didn't do a day's work in her life,
 She should never be ruled by **he**

This old rhyme later became a traditional folksong called "Father Grumble," which has been popular for many years in Britain and America. In the 1960s, I first learned this great song (with a new title "Little Phoebe" and updated lyrics) from James Leisy's folksong book *Hootenanny Tonight* (190). This funny old rhyme is now available from many online sources.

You'd think after the man heard the long list of things to do that he'd stop right there, but no. He gave way to pride and stubbornness.

allow A dialectal term, it was short for "allow me to have my say."

stead place. A very old word (from Old English "stede," akin to Old High German "stat," place) and mostly obsolete now, though it is still used as part of the word "instead."

Tidy cow (an obsolete Scots expression) a cow giving milk. The term "tidy" comes from Middle English "tid," time, a fixed point in time. So, a "tidy" or "timely" cow would be ready for milking at the same time each day. The noun "tide" originally referred to the set times of the day for high tide and low tide.

high ... ho From the 15th century, "high" was an alternate spelling for "hi" and both were originally used to attract attention. The other exclamation "ho" was used in the same way, to get attention, but also as a demand for silence. Since the 17th century, a later version, "whoa" has been used when getting the attention of animals, carrying or pulling a load, to stop.

sore very much. Now archaic or dialectal, this term was once used to intensify the idea of dislike or reluctance, or an action done against one's will.

Compare this to the expressions "sore sick" for very sick and "full sorely," indicating much distress (page 30).

he (?) This may be a special form of "him" used here to rhyme with "tree."

Blacksmithing:

Blacksmiths were once as common as car mechanics are today.

> **Father** Short came down the lane,
> Oh, I'm **obliged** to hammer and smite
> From **four in the morning** till eight at night,
> For a bad master and a worse **dame**.

Occupations

Father a title that was given to a man of advanced age, or position, or both. Announcing that Father Short was coming was probably a warning to the other workers: "Here comes the boss!"

obliged required, under obligation. In this case, it was probably a legal obligation. Apprentices were bound by legal agreement to serve an employer in a trade or handicraft for a certain number of years, sometimes 4 but as many as 7 years, in order to learn its details and duties. The employer, in turn, was legally bound to instruct them.

four in the morning This was no exaggeration. To quote again from the 17th century writer, Breton: "It is now the fourth hour. [Now is] the milkmaid gone to the field, and the spinner at the wheel . . . and the cunning workman will be trying of his skill." (as recorded in *Life in Shakespeare's England* (348).

dame a lady of rank. In this poem, it would be the master's wife.

> "Robert **Barnes**, my fellow fine,
> Can you shoe this horse of mine?"
> "Yes, good sir, that I can,
> As well as any other man.
> There's a nail, and there's a **prod**.
> Now, good sir, your horse is shod."

This was a very popular rhyme. There are over twenty (should I say "four and twenty?") variants of this poem. The nursery rhyme on the next page is one of them. This poem has been used for baby games— knee bouncing and toe tapping— and for getting children to put on their shoes. Opie said, "This rhyme is heard particularly in Scotland and the north country." (366)

Barnes As a Scots surname, this may well have come originally from "bairn," (*child*). (Reaney, *A Dictionary of British Surnames*). The form "barne" was used from the 14th to the 17th century, for example in Shakespeare: "they say barnes are blessings" (*All's Well That Ends Well*, 1.3.27); and "barn" still survives in northern England as a word for "child."

prod probably a kind of nail. Opie defines it as "an iron pin used in making patterns." (366). In smithery, a pattern is the full-scale model used for making a sand mold into which molten metal is poured to form a cast.

> Is John **Smith** within?
> Yes, that he is.
> Can he set a **shoe**?
> Aye, **marry, two**.
> Here a nail and there a nail,
> **Tick, tack, too.**

Smith This name was ultimately derived from "smith" or "smithy," a blacksmith.

shoe It was usually spelled "scho(o)" from the 14th to the 16th century and was pronounced like "show" in some northern dialects. Around 1512, the poet John Skelton rhymed "shoes" with "hose" and "foes." However, by the second half of the 16th century, "shoe" had acquired its present pronunciation.

two (OE *twa*) two). The word "two" formerly rhymed with "grow," but by the 1500s, it rhymed with "grew."

too This was an alternate spelling for "toe" between the 14th and 16th century. It's not certain how it was pronounced during this period, but it may have rhymes with "flow."

Therefore, based on the historical spelling and phonetic facts of *shoe*, *two*, and *too*, this nursery rhyme probably originated sometime between 1350 and 1550.

The interesting thing about the spelling and phonetics of *shoe*, *two* and *too* is that before the early 1500s, they all probably rhymed with "flow," and after 1600, all of them came to rhyme with "flew." But later, the spelling of *too* (the digit on the foot) became *toe*, and it once again rhymed with "flow." Words can be such wild mavericks, can't they?

marry (archaic and dialectal) an exclamation of surprise. Once a common term, it was often used in answering a question and implying surprise that it was even asked. The sense is: "Indeed!" or "Yes, of course! He can set one or two shoes with no problem."

Originally, this *marry* came from the name of the Virgin Mary, used as an oath. The earliest known record of it in writing was in 1350.

tick Originally, this word meant: a light touch, a tap, or a pat.

So, the full meaning of **Tick, tack, too** might have been: With a gentle **tick**, the blacksmiths can **tack** a shoe onto the **toe** (hoof) of the horse.

Of course, Tick-tack-toe has since become the name of a game. The British dictionary OED describes it as "a children's game played on a slate, consisting in trying with the eyes shut to bring the pencil down on one of the numbers of a set, the number hit being scored."

In the U.S. it's better known as the name of the game in which two players put either crosses or circles on a grid of nine squares; the first to get three in a row wins. This game may have been named after the tapping sound of jotting down the marks. Or maybe it was once the practice for the winner to say, "tick, tack, toe" while tapping each of the three marks of the winning row. In other dialects, the game is spelled: "tit-tat-toe" or "tip-tap-toe."

Jack Jingle **went prentice**
To make a horseshoe.
He **wasted** the iron
Till it would not do.

His master came in
and began for to **rail**.
Says Jack, "The shoes's spoiled,
But 'twill still make a nail.

He **tried at** the nail,
But **chancing** to miss,
Says, "If it won't make a nail.
It shall yet make a hiss.

Then into the water
Threw the hot iron, smack!
"Hiss," **quoth** the iron.
"I thought so," says Jack.

This is probably part of a chapbook series on the adventures of Jack Jingle. Chapbooks were cheap books (from the Old English noun *ceap*, sale, goods). They were sold for pennies on the streets by *chapmen*. (The short form *chap* is still used in England for *fellow*.)

went prentice went to be an apprentice, became bound as an apprentice. Sometimes, unstressed vowels at the beginning of words were dropped (as in *lone* from *alone* or *squire* from *esquire*).

The short form, *prentice*, appeared in 14th century Middle English as early as the full word did, and for several centuries it was the usual form.

The word comes from Old French *apprendre*, "to learn" and originally from Latin *apprehendere*, "to take hold of," from which we also get *apprehend* and *prehensile*.

wasted overworked, worn away.

rail (in use since the late 1400s) to speak vehemently and bitterly, to complain loudly. The term is still used in some expressions, such as, "He was ranting and *railing* all day about our political problems."

tried at Originally, this may have been *tried out*. In the 16th and 17th centuries, to *try* or *try out* metal was to refine it or remove the dross (the scum on the surface of molten metal) by heating it.

chancing happening. This term was used from the 1400s to the 1800s, as was the following word:

quoth said. When I was about nine years old, I found a small leather-bound book on my uncle's dresser. It was Edgar Allan Poe's 1845 poem "The Raven." I couldn't understand many of the words, but I loved their sounds! And I'll never forget the phrase:
"Quoth the Raven, 'Nevermore.'"

Seafaring:

I saw a ship a-sailing,
A-sailing on the sea.

And, oh! it was all laden
>With pretty things for thee!

There were **comfits** in the cabin
>And apples in the hold.
The sails were made of silk,
>And the masts were made of gold.

The four-and-twenty sailors
>That stood **between the decks**,
Were four-and-twenty white mice
>With **chains about their necks**.

The captain was a duck,
>With a **packet** on his back.
And when the ship began to **move**,
>The captain said, "Quack, quack!"

comfits pieces of candy made of fruits, roots, or seeds, preserved with sugar and dried. This word, like "confectionery," comes from the Latin "confi-care," meaning "to prepare."

between the decks amidship, down between the foredeck and the stern deck, where most of the masts and rigging were located, so where most of the work is done. Naval Academy cadets, men or women, training to be officers are still called "midshipmen."

chains about their necks Apparently, these do not refer to the chains of slavery or bondage, nor even of decoration (necklaces), but rather to the chains used aboard a sailing vessel to carry the lower shrouds of a mast outside the ship's sides where, once fastened, they increase the firmness of the mast.

packet In earliest use, this referred to a mail bag. (In fact, the word "mail" originally meant "bag.") The captain may have carried the most important international letters and dispatches on his own person to ensure their safety.

The boats that were maintained for carrying "the packet" became known as "packet-boats." The term later applied to any ships carrying mail, goods, and passengers between two ports at regular intervals. The most famous of these were the sleek American packet-ships of the early 1800s. One Englishman noted in 1824 that "any one who will walk through the docks at Liverpool . . . will see the American ships, long, sharp built, beautifully painted and rigged, and remarkable for their fine appearance and white canvas." (Bane, as quoted by Morison & Commager in *The Growth of the American Republic*, 499) The first such ship, the "James Monroe," left New York for Liverpool in 1818 with her hold filled mostly with apples and flour. (And comfits in the cabin, no doubt.)

move move off, depart from the port.

Hunting:

Tomorrow the fox will come to town,
Keep, keep, keep, keep, keep.
Tomorrow the fox will come to town,
O keep you all well there.

I must **desire** you, neighbors all,
To **hallo** the fox out of the **hall**,
And cry as loud as you can call,
Whoop! Whoop! Whoop! Whoop! Whoop!

Formal fox-hunting began in England in the 1500s, but has been banned in Britain since 2005 and in the U.S. since 2004. However, enforcement of the ban has been weak or non-existent because several of the wealthy insist it should be maintained as a "traditional sport," in which they use their red coats, white pants, black hats, horses, and hounds. In the Middle Ages, fox-hunting became a sport reserved for noblemen. Of course, there have always been professional hunters and people who hunted game to help feed their families.

In this rhyme, the chase seems to be a community affair, with the townspeople assisting the hunters. Foxes eat rodents, beetles and other pests in the wild, but have been known to "come to town" for such domestic fare as grapes, honey, eggs, and poultry.

Hunting, like any occupation, had its own jargon. The familiar "tally-ho," for example, was a cry to signify that the fox has been sighted.

Occupations

keep A cry to "Keep your eyes alert! Be on the lookout!" (From the Old English verb "cepan," pronounced like /capon/ "to behold, watch out for.") This particular sense of the word survives primarily in combinations, such as: *gamekeeper*, *beekeeper*, *zookeeper*, and *gatekeeper*, with the idea of "one who keeps watch over."

desire to ask someone to do something as a favor.

hallo apparently a variant of the hunter's "halloo," an exclamation to incite dogs to the chase. And, judging from this poem, the word was also used as a verb, just as "cheer" can be a noun or a verb.

hall This probably refers to the nobleman's estate. (For more information on the pronunciation of *all*, *hall*, and *call*, see Afterword.)

whoop a shortened form of "whoo-whoop," the shout of huntsmen at the death of the game.

> **Bye**, Baby **Bunting**,
> Daddy's gone a-hunting,
> To get a little rabbit's skin
> To wrap his Baby Bunting in.

bye This word means "sleep" and is found in several lullabies, for example, "Hush-a-bye, baby," "Rock-a-bye, baby," and "Bye, O my baby" (Opie, 19). One definition of "bye-bye" that the OED gives is "a sound to lull a child to sleep." The word "bye" may come from the expression "good-bye" (a shortened form of "God-be-with-ye.")

However, it's interesting to note that "bye" (or "by") is the last syllable in the word "lullaby." The first part of this term is from the word "lulla" (also spelled "lullay" or "lully"), formed from the verb "lull." "Lullay" is still heard at Christmas time in the beautiful old Coventry Carol, "Lullay, Thou Little Tiny Child." A lullaby, of course, is used to lull a baby to sleep, and "lulla" was often *preceded* with "by," as in this part of the Coventry Carol: "By, by, lully, lullay." In the 16th century "Lullaby" was also used for *farewell* or *good-night*, as in Shakespeare: "Marry, sir, lullaby to your bounty till I come again." (*Twelfth Night* 5.1.48)

bunting As an adjective, this word is defined in the OED as: "short and thick... as a plump child." Was this word being used here as a noun, referring to the child to whom the mother was speaking? Perhaps. Another source indicates that the term, as used here, was an old form of endearment. (Baring-Gould, 226)

As a noun, "bunting" also refers to "a sleeping bag for infants, a garment of soft, warm cloth made into a kind of hooded blanket that can be closed so only the face is exposed." When I tried to find the origin for this use of the word, I didn't get very far because most of the dictionaries that I consulted said that this word came "from 'Bye, Baby Bunting,' a nursery rhyme."

Another use of the noun "bunting" refers to the coarse, open fabric used in making flags. That doesn't fit here, does it?

Actually, there's one more meaning of "bunting" that would fit this rhyme very well: There are over two dozen songbirds in North America and Europe with the name "bunting," including the Indigo Bunting, the Painted Bunting, and the Snow Buntings. Do you suppose the mother birds enjoys tucking each little bunting bird into its nest?

Street Vending:

If I had as much money as I could spend,
I never would cry, "Old chairs to mend!
Old chairs to mend! Old chairs to mend!"
I never would cry, "Old chairs to mend.!"

If I had as much money as I could **tell**,
I never would cry, "Old clothes to sell!
Old clothes to sell! Old clothes to sell!"
I never would cry, "Old clothes to sell!"

The repetitions of the phrases indicate this poem may well have once been used as a song, a fact that is true of many nursery rhymes.

tell count. This verb was used in the old expression "to tell beads" when reciting the rosary. The word survives today in a noun because the person at a bank who counts the money is called a "teller."

Occupations

> There was a little woman,
> As I've been told,
> Who was not very young,
> Nor yet very old.
>
> Now this little woman
> Her living got
> By selling **codlins**,
> Hot, hot, hot

codlins roasted apples, once commonly sold on the streets of London. The Oxford English Dictionary gives as an example: "1825, popular song: 'A little old woman her living she got, By selling hot codlins, hot, hot, hot.'"

"Codlin" was a shortened form of "codling." This happened because in Early Modern English the /ng/ sound at the end of words was often pronounced as /n/ (see "warning" above, page 55). This frequently happens today in informal English: ("I know who did it, but I'm not sayin' a word.")

The French called this long, greenish cooking apple "coeur de lion," literally 'lion's heart,' because of its hard core. In fact, one meaning of "coeur" is "core," and yes, our English word "core" does come from "coeur." Similarly, the French phrase "dent de lion" (lion's tooth) gives us the English word 'dandelion,' after its tooth-shaped leaves. However, today's French word for *dandelion* is "pissenlit," because the dandelion leaf, used in tea or salads, is a strong diuretic and could make us wet the bed.

Well, getting back to "coeur de lion." In 1066, the French from Normandy, led by William the Conquerer, defeated the English at the Battle of Hastings, and they stayed in England. In fact, many of them went back and brought their families over. They also brought their language with them, and Old English changed into Middle English with many new words. People no longer ate pig or cow for dinner; they had pork or beef. And that green cooking apple, "coeur de lion," was called "querdelyon" in Anglo-French and then later became "querdling" in English, which eventually became spelled as "codling" because it may have been influenced by the English word *coddle*, meaning "to stew or bake."

> There was an old man, and he lived in a wood,
> With a **bill** and a **stump** for making of brooms.
> And his lazy son Jack would **snooze** till noon,

Nor follow his trade, although it was good,
With a ball and a stump for making of brooms, **green brooms**.

One morn in a **passion** and **sore** with vexation,
He swore he would **fire** the room,
If he did not get up and go to his work
And **fall to** the cutting of brooms, green brooms,
And fall to the cutting of brooms.

Then Jack he arose and slipped on his clothes,
And **away** to the woods very soon,
Where he made up his pack and put it on his back,
Crying, "**Maids**, do you want any brooms, green brooms?
Maids, do you want any brooms?"

bill short for "billhook," a heavy knife with a curved end, a sickle, or a brush hook, used for cutting twigs.

stump the chopping block where the twigs were trimmed with the billhook, then tied to the wooden broom handle with strips of cane.

snooze A common word today for "take a nap," but it's not a very old English word. Its origin is unknown, and it did not appear in written form until 1788. So, unless there was an older variant of the rhyme that used a word like "sleep" in this line, it may be assumed that this poem was composed no earlier than the late 1700s.

green brooms The brooms were made from the green, slender, stiff branches of the "broom" plant (a.k.a. "besom"), a member of the pea family), and it is known in America as Scotch broom. The finished tools have been called *brooms* or *besoms* since Old English times.

When I lived in northern San Diego County in the 1970s, I could look at the broom plant outside our den window. It stood about four feet high and had many small, green leaves. But due to the poor soil and the gophers, it sometimes failed to produce its bright yellow flowers in the spring.

American wooden brooms are not made from Scotch broom, but from broomcorn, a variety of sorghum. Today's modern synthetic brooms may never replace the cheaper (and, some say, better) natural brooms, which are still very popular.

The word "broom" (from Old English "brom," *brushwood*) is closely related to the word "bramble," which originally was formed from "broom": "bram-el." (Our word "kernel" developed the same way from Old English "corn.") One of the countless superstitions about brooms is never take an old broom into a new house. The old dirt and bad luck will come with it. Also, for good luck, dip your broom in cinnamon water before using it, no doubt making the floors smell nice and, some believed, bringing good luck and property as well.

passion an outburst of emotion.

sore fierce, very emotional.

fire set fire to

fall to begin. It has the same sense as "get down to the business of." (See above, "fell," page 100.)

away went away (archaic). Sometimes "away" was used without a verb. In 1740, Dyche & Pardon defined "away" in their *New General English Dictionary* as "be gone, depart, quit, or leave the place." This one word is still occasionally heard in some expressions, for example:

"Away with you!" In 1967, people were encouraged to go up in a hot air balloon with the popular song, "Up, Up, and Away!" In the 1950s and 60s, the comedian Jackie Gleason always liked to begin his TV show by saying, "And away we go!"

maids Since the late 12th century, the word "maid" (an alternate form of "maiden") has had different denotations through the centuries:

- At first it simply meant a young woman
- Later, it referred to an unmarried woman, (usually young, although the term "old maid" is still around)
- "Maid" has also been used for a female domestic servant (It's sometimes connected to another word, for example: *chambermaid* or *housemaid*.)

Any of these meanings would fit this nursery rhyme.

Various Trades:

Little **Tom Dogget**,
What dost thou mean,
To kill poor **Dolly**
Now she's so lean?

Chorus (?):   Sing, oh, poor Colly,
Colly, my cow,
For Colly will give me
No more milk now.

I had better have kept her
Till fatter she had been,
For now, I confess,
She's a little too lean.

First in comes the tanner
With his sword by his side,
And he bids me five shillings
For my cow's **poor** hide.

Then in comes the **tallow-chandler**,
Whose brains were but shallow,
And he bids me two-and-sixpence
For my cow's **tallow**.

Then in comes the huntsman.
So early in the morn,
He bids me a penny
For my cow's **horn**.

Then in comes the **tripe-woman**,
So fine and so neat,
She bids me three half-pence
For my **cow's feet**.

> Then in comes the butcher,
> That nimble-tongued youth,
> Who said she was **carrion**,
> But he spoke not the truth.
>
> The skin of my **cowl**
> Was softer than silk,
> And **three times a day**
> My poor cow would give milk.
>
> She every year
> A fine calf did me bring ,
> Which **fetched** me a pound,
> For it came **in the spring**.
>
> But now I have killed her,
> I can't her recall.
> I will sell my poor Colly,
> Hide, horns, and all.
>
> The butcher shall have her,
> Though he gives but a pound,
> And he knows in his heart
> That my Colly was sound.
>
> And when he has bought her,
> Let him sell all together
> The flesh for to eat
> And the hide for leather.

 Cattle have been an important part of English life for centuries and were highly prized possessions. In fact, in Old English times, *property* and *cattle* were both represented by the same word: "ceap" (pronounced like /chay-ahp/).

 Not only were these animals an important commodity in the marketplace, but they could also be used towards the dowry of some young woman eligible for marriage, as illustrated by this Scottish nursery rhyme:

> A cow and a calf,
> An ox and a half,
> Forty good shillings and three.
> Is that not enough **tocher** (dowry)
> For a shoemaker's daughter,
> A bonny lass with **a black e'e**? (dark eyes)

The loss of one cow for a well-to-do farmer with a large herd would not be an event of any special significance—certainly not enough to compose a lengthly poem about her. But for poor country folk whose only livestock consisted of the family cow and perhaps a few pigs and chickens, often living within the house, the sudden loss of "poor Colly" would be as tragic as losing a beloved pet dog or cat.

Not only would the cow often be a family companion with a name, but she was no doubt their sole source of milk, cream, cheese, butter, curds, and whey. She provided some additional income each year by giving birth to "a fine calf" in the spring. Even her manure was used, to fertilize the garden. But if the annual calf had already been sold, there would be no young cow to replace the one lost.

Tom Dogget It is not known what connection, if any, this Tom Dogget had with the successful 18th century Irish actor, Thomas Doggett of Dublin. Probably none.

colly a term of endearment for a cow (akin to the Old Norse word for a cow, "kolla.")

poor meaning "unfortunate," rather than "in bad condition," because later in this poem, Tom describes Colly's hide as "softer than silk."

tallow-chandler a candle maker or seller. (The word is related to "chandelier," the ceiling fixture designed to hold candles.)

tallow the hard, coarse animal fat, obtained from the parts around the kidneys of cattle and sheep, used in the making of candles.

horn Hunters used cow horn either as a *hunting horn* (a bugle for blowing signals during the hunt) or as a *powder horn* or *gunpowder flask*.

Occupations

tripe-woman Sarcastically described here as "**so fine and so neat**" because she had a very messy job, using body parts that the butcher didn't want, such as **tripe** (the tough stomach tissue, no long a popular food in England or the U.S., but still commonly eaten in other countries) and *cow's feet*. (The hooves were simmered slowly, then added as flavoring for stews and soups.)

carrion decaying flesh of a dead body.

cowly Cowly leather has the fur remaining on it, with the mottled pattern of the cow's hide still visible. It has been used for rugs or for couch covers.

three times a day Cows are usually milked twice a day, but occasionally three times a day, either to ease the pressure on older cows' udders and/or to increase the daily yield of milk. The natural life span of a cow is approximately twenty years. However, on today's dairy farms, when a cow's daily output drops too low, after she is between 4.5 and 7 years old, she's sent out to be slaughtered.

fetched (dialectal) brought as a price.

in the spring Calves born at that time of the year get bigger and stronger more quickly because they feed on the lush verdant springtime pastures.

So, did Tom get much money for his cow? The total amount that he was paid came to less than one and a half British pounds. It doesn't sound like much (A pound is worth about $1.15 today) but because of inflation, a penny 400 years ago would equal a pound today. So if Tom sold his cow tomorrow, he'd get about $300 for her, which sounds like a lot, but a cow sells now for $2,200 to $5,200.

> **Muley** cow, muley **cow**, why do you **low**?
> Has butcherman taken your baby, poor cow?
> Oh! It was cruel to take it away!
> But veal is good eating, the marketmen say.

muley in British dialect: any cow. In the U.S., where the word is more common, it means a hornless cow. It's pronounced like /moo-lee/ or /muh-lee/, but not like /mule-lee/ because the word does not come from "mule," but instead from the Scotch and Anglo-Irish word "moiley," meaning *bald*, hence the alternate spellings: "mooley" and "mully."

cow . . . low These two words don't seem to rhyme, but they do in certain British dialects, sounding like /cuh-oo/ and /luh-oo/.

(Yes, some of these poems make a plant-based diet seem more viable.)

> The miller he grinds his **corn**, his corn.
> The miller he grinds his corn, his corn.
> The little boy blue comes **winding** his horn,
> With a **hop, step, and a jump**.
>
> The **carter** he whistles aside his team.
> The carter he whistles aside his team.
> And **Dolly** comes **tripping** with nice **clouted cream**.
> With a hop, step, and a jump.
>
> The **nightingale** sings when we're at rest.
> The nightingale sings when we're at rest.
> The little bird climbs the tree for his nest,
> With a hop, step, and a jump.
>
> The **damsels** are churning for curds and whey.
> The damsels are churning for curds and whey.
> The lads in the field are **making the hay**.
> With a hop, step, and a jump.

corn As Web NC tells us, the word "corn" is often specifically used for the important cereal grain of a given region; thus, in England it refers to wheat, in Scotland and Ireland to oats, and in the United States, Canada, and Australia to Indian corn or maize."

winding blowing (archaic). The noun "wind" (the movement of air) originated in Old English, but the verb "wind" (to blow) is a fairly recent word (first used in the late 16th century, and from that time through the 17th century) it usually rhymed with "find." So, in the first verse of this poem, the phrase "winding his horn" probably rhymes with "grinding his corn."

Therefore, this fact gives us an approximate date for the origin of this nursery rhyme: sometime between 1550 and 1700.

The other verb "wind" (which also rhymes with "find") has a different meaning: "to twist or turn," as in winding up a toy or a clock, and it comes from a different Old English word, "windan."

hop, step, and a jump This nursery rhyme was probably a chant or a song with 4 beats in lines 1, 2, and 3, but 3 beats in line 4. This poem goes with a jumping game, also known as "hop, *skip*, and jump," which children have been enjoying for hundreds of years. In 1896, Hop, Skip, and Jump became an Olympic event; it was later renamed the Triple Jump. The athletes run to the takeoff board where they begin the "hop" by leaping off with one foot; they must land on the same foot and use it again to begin the "skip" part; then they land on the opposite foot and use it to leap into the "jump" before landing in the sand pit with both feet. The record distance for men is 59' 4" (in 1996) and for women 51' 4.75" (in 2021).)

carter one who drives a cart (as in "teamster," one who drives a team of horses, oxen, etc. Drivers of motor trucks have been called "teamsters" since 1907.)

Dolly a short form of "Dorothy" or "Dorothea." The word for the child's toy "doll" came from the same name around 1700.

tripping Usually when we use this word, we think of catching a foot on something and stumbling. However, "tripping" can also mean "dancing or skipping with light quick steps," which is what Dolly is doing here. In 1688 the poet John Milton wrote: "Come and trip it as ye go, / On the light fantastic toe." And "trip the light fantastic" is still a very common phrase.

clouted cream First written down in 1540 as "clouted cream," this expression had changed to "clotted cream" by 1800. It refers to the cream that is thickened by scalding or heating.

nightingale a small brown bird of mainland Europe and southern England, living in dense woods, thickets, and parks, well-known for its beautiful, melodic song which the male sings at night as well as in the day. (To hear it, just Google "nightingale song.")

damsels country girls, maids, and—as used here—milkmaids. Originally, however, the word "damsel" referred to an unmarried lady of the titled aristocracy (nobility) or of high social status (gentry); such were the medieval "fayre damsels in destresse." Later, it lost all connection with rank. It has not been in ordinary speech since the 17th century, except in literature or in playful speech. (It comes from the Latin "domina," a lady, a mistress of a household.)

making the hay Farmers have to *cut* it (with a sickle or scythe), *ted* it (dry it) by spreading it into *windrows* (long line), then pitchfork it into *haymows* (large stacks) to store it. The old proverb "Make hay while the sun shines" teaches us not to miss good chances.

> Who lives so merry in all this land
> As does the poor widow that **selleth** the **sand**.
> And ever she singeth, as I can guess,
> "Will you buy any sand, any sand, Mistress?"
>
> The broom-man maketh his living most sweet
> With carrying of brooms from street to street.
> Who would describe a pleasanter thing
> Than all the day long to do nothing but sing?
>
> The chimney-sweeper all the long day,
> He singeth and sweepeth the soot away.
> Yet when he comes home, although he be weary,
> With his sweet wife he maketh full merry.
>
> The cobbler he sits cobbling till **noon**
> And cobbleth his shoes till they be **done**.
> Yet doth he not fear, and so doth say,
> For he knows his work will soon **decay**.
>
> The **serving-man** waiteth from street to street,
> With blowing his nails and beating his feet.
> And serveth for forty shillings a year,
> That 'tis impossible to make good cheer.

Occupations

> The **husbandman** all day goeth to **plough**.
> And when he comes home, he serveth his sow.
> He **moileth** and toileth all the long year.
> How can he be merry and make good cheer?
>
> The merchantman doth sail on the seas,
> And **lie** on the shipboard with little ease:
> Always in **doubt** the rock is near.
> How can he be merry and make good cheer?
>
> Who liveth so merry and makes such **sport**
> As those that be of the poorest sort?
> The poorest sort, wheresoever they be,
> They gather together by one, two, and three.

This seems to be an ode to the working class who, despite long hours and low pay, always have high spirits. Nice idea, though somewhat naive.

selleth sells. The -eth ending for verbs was used throughout Middle English and continued for a time in Early Modern English, especially in southern England, during the late 1500s and early 1600s. The *King James Bible* (1611) used the -eth ending (for example in Psalm 23: "He leadeth me beside the still waters.") During Shakespeare's lifetime (1564–1616) he used both the -eth and the -s endings for verbs (as did the composer of this nursery). In *The Merchant of Venice* (1596) Portia says, "The quality of mercy is not strained . . . It bless**eth** him that give**s** and him that takes." (4.1.184, 187).

sand Good clean sand was used with soft soap to scour pots, pans, walls, floors, etc. Also, a fine white sand was used to sprinkle over writing to dry the wet ink marks.

noon . . . done This would be a full rhyme in northern Britain. One of the Scots spellings for "done" is "dune." Also, in the 1400s and 1500s, "done" was sometimes spelled as "doone."

decay be destroyed or ruined, worn out. This was a common Elizabethan use of the word, as in Shakespeare: "And every day that comes comes to decay / A day's work." (*Cymbeline* 1.5.56)

serving-man (archaic) This word was used often in the 1500s and 1600s. Here it perhaps refers to a footman—either one who waits on his master by running errands "from street to street" or one who waits outside with the carriage in all kinds of weather.

husbandman (archaic or poetic) a farmer. The word is related to "husbandry," a term still used for the scientific management of farming, especially of domestic animals. These words, along with "husband," all come from Old English "husbonda," a householder.

plough the British spelling of "plow." On page 48, the rhyme "My father he died" has the word "plow" at the end of the second line, denoting an American editor, whereas British editors of that rhyme used "plough."

moileth to work hard, to drudge, or to work in wet and slime. The phrase "to moil and toil" is a very common dialectal expression.

lie Perhaps this is a pun on the nautical term *lay*. Richard Dana, in his 1840 novel *Two Years Before the Mast* (26) tells us: "This word *lay*, which is in such general use on board ships, being used in giving orders instead of *go*; as, 'Lay forward!' 'Lay aft!' 'Lay aloft!' etc., I do not understand to be the neuter verb *lie*, mispronounced, but to be the active verb *lay*, with the objective case understood; as, 'Lay *yourselves* forward!' 'Lay *yourselves* aft!' etc." (italics mine)

For centuries, many of the best authors had an excellent understanding of grammar.

doubt an obsolete use of the word; here it means *fear* or *apprehension*.

For hundreds of years, it was spelled the way it's pronounced (for example, 15th century: *doute*). However, then in the 17th and 18th centuries, along came the pedantic grammarians of the Age of Enlightenment who noticed that the word came from the Latin *dubitare*, (to waver in opinion), and they felt obliged to "correct" the spelling by re-inserting the letter **b**.

The same thing happened with the word *debt*. The historical spellings (*det, dett, dete, dette*) reflected the way it was spoken. But since it came from the Latin *debitum*, the erudite grammarians insisted on putting the **b** back in.

CHAPTER 14

Myth and Legend

For many centuries, myths and legends, either as far-out fantasies or as realistic fiction, have been extremely popular with children and adults. Sometimes they were used to teach children a lesson; other times they were used just to entertain them. Of course, the best ones can do both.

> A **moony** old cat that **lived on the dew**,
> Had six little kittens that never would mew.
>   She bought a big bellows and blew in their ears.
>   Then all mewed so loud, it brought her to tears.
> Now when they were bad, she found it was **good**
> To **blow** them all **up**, and give them no **food**.
>   It filled them so full, they seemed overfed,
>   But it was only a hoax to get them to bed.
> Now as they grew older, their tails had a quirk.
> Down their throats went the bellows—
> They flew stiff with a jerk.
>   At last, she got mad and blew them so high
>   They never came down, but stuck in the sky.
> they turned into stars. Any night that you please
> You can see them so easy. They are called "**Pleiades**."

moony inclined to moon, to spend time idly day-dreaming.
As my parents used to say, "Is she still mooning over her boyfriend?

lived on the dew drank the dew for sustenance.

good . . . food In northern England and Scotland, these would make a full rhyme, having the same vowel sound as "mood."

blow . . . up This was a play on words. To "blow up" was once a colloquial expression meaning "to scold severely," which was what the cat was doing to her kittens in this verse. But the meaning shifted in the next verse, indicating that she blew them up like balloons.

Pleiades The Seven Sisters is a group of stars forming a very small "dipper" in the constellation Taurus. Only six of them are visible to the naked eye. The seventh is very dim and hard to see without a telescope.

This nursery rhyme is Mother Goose's story of how they got there. The ancient Greeks told it differently. Actually, there are several versions of the way they told the myth, so I've culled elements from all of them. The story is essentially this:

The Pleiades were the seven daughters of Atlas. Orion, the hunter, fell in love with them and chased them for five years, but was never able to catch them! Zeus finally changed all of them into stars and put them into the heavens. There they can still be seen: Orion, followed by his dog, is chasing them across the sky.

> **Little lad**, little lad, where **wast thou** born?
> Far off in **Lancashire**, under a **thorn**.

For the above short rhyme, other sources have added a third line:
> Where they sup sour milk with a ram's horn. (Halliwell, 191)

And an even earlier version has two more lines:

> And a **pumpkin** scoop'd with a yellow rim
> Is the bonny bowl they breakfast in. (Baring-Gould, 83)

And from all these lines, Baring-Gould then concluded that the **little lad** was "one of the Little People—and it is one of the very rare mentions of fairies to be found in the older nursery rhymes." (Hmmm. I wonder why. They were quite popular in traditional stories, *fairy* tales.)

Myth and Legend

In England **pumpkin** refers to any large squash. In the U.S. *pumplin* refers only to the large, orange gourd (*Curcurbita pepo*) which is native to America.]

wast thou This phrase for "were you" was still common in the 1600s: "Where wast thou . . . ?" (Job 38.4, *King James Bible*, 1611)

Lancashire a northern English county on the Irish Sea, south of Cumberland, near Scotland.

thorn a thorn bush. In England, it is also called *gorse, furze*, or in northern Britain, *whin*.

> **Fa fe fi fo fum!**
> I smell the blood of an English**man**.
> Be he alive or be he dead,
> I'll grind his bones to make **me** bread.

Fa fe fi fo fum Many of us remember this phrase as "Fee fie fo fum," spoken by the giant in "Jack and the Beanstalk." But this five-part version is found in two other sources: *Mother Goose* (329) and *Book of Nursery and Mother Goose Rhymes* (59).

So, what do the words in this exclamation mean?

fa from Old English "fah," *hostile*. (The spelling of *fah* was still used in the 16th century.)

fe It sounds like /fee/ but it's probably a variant of "fie,"

fi A Middle English homonym of "fie," an exclamation of disgust.

fo "ugh!" Probably a 16th or 17th century form of "faugh" (pronounced like /faw/) or a Middle English variant of "foh," meaning *enemy* and spelled as "foe" in Modern English.

fum a noxious smell, a Middle English form of "fume," *smoke*. However, here the sense is probably more like *stench* or *stink*.

In early Modern English, "fumous" meant *creating wind* (as in passing gas). For example, in 1624, one writer stated, "He must abstaine from garlicke, onions, mustard, and such like fumes things." (Nares, *A Glossary*, 340) And *Johnson's Dictionary* (1963) defined "fumette" as "a word introduced by cooks . . . for the stink of meat."

One meaning of Modern French "fumee" is *reek*. Also, in Modern English, "fume" still refers usually to an offensive vapor or gas.

So, loosely translated, the phrase "Fa fe fi fo fum" means something like: "Oh! Yuk! Phooey! Ugh! The stink!"

The words "Fee fie foe fum" were used in a number of folk tales, including "Jack and the Beanstalk" and "Jack the Giant Killer."

Elements of these phrases, scholars have traced back to "Beowulf" and to other European languages, where some non-English people may have been enemies of Englishmen.

One version of this line was used by Shakespeare in *King Lear* (3.4.189–190): "Fie, foh, and fum! / I smell the blood of a British man"

-man In the second line of this nursery rhyme, the last vowel in "Englishman" had an /uh/ sound, as in m**o**nth. So, "Englishman" rhymes with "fum" at the end of the first line. Many unstressed vowels began to shift in Old English, and later in Middle English, to a more relaxed /uh/ sound. For example, the vowel before the letter **m** in "welcome" had an /oo/ sound (like "c**oo**l) in Old English "wilcuma," then shifted to an /oh/ sound (as in "c**o**mb) in Middle English "welc**o**me, and finally to the /uh/ sound of Modern English.

me This is probably a carryover from Middle English, when the word "my" was pronounced like "me," or it could be a shortened form of "min" (sounded like "mean") the OE word for "my" and "mine."

This last line of the poem could also be another clue to the ancient age of the rhyme. Before the 12th century, when large windmills started coming into use, it was the usual practice for people to grind their own flour for bread.

Myth and Legend

> Robin Hood, Robin Hood
> Is in the **mickle wood**!
> Little John, Little John
> He to the town **is gone**.
>
> Robin Hood, Robin Hood
> Is **telling his beads**,
> **All** in the green wood,
> Among the green **weeds**.
>
> Little John, Little John
> If he comes no more,
> Robin Hood, Robin Hood,
> He will fret **full sore**!

According to Baring-Gould (143), in the 14th and 15th centuries, Robin was a "favorite figure in ... English ballads ... Robin Hood was supposed to have lived in the 12th century ... he may have been one of last Saxons to hold out against the Normans." However, Hazelton Spencer, editor of *British Literature*, says that "Robin Hood is even less historical than King Arthur. There is no reason to suppose there ever was any such person; but the ballad-makers who invented him provided the common people with a yeoman hero after their own hearts." (vol. I, 202) Spencer also stated that the earliest mention of him in literature goes back to about 1377 in *Piers Plowman* in which Sloth admits that he doesn't know his Paternoster (The Lord's Prayer), but says he knows rhymes of Robin Hood. (vol. I, 78). This reminds me of some people who can't quote many lines from the Bible, but they sure can quote many lines of Luke Skywalker in *Star Wars*!

mickle big, great. (obsolete, except in British dialect). This term, like our word "much," comes from Old English "micel" (pronounced like /mitchel/) and meant *great, large, much*.

is gone has gone (for more information on this, see "is grown" on page 84)

wood a dense growth of trees. Today this word is usually used in the plural (as in "He got lost in the woods.") Whether singular or plural, both words have the same meaning: tree-filled land, larger than a grove but smaller than a forest.

telling his beads counting his rosary beads. These words indicate that the poem—or at least this stanza—was probably composed before the 16th century's Protestant Reformation, but not earlier than the 13th century because, according to Roman Catholic tradition, the practice of using the rosary was introduced by St. Dominic about 1208.

all deep, entirely, completely (as in "She's all by herself.")

weeds This referred not so much to little plants, but to wild, luxurious growth, like underbrush.

full sore very intensely. These words were used to help express strong emotions, such anger, grief, annoyance, etc. (See also above, page 30.)

CHAPTER 15

Food

The three principal necessities of life are food, clothing, and shelter. But, as many growing children will tell you, food is far and away the most important. So, we find many nursery rhymes mentioning food. Often, they evolved from requests for food or answers to such requests.

>**Simple Simon** met a pieman
>>going to the fair.
>Says Simple Simon to the pieman,
>>"Let me taste your **ware**."
>
>Says the pieman to Simple Simon.
>>"Show me first your penny."
>Says Simple Simon to the pieman,
>>"Indeed, I have not any."
>
>He went to catch a **dickey bird**,
>>And thought he could not fail,
>Because he'd got a little salt
>>**To put upon his tail**.
>
>He went to take a bird's nest
>>'Twas built upon a **bough**.
>A branch gave way and Simon fell
>>Into a dirty **slough**.

> He went to shoot a wild duck,
> > But the wild duck flew away.
> Says Simon, "I can't hit him,
> > Because he will not stay."
>
> He went for to eat honey
> > Out of the mustard pot.
> It bit his tongue until he cried.
> > That was all the good he got.
>
> Simple Simon went a-fishing
> > For to catch a whale.
> All the water he had got
> > Was in his mother's pail.

Still another verse is provided by Opie (p. 385):

> Simple Simon went to look
> > If plums grew on a thistle.
> He pricked his finger very much,
> > Which made poor Simon whistle.

As you can see, only the first two verses of this nursery rhyme have any connection with each other. It probably is a *paratactic* poem, which means—literally—that the different verses are *arranged beside* each other. So, a paratactic poem is not a story by one composer, but rather a collection of verses that have been added one by one down through the years. The final product, therefore, is often the work of several authors. Many folk songs develop the same way.

For another paratactic poem, see "Jack Sprat," below (156–58).

The advantage, of course, is that verses can be added, deleted, or even forgotten without spoiling the effect of the poem. People just say, "Oh, that's good, but it's not the way I heard it."

Although they come from different sources at different time, the verses of paratactic poems always have one thing in common: the underlying theme or idea of the poem itself. The theme of "Simple Simon" is, of course, foolish ways of getting food.

Simple Simon One source speculates that "Simon . . . may have been a name for a simpleton for several centuries." Tales of Simple Simon were known at least from the late 1600s, and some say that Simple Simon was a chapbook character of Elizabethan times. (Opie, 385). So, the late 1500s may have been its origin.

dickey bird a small bird, especially a caged bird. (If it were in a cage, then Simon's attempt to catch it is even more ridiculous.)

salt / to put upon his tail Back in the early 1970s, our family went camping in the mountains, and our six-year-old daughter just about emptied the salt shaker, thinking she could catch a blue jay if she could just get close enough to its tail. She came by the belief honestly. My parents and my wife's grandmother got us to try the same thing when we were kids in the 1940s.

I wonder just how old the joke is. *The Oxford Dictionary of English Proverbs* quoted a 1580 source: "It is a . . . foolish bird that staieth [stays still and puts up with] the laying salt on his tail." (697)

Indeed, if any bird ever let you get that close, you could practically pet it!

bough rhymes with "how" and makes an end-rhyme with **slough**:

slough a swamp or marsh, a quagmire, an impassable muddy place. In Britain, it rhymes with "plough" ("plow"). In Canada and the U.S., it rhymes with "stew," so it sometimes is spelled "slew" or "slue."

A slough can be as small as a reed-filled pond, or as big as an inlet, a backwater, or even a lake. There is a body of water like this in California near Los Angles Harbor. It was called Bixby Slough, but when the area around it was turned into a park, it was renamed with the insipid title "Harbor Lake." But then I suppose most people who lived around the park would prefer to have "lake-front homes" rather than "slough-front homes," even if they did have to pay higher taxes.

> **Polly** put the kettle on,
> Polly put the kettle on,
> Polly put the kettle on,
> We'll all have **tea**.

> **Sukey** take it off again,
> Sukey take it off again,
> Sukey take it off again,
> They've all gone **away**.

Apparently, this was a popular 18th century song and dance. In the following century, it was uttered by Grip, the raven in Charles Dickens's *Barnaby Rudge* (1848). Even later, "around 1870 'Polly put the kettle on and we'll all have tea' was a much-repeated catch phrase." (Opie, 353)

Polly As indicated above (page 107), *Polly* was a nickname for *Mary*.

tea . . . away Here, "tea" was pronounced like /tay/ and rhymed with "away." (For more about this, refer to page 107 above)

Drinking tea has been a highly regarded custom in Britain for centuries. However, tea and coffee were not sold in England until the second half of the 17th century. At first, both beverages were quite expensive, but when the government reduced the tax on tea, it soon became more affordable for more people, and shortly thereafter, it was the most popular hot beverage in Britain.

By the early 1800s, it became customary to take a break between 3 and 4 p.m. for "tea time," when hot tea was served with light refreshments. In 1963 a friend and I went into a small cafe in London to enjoy a nice cup of tea. It was between 5 and 6 in the afternoon. When we gave the waitress our order, she frowned and said, "Tea time is over." We Americans were a little confused and asked if we could have coffee. "Yes. You can have coffee." That day we both learned about the proper time to "put the kettle on."

Sukey a nickname for "Susan." (rhymes with "kooky" or "blue key") This name, like "Polly," was very commonly used by the lower classes, especially among servants, in the 18th century. Also, a "sukey" or "black sukey" was a colloquial term for a kettle until at least the early 1800s.

> A little bit of **powdered** beef,
> And a great **net** of cabbage,
> The best meal I have had today
> Is a good bowl of **porridge**.

powdered (obsolete) seasoned or sprinkled with salt or spice.

net a large mesh used to hold cabbage while it's being boiled.

porridge This dish was made from grain, usually a meal made of oats, boiled in milk or water; now commonly called "oatmeal." Sometimes meat or vegetables were added for a more nutritious meal, as here.

> Upstairs, downstairs, upon my lady's window,
> There I saw a cup of **sack** and a **race** of ginger.
> Apples at the fire and nuts to crack,
> A little boy in the cream-pot up to his neck.

This rhyme comes from Hook's *Original Christmas Box* (Opie, 191). The foods mentioned here sound as if they might be the ingredients for a Yuletide treat—perhaps baked apples, filled with chopped nuts, flavored with wine and ginger, and served with rich cream. Yum!

sack This was the term used in the 16th century to refer to the dry, rough, light-colored wine imported to England from Spain and the Canary Islands. During the 17th century, the word also came to be used for all strong white southern wines, distinguishing them from the northern Rhenish and red wines. It was very similar to what we now know as sherry. Many believe it to be more palatable with a little sweetening. As Falstaff states in Shakespeare's *King Henry the Fourth*, "If sack and sugar be a fault, God help the wicked!" (2.4.17)

The word "sack" comes from the French "sec," originally "vin sec," (dry wine). So, as any wine steward would tell us, today's sec is a sparkling dry wine, somewhat sweet, having between 17 to 32 grams of sugar per liter.

race a root (of ginger). The word comes from Old French "rais" and ultimately from Latin "radix," which is also the base for "radish" (a *root* vegetable) and for the "radical sign," the mathematical symbol √ used to find the square *root* of a number.

> **Dibbity**, dibblty,
> Dibbity, **doe**.
> Give me a pancake
> And I'll go.

> Dibbity, dibbity,
> Dibbity, **ditter.**
> **Please to give** me
> A bit of a **fritter.**

dibbity This word for "pancake" was formerly used in various British dialects, but by the mid-1800s "dibbity" was archaic or obsolete. None of my sources listed an origin for the word, but it seems to be related to "dibble" or "dib" (both of which come from "dab," 'to pat lightly,') from the patting into the shape of dibbity dough.

doe a 17th century spelling of "dough."

ditter This word was used as a noun "a children's game of tag" and as a verb, "to confuse, bewilder." It might also have been an alternate spelling of "didder," a variant of "dither," to *tremble, shake, vibrate,* as used in several British dialects. But none of these definitions make much sense here. "Ditter" was probably just a nonsense word thrown in to rhyme with "fritter."

please to give "Please" used with "to" + a verb was a common construction in Early Modern English.

fritter a small quantity of batter or batter-covered fruit, corn, etc.
    My father, born in 1900 in the northern New York dialect region, used the word "fritter" for a doughnut (donut), which he sometimes called a "fried cake" or a "cruller," either plain or filled. When we teased Dad for eating them, his reply was always, "Donut be so cruller!"
    In the 17th century, "fritter" was apparently synonymous with "pancake." The OED gives sample definitions from 1634: "pancake or fritter or flapjack" and from 1664: "Home to supper to a good dish of fritters."
    We can be certain that fritters were prepared by frying because of their linguistic history (etymology):

- Both "fry" and "fritter" originated from the same Latin root: "frigere," 'to fry.'
- Later, the English word "fry" developed from the French verb "frire," 'to fry.'
- And "fritter" came from the French word "friture," 'frying.'

CHAPTER 16

Love and/or Marriage

As noted before, nursery rhymes, as folk literature, deal with all aspects of life. Children are introduced early to the joys and the tribulations (and antics) of adulthood through a great number of rhymes. Some of these poems may be snatches from old songs or ballads. Most of them illustrate—with or without humor—the behavior and customs that were used during courtship or the practical arrangements that were thought to be good for a successful marriage.

> Did you see my wife, did you see, did you see,
> Did you see my wife looking for me?
> She wears a straw bonnet, with ribbons on it,
> And **dimity** petticoats over her knee.

dimity a thick cotton fabric, woven with raised stripes or fancy figures; usually used for beds and bedroom hangings and sometimes (as here) for garments.

> Old woman, old woman, shall we go **a-shearing**?
> Speak a little louder, sir. I am very **thick** of hearing.
> Old woman, old woman, shall I kiss you **dearly**?
> Thank you, kind sir, I hear you very clearly.

This poem is definitely one of my favorites. It's from an old English folksong. The earliest version that can be found in writing was published in

1776 in David Herd's *Scots Songs and Ballads* (Opie, 429). It's more effective, of course, if the first question is spoken strongly and the second one very softly.

a-shearing Cutting the woolen fleece off sheep has never been an easy task, one which an old woman would have gladly avoided.

For thousands of years it has been done by hand, beginning in the Bronze Age with sharp-edged blades. These were used until about 400 BC when mechanical shears were invented in Italy. An expert shearer needs a great deal of strength, dexterity, and experience. The speed record for hand shearing was set over 100 years ago by someone who sheared 321 sheep in only 7 hours and 40 minutes (averaging 1 minute 26 seconds per sheep!)

The process became somewhat faster after 1888 when electric shears were invented. The speed record for that kind of shearing (37.9 seconds) was set in 2021.

thick (dialectal) weak or dull in perception. Here it would mean "hard of hearing," but it also was used to describe other problems (such as "thick-eyed" or "thick-sighted"). Today we still use "thick-headed" in referring to a dull thinker.

dearly affectionately. (Now used mostly with the verb "love" or its equivalent), as in the expression, "I love you dearly."

> Oh, **rare Harry Parry**,
> When will you marry?
> **When apples and pears are ripe**.
>
> I'll come to your wedding
> Without any **bidding**,
> And dance and sing all the night.

The last line of the earliest version (1780) wasn't quite so tame: "And lye with your bride all night." (Opie, 235)

rare wise, remarkably good. Used colloquially, the term is more casual, as today when we mean something is okay, we often say that it's "fine, good, nice," or—informally—as "cool." This use of the word was common in the

17th century. Shakespeare used "rare" as an exclamation and as an adjective in his play *King Henry the Fourth, Part One* (1.2.71–76) when Falstaff asks Prince Hal if he would hang a thief, if he were king:

Prince: "No; thou shalt."

Falstaff: "Shall I? O *rare*! By the Lord, I'll be a brave judge."

Prince: "Thou judgest false already. I mean, thou shall have the hanging of thieves and so become a *rare* hangman."

Harry Parry I don't know for sure who Harry Parry was, but since "Harry" was used as a nickname for either Harold or Henry, this might be a reference to Henry Parry, the personal chaplain of Queen Elizabeth and was present at her death in 1603. James the First appointed him dean of Chester in 1605.

In 1607 he became bishop of Gloucester and, three years later, bishop of Worcester. Coincidentally, all three of these cities are near the eastern border of *Wales*.

Parry died in 1616, the same year that Willian Shakespeare did. (William was 52; Henry was 55.) Parry had never married. Queen Bess had an aversion to married clergy, and she would certainly never have had a married cleric for her personal chaplain. In general, celibate clergy received quicker and higher promotions from her than married ones did.

When apples and pears are ripe In this poem, Harry Parry shows "rare" good sense by putting off marriage until after the harvest was in. Or perhaps this was just a proverbial phrase for postponing an event. My parents had similar expressions, such as, "He'll be late if he waits till the cows come home."

bidding This word may have meant "an invitation." However, it might have been a Welsh term for "a wedding gift." Until the mid-1900s, a "bidding" ceremony was held on wedding days in *Wales*. Friends, neighbors, and relatives would bring money and gifts to help the young couple set up house. (Opie, 200) If that was the intended meaning here, then this poem may have originated in *Wales*.

The next nursery rhyme about Jack Sprat is very long: a 15-verse story! So long, in fact, that it's probably another *paratactic* poem in which different verses were added by different people at different times. The same kind of construction happened with the poem about Simple Simon (see above, page 147). Today's nursery rhyme books usually contain only the first two lines of the Jack Sprat poem—the only ones I knew as a child. The version below is from Dorothy J. Snow's *Mother Goose*, published in 1941.

> **Jack Sprat** could eat no fat; his wife could eat no lean.
> And so, between them both, they licked the platter clean.
> Jack ate all the lean; Joan ate all the fat.
> The bone they picked clean, then gave it to the cat.
>
> When Jack Sprat was young, he dressed very smart.
> He courted **Joan Cole** and gained her heart.
> In his fine leather **doublet** and old **greasy** hat,
> Oh, what a **smart** fellow was little Jack Sprat!
>
> Joan Cole had a hole in her petticoat.
> Jack Sprat to get a **patch** gave her a **groat**.
> The groat bought a patch which **stopped** the hole.
> "I thank you, Jack Sprat," says little Joan Cole.
>
> Jack Sprat was the bridegroom; Joan Cole was the bride.
> Jack said from the church his Joan home should ride.
> But no coach could take her, the lane was so narrow.
> Said Jack, "Then I'll take her home in a wheelbarrow."
>
> Jack Sprat was wheeling his wife by the ditch.
> The barrow turned over, and in she did **pitch**.
> Says Jack, "She'll be drowned," but Joan did reply,
> "I don't think I shall, for the ditch is quite dry."
>
> Jack brought home his Joan, and she sat in a chair,
> When in came his cat, which **had got** but one ear.
> Says Joan, "**I'm come home**, Pussy, **pray**, how do you do?"
> The cat wagged her tail and said nothing but, "Mew."
>
> Jack Sprat took his gun and went to the **brook**.
> He shot at a **drake**, but he killed the **duck**.

He brought it to Joan, who a fire did make
To roast the fat duck while Jack went for the drake.

The drake was swimming, with his **curly tail**.
Jack Sprat went to shoot him, but happened to fail.
He let off his gun, but missed the **mark**.
The drake flew away, crying "Quack, quack, quack."

Jack Sprat, to live **pretty**, now bought him a pig.
It was not very little; it was not very big.
It was not very lean; it was not very fat.
It will serve for a **grunter** for little Jack Sprat.

Then Joan went to market to buy her some fowls.
She bought a **jackdaw** and a couple of owls.
The owls they were white; the jackdaw was black.
"They'll make a **rare** breed," says little Joan Sprat.

Jack Sprat bought a cow, his Joan for to please,
For Joan she could make both butter and cheese,
Or pancakes or **puddings** without any fat.
A **notable** housewife was little Joan Sprat.

Joan went a-brewing a barrel of ale.
She put in some hops that it might not turn stale.
But as for the **malt**, she forgot to put that.
"This is **brave**, **sober** liquor," said little Jack Sprat.

Jack Sprat went to market and bought him a mare.
She was lame of three legs, and how she could **stare**.
Her ribs they were bare, for the mare had no fat.
"She looks like a racer," says little Jack Sprat.

Jack and Joan went **abroad**; puss took care of the house.
She caught a large rat and a very small mouse.
She caught a small mouse and a very large rat.
"You're an excellent hunter," says little Jack Sprat.

> Now I have told you the story of little Jack Sprat,
> And little Joan Cole, and the poor one-eared cat.
> Now Jack has got rich and has plenty of **pelf**.
> If you know any more, you may tell it yourself.

The first six verses give the account of Jack's courtship and wedding. The other events are in no particular order and could have been added at any time. This poem is very similar to an 1873 edition, but other variants are much older. Some of the extra verses may have been added in the 17th and 18th centuries to fill in a chapbook's sixteen pages.

Jack Sprat Was Jack Sprat a real person? A 1659 version of the first verse begins: "Archdeacon Pratt would eat no fat." But the DNB has no mention of an Archdeacon Pratt. Apparently, in the 1500s and 1600s, "Jack Sprat" was a term for *dwarf*, an earlier form being "Jack Pratt." (Opie, 238)

Joan Cole Likewise, we don't know if Joan Cole was a real person. The English name 'Cole' is a very old personal-name (from Old English "col," meaning *coal-black, swarthy.*) Many British names come from OE personal-names. The origin of family names is a field in itself. (See Reaney: *A Dictionary of British Surnames*).

doublet a tight-fitting jacket, with or without sleeves, worn by men in the Renaissance (from early 1300s to the early 1600s).

greasy In Shakespeare's time, this word meant not just *grimy*, but *despicably, disgustingly dirty*, as in the play *As You Like It* (2.1.55): " . . . you fat, greasy citizen."

groat a silver coin worth fourpence. It was not minted after 1662.

stopped (obsolete) mended a garment of cloth with an inferior material.

pitch (obsolete) to fall headlong heavily, to land on one's head. (The term has also been used to describe the action of a ship's bow as it plunges headlong into a stormy sea.)

had got probably, had gotten at birth, had been born with.

I'm come home the archaic present tense. Today we'd say "I've come home." (see "is grown," above, page 84).

pray short for "pray tell me," which is archaic for "please tell me" or just "so tell me."

brook . . . duck In the 15th and 16th centuries, these two words rhymed because they shared the same vowel sound that is heard in "broom" or "spook" or "doom."

drake . . . duck These words for the birds refer to the male and female genders, just as "gander" and "goose" refer to the male and female. As the OED explains it, "in the domestic state the female greatly exceeds in number; hence *duck* serves at once for the name of the female and of the race, *drake* being a specific term of sex."

curly tail Usually, only the male ducks have curly feathers at the end of their tails. There are over 20 species of ducks in Britain. The most common are the mallards, which are found "anyplace there is water!"

In fact, as Roger Tory Peterson tells us, most domestic ducks, "even though they are sluggish, pot-bellies, and white, are descended from the handsome, green-backed wild mallard." (*The Birds*, 166)

Did **mark** rhyme with **quack**? Post-vocalic **r** was often silent in common speech after 1400, but not in "King's English" until the mid-1700s. So, **mark** came to sound like "mock." And **quack**, early on, probably rhymed with "clock" (The same sound is heard in the German "quack" and the Dutch "kwak.")

pretty fine, nicely, good.

It will serve It will do. It will be good enough.

grunter Beginning in the 17th century, a "grunter" was a suckling pig. In the 19th century, after 1840, a sixpence coin was variously referred to as a "grunter," a "sow's baby," or "half a hog."

jackdaw the common name for the "daw," smallest of the crow family, often nests in barns, steeples, etc. Like other corvids (ravens, rooks, magpies, jays, and others), it can imitate human words. A poetic line from the early 1500s goes: "Tush, hold your peace, ye speak like a daw." (Skelton, *The Complete Poems*, 208). It is also famous for pilfering small objects.

With animal names, "jack" sometimes means *male*, as in "jackass." Other times it can mean *small*, as in "jackdaw" or "little Jack Nag" (page 83). However, I've also heard it used in fishing to signify "large, of impressive size," as in the term "jack perch."

rare unusual, special, excellent.

puddings sausages (see "pudding-stick" page 47).

notable This word was applied to a woman who was *capable*, *clever*, and *industrious* in household management. The term was common from about 1750, but dropped out of use in the early 1900s.

When used in this sense, the **o** had an /aw/ sound, making "notable" rhyme with "audible." Since this use of the word "notable" was not common *before* 1750, and "groat" was not used *after* the 1600s, we have strong internal evidence: the verses in this poem began in the mid-1600s and continued to be added for many years.

brave good, fine. (The word was probably used ironically here.)

sober subdued. The malt was needed to ferment the sugars and create alcohol. In Elizabethan times "sober" had not yet acquired the meaning of "temperate, abstaining from alcohol." However, "brave" still meant "good" or "fine" in the 19th century (OED: "Knowledge is a brave thing," 1834). So, if this verse were added in the 1800s, we'd have a very funny pun here.

stare When a horse's coat was frizzy, it was said to "stare," to stand out in all directions (kind of like the way my hair looks after a sleepless night). The German word "starren" has a similar meaning: to *bristle*, to *stand on end*."

abroad outside the house, outdoors.

pelf money, wealth, riches. In former times, this word had a more general meaning of *property, possessions, goods*. (This is from the Old French word "pelfre," *booty*, which was also the origin of our verb *pilfer*, to steal goods.)

> Old **Mother Niddity Nod**
> Swore by the **pudding-bag**
> She would go to the **Stoken Church Fair**.
> And then Old **Father** Peter
> Said he would meet her,
> Before she got half-way there.

(I love to hear of love between the elderly.)

Mother . . . Father These were titles given out of respect for elderly people (as with "Father Short," above, page 120). My aunt, Elnora Burke, was affectionately referred to as "Ma Burke" by the children in her neighborhood.

Niddity Nod In 1898, the *English Dialect Dictionary* defined "niddity-nod" as "a foolish person." The expression apparently came from "niddle-noddle" which, as a verb, meant "to do anything in a dreamy, bewildered way; to walk slowly; to dawdle," and as a noun "a foolish person; anything wavering or unstead," (similar to "nod," see also "noddle," above, page 43).

pudding-bag the bag or gut used in making sausage. (See "pudding-poke," above, page 113.) The plural form "bags" is used in Scotland and northern England dialects for *entrails, guts, stomach*.

There is a vowel rhyme here with "nod" and "bag," which were pronounce something like /nawd/ and /bawg/ (see page 207).

Stoken Church The town of Stokenchurch is about 15 miles ESE of Oxford. Its name comes from Old English "stocce cerise," which means *church built of stocks* or t*imber church*, (probably made of logs).

Fair The town of Stokenchurch still has a Christmas Fair in December, as well as a Summer Fete in June. Village fairs have been a strong tradition, for they are still very common in Britain. Now they are usually called "fetes" (according to Norman Schurr, in his 1974 book, *British Self-taught: with Comments in American*), and they are "an important part of English life.

Not only churches and organizations . . . but apparently every village in England, down to the smallest, organizes a *fete*. The village fete is annual and is a small-scale country fair, sometimes preceded by a parade with floats. Attendance at a village fete has been spotty in many cases, and in some villages dire talk of discontinuing the practice is almost as regular as the fete itself." (Schurr, 142–43).

>Margaret wrote a letter
>**Sealed it with her finger**,
>Threw it in the **dam**
>For the dusty miller.
>
>Dusty was his coat,
>Dusty was his **siller**,
>Dusty was the kiss
>I'd from the dusty miller.
>
>If I had my pockets
>Full of gold and siller,
>I would give it all
>To my dusty miller.

Sealed it with her finger She was probably sealing the wax with a signet ring which would reveal the identity of the sender.

dam Many gristmills were powered by a waterwheel which was turned by water spilling in from a millpond. To keep the water level high enough, a dam was built across a stream or small river. I'm not sure why Margaret tossed her letter *in* the dam instead of *on* it, but the dam's pond was probably called a "dam."

siller a Scots word for silver or money.

>The daughter of the **farrier**
>Could find no one to marry her,
>Because she said
>She would not wed
>A man who could not carry her.

> The foolish girl was wrong enough
> And had to wait quite long enough,
>> For as she sat,
>> She grew so fat
> That nobody was strong enough.

farrier (from the Latin "ferrum," iron). A farrier now refers to a blacksmith who shoes horses. However, before the advent of modern veterinary medicine, a farrier was sort of a horse doctor as well, one who treated all kinds of equine ailments.

(Since this unkind poem is jeering obesity, it would also fit in the chapter on Taunts and Satire.)

> On Saturday night
> Shall be all my **care**
> To **powder my locks**
> And **curl** my hair.
>
> On Sunday morning
> My love will come in
> When he will marry me
> With a gold **ring**.

care We think of "care" as concern, solicitude, carefulness, even worry. The meaning here was just as strong, if not more so, as defined in a dictionary published in 1740 by Dyche and Pardon: "the doing a thing with prudence, diligence, caution, observation, and consideration."

powder my locks In the 1700s, a scented powder made of fine flour or starch was used in hairdressing by women and men for sprinkling on the hair or wig.

curl For hundreds of years, of course, there were no electric curling irons, but curling irons with wooden handles were available. They were set near the fire in a fireplace or put on top of a wood-stove. The obvious danger of using an iron that was too hot was that your skin could get burned and/or the hair could be so badly damaged it would just fall off. So people definitely would need to use all their "care" to curl their hair.

ring This was probably pronounced like "rin" and it would rhyme with "in" at the second line of this verse. In Early Modern English, -**ng** at the end of words often became **n**. (For example, "thing" would become "thin") This happened most frequently in unstressed syllables.

(See above with "warnin" on page 55 and "codling" page 129). Today, with informal English, dropping the **g** in unstressed syllable is still very common: ("I do my best thinkin' when I'm drinkin' lemonade.")

> **It's once** I courted as pretty a lass
> As ever your eyes did see.
> But now she's come to such a pass,
> She never will do for me.
>
> She invited me to her own house,
> Where **oft** I'd been before.
> And she tumbled me into the **hogtub**,
> And I'll never go there any more

It's once It was once upon a time.

oft often. The word "oft" or "ofte" is from Old English. The word "often" is a later variant and became more common in the 1500s.

Should the **t** in "often" be pronounced? For hundreds of years, it was not, but during the 1800s, as more people became literate and learned that "often" had a **t**, some decided to give it a "spelling pronunciation." Most descriptive dictionaries (that record how English "is" spoken) give both pronunciations. Many prescriptive dictionaries (that record how English "should" be spoken) give only the silent **t** version.

The natural thing for people to do is to use pronunciations that are easier. For example, the **t** in "most" is clearly heard before vowels, as in "Most apples are red." But the **t** is virtually silent before consonants, as in "Most cherries are red too." Actually, in the compound word "oftentimes" that **t** is never pronounced.

(For more information on words with a silent **t**, there is a good blog in *grammarphobia.com*.)

hogtub This word sounds a lot like "hot tub," doesn't it? Except a hogtub is definitely not a pleasant place to be, even if a pretty lass tumbled you into it. A hogtub was a trough into which all kinds of sloppy garbage were thrown to feed the pigs. Another name for it was "hogwash," a word that has been extended to refer to anything disgusting or ridiculous. I like the OED's definition: "Contemptuously applied to weak inferior liquor or any worthless stuff."

Occasionally we find animals in love ballads who are personified in human-like situations, behaving and talking like people. Scholars refer to this as anthropomorphism (from the Greek "anthropos," human being + "morphe," form).

Two of the most famous stories deal with the romance between Jenny Wren and Cock Robin and between Mr. Frog and Miss Mouse:

Brace yourself. The first romantic rhyme rambles on for *thirty-six* verses! For long ballads like this, it's better to read the whole story first, and then go back to examine the high-lighted words.

> It was on a merry time,
> When **Jenny Wren** was young,
> So neatly **as** she danced,
> And so sweetly as she sung —
>
> **Robin Redbreast** lost his heart.
> He was a gallant bird.
> He doff'd his hat to Jenny,
> And thus, to her he said:
>
> "My dearest Jenny Wren,
> If you will but be mine,
> You shall dine on cherry pie
> And drink nice **currant wine**."
>
> "I'll dress you like a **Goldfinch**
> Or like a peacock **gay**.
> So, if you'll have me, Jenny,
> Let us appoint the day."

Jenny blush'd behind her **fan**,
And thus declared her **mind**.
"Then let it be tomorrow, **Bob**,
I take your offer kind."

"Cherry pie is very good,
So is currant wine;
But I'll wear my **russet** gown
And never dress too **fine**."

Robin rose up early,
Before the break of day.
He flew to Jenny Wren's house
To sing a **roundelay**.

He met the Cock and Hen,
And **bade** the Cock **declare**
This was his wedding day
With Jenny Wren the fair.

And first came Parson **Rook**,
With his spectacles and **band**.
And one of **Mother Hubbard's books**
He held within his hands.

The Sparrow and **Tom-Tit**,
And many more were there.
All came to see the wedding
Of Jenny Wren the fair.

Then follow'd him the Lark,
For he could sweetly sing,
And he was to be the **clerk**
At Cock Robin's wedding.

He sang of Robin's love
For little Jenny Wren,

And when he came unto the end.
Then he began again.

The Goldfinch came on next
To give away the bride.
The **Linnet**, being bridesmaid,
Walk'd by Jenny's side.

And as she was a-waiting,
Said, "Upon my word,
I think that your Cock Robin
Is a very **pretty** bird.

The Blackbird and the Thrush,
And charming **Nightingale**,
Whose soft "**jug**" sweetly echoes
Through every grove and dale.

The **Bullfinch** walked by Robin,
And thus, to him did say,
"Pray **mark**, friend Robin Redbreast,
That Goldfinch dressed so gay;

What though her gay apparel
Becomes her very well,
Yet Jenny's modest dress and look
Must **bear away the bell**."

Then came the bride and bridegroom.
Quite plainly was she dressed,
And blushed so much her cheeks were
As red as Robin's breast.

But Robin cheered her up.
"My pretty Jen," said he,
"We're going to be married,
And happy we shall be."

"Oh, then," says Parson Rook,
"Who gives this maid away?"
"I do," says the Goldfinch,
"And her **fortune** I will pay:

Here's a bag of grain of many sorts,
And other things beside.
Now happy be the bridegroom,
And happy be the bride!"

"And will you have her, Robin,
To be your wedded wife?"
"Yes, I will," said Robin,
"And love her all my life!"

"And will you have him, Jenny,
Your husband now to be?"
"Yes, I will," said Jenny,
"And love him heartily!"

Then on her finger fair
Cock Robin put the ring.
"You're married now," says Parson Rook,
While the Lark aloud did sing:

"Happy be the bridegroom,
And happy be the bride!
And may not man, nor bird, nor beast
This happy pair divide!"

The birds were asked to dine—
Not Jenny's friends alone,
But every **pretty songster**
That had Cock Robin known.

They had a cherry pie,
Beside some currant wine,

And every guest brought something,
That sumptuous they might dine.

Now they all sat or stood,
To eat and drink.
And everyone said
What he happened to think.

They each took a **bumper**,
And drank to the pair,
Cock Robin the bridegroom
And Jenny the fair.

The dinner things removed,
They all began to sing,
And soon they made the place
Near a mile around to ring.

The concert it was fine,
And every bird **tried**
Who should sing for Robin
And Jenny Wren the bride.

When in came the **Cuckoo**,
And he made a great **rout**.
He caught hold of Jenny
And pulled her about.

Cock Robin was angry,
And so was the Sparrow,
Who fetched in a hurry
His bow and his arrow.

His aim then he took,
But he took it not right.
His skill was not good,
Or he shot in a fright;

> For the Cuckoo he miss'd.
> But Cock Robin he kill'd!
> And all the birds mourn'd
> That his blood was so spill'd

Yes, a very sad ending, but the use of tragic, melodramatic endings was common in the old poems, songs, and stories of folk literature for hundreds of years—even until the early 1900s.

The mating of a robin and a wren is also a centuries-old tradition. In 1906, the nursery rhyme scholar Lina Eckenstein wrote: "It was the custom in many parts of England to regard the robin as the male and the wren as the female. One such rhyme in Lancashire goes: 'The robin and wren / Are God's cock and hen.'" She went on to say that "bird wedding stories were also popular in France and Spain, [but that] the feast is always spoiled by the cat rushing in." (*Comparative Studies in Nursery Rhymes*, 205–07)

This poem, however, ends differently. The ending was apparently taken from an older, very popular poem concerning the death of Cock Robin which begins: "Who killed Cock Robin? / I, said the Sparrow, / With my bow and arrow, / I killed Cock Robin."

(For the complete text of this poem, including various theories about its origin, see Opie, 130–33.)

I was not able to discover where or when this much longer thirty-six-stanza version originated.

Jenny Wren For many years, this name for the wren had been popular, especially in nursery rhymes for young children. "Jenny" is a nickname for "Jane" and was often used to denote a female animal, for example a "jenny-ass" for a female donkey and a "jenny-hooper" or a "jenny-tit" for some female birds.

as (archaic) in the manner that. The sense here is: "so neatly in the way that she'd danced, / And so sweetly in the way that she'd sung."

Robin Redbreast The European robin (*Erithacus rubecula*) is a small bird, only an inch or two bigger than the wren. It's very different from the North American robin (*Turdus migratorius*), which was so called by early colonists because it also has reddish-orange breast feathers. (These brightly marked feathers are higher on the European robin, covering its face, throat, and breast; on the American robin they cover the breast and the entire abdomen.)

On the European continent, the robin is generally called "redbreast" or "redthroat." But in English, an interesting name change has taken place. At first, the Middle English word for the robin was "redbrest." Then the nickname "Robin" (a variant of "Robert") was given to the bird apparently sometime in the Middle Ages, and for centuries thereafter the two words were often used together (as my parents sometimes did in the mid-1900s). Today "robin," the former nickname, is the accepted name for the bird; and "redbreast," the former name, is now sort of a tagged-on nickname.

currant wine I discovered that there are two kinds of currants. The kind bought in the grocery is a small seedless grape, dried like a raisin. As far as I know, it's used only in cookies. For centuries it was imported to Northern Europe from the Mediterranean region, particularly from Corinth—hence its name "currant," from the French term for the fruit "raisin de Corinthe" (in France "th" is pronounced /t/.)

The other kind of currant (so named because it resembles the first kind) is a small, sour berry with a red, black, or white color. It grows on a prickly shrub and belongs to the same genus as the gooseberry. It is used in jellies and jams. But before the 1970s, I had never heard of it used for making wine.

First, I searched for it in books on wine. No luck. Then I tried general reference books. The only thing I could find was a brief quotation in the OED from a 1648 recipe: "Currants-wine, take a pound of the best currants." Had it become a thing of the past? I wondered what it had tasted like. Could it be made from scratch? Not being a wine-maker myself, I decided to try to buy some.

If you want to "throw a curveball" to a wine-shop proprietor, just call up and ask for currant wine. But finally, much to my delight, there was one dealer in San Diego County who found ("down in the cellar") a bottle of black currant wine imported from Denmark—and only $3.10 a fifth! Sound cheap? Mind you, this was in 1973. I bought a bottle the same day. (Today you can buy it online for about $9 a fifth.)

Black currant wine is very dark, almost opaque. It's a little pulpy, like country-brewed raw apple cider. It's a good, sweet wine with a strong, robust flavor. The alcohol content (18%) is higher than that of most wines. I don't know if it's still used anywhere as a wedding wine, but the inscription on the back of the bottle said: "A perfect gift for Mother and for all festive occasions."

Goldfinch A small brightly colored European finch (*Cordless caruelis*). The goldfinch was so called from the yellow on its wings. It was often kept as a caged bird.

fan After about 1650, France took Italy's place as the principal producer of luxury wares. It was then that Paris became the center of fashion. The folding fans, with printed or painted scenes, and used by English women, were thus imported from France.

By the 18th century, the fan was considered to be a necessary part of a lady's public appearance. During the first three decades of the 19th century, when the narrow, light empire style was in fashion, very small fans (about eight inches in radius) were popular.

mind (obsolete) a wish, desire, opinion. Shakespeare used the noun in this sense; for example: "it is my father's mind that I repair to Rome" (*Titus Andronicus* 5.3.1) Today it's used only when an upset person is expressing a strong *intention*, as in "I've got a good mind to tell him what I think of him."

Bob "Robin" was originally a diminutive form of "Robert," and the nickname "Bob" was used for both names. In the 13th century, the name "Robin" was so popular that it was more common than "Robert" itself. Today, "Robin" is often used as an independent name (for boys or girls) and "Bob" is usually a nickname only for "Robert."

russet a coarse, homespun, woolen cloth of reddish-brown, grey, or neutral color, formerly worn by peasants and country-folk.

fine showy, ostentatiously elegant.

roundelay a short, simple song with a refrain. It was also used specifically to refer to a bird's song. For example, the OED quotes from Sir Walter Scott's 1813 work *Rokeby* (II, XVI):

"While linnet, lark, and blackbird gay / forth the nuptial roundelay."
Note that here, as with Cock Robin, the roundelay was a mating song.

bade (past of "bid") obsolete for *asked* but now means *commanded.* The pronunciation of this word can rhyme with "fad" or with "fade."

declare make a formal announcement or proclamation.

Rook an abundant European corvine bird, about the size and color of the American crow.
  His thievery habits probably led to the use of "rook" as a verb, meaning "to swindle or cheat," as in "I thought it was a fair exchange, but I got rooked."

band a clerical collar; a white cloth strip hanging down from the neck in front. (called "bands" after about 1800.)

Mother Hubbard's books A "bible" for many youngsters, the first children's book about Mother Hubbard was called *The Comic Adventures of Old Mother Hubbard and Her Dog*, published in 1805.
  This means that this verse could not have been written before 1805. However, other verses in this rhyme are older. For example, we know that the ending was derived from 18th century chapbook stories about the death of Cock Robin.

Tom-Tit a pet name for the "titmouse." (See "tom-tit" above, page 63.)

clerk (rhymes with "lark") a parson's assistant who sang the responses.

Linnet a small finch, not found in the United States, but common in Europe. The Linnet (from Old French "linette") feeds on flax seeds, which are also used to make linen (from Old French "lin," flax).

Nightingale The male of this European thrush is noted for his melodious mating song, which it can perform at night *or* day. The name literally means "night singer" and comes from Old English "nihtegale" from "niht" (night) and "galen" (to sing).

jug a word for the nightingale's sound, first used in the 1530s.

Bullfinch This small Old-World bird is well known for its soft, warbling song. It is related to the grosbeak.

mark notice, pay attention

what The sense here is "*even* though." But nowhere could I find "what" defined as *even*. So perhaps the word "what" was just an interjection (like *lo*, *now*, or *well*) which was used only to begin or call attention to the rest of the sentence (although the latest OED example of it being used this way was from Chaucer in the 1300s).

bear away the bell take first place. The OED conjectures that it originally meant "to carry off the prize," perhaps a gold or silver bell given as a prize in races or the like. The phrase has been popular for centuries. It was known and used by Chaucer. The earliest mention of it that I found was written around 1303 in a book called *Handlyng Synne* [Handling Sin]: "Yn alle sloghness he bereth the bel." ["In all slough-ness, he bears the bell."] To paraphrase: In all manner of sinking into muddy sin, he takes the cake. (As recorded in Whiting's book *Proverbs*, 37)

fortune dowry.

pretty When describing the wren as "pretty Jenny," it just means *attractive*. But here, "pretty" means a *skillful* or *clever* songbirds.

songster a songbird, or anyone who sings, especially one who sings skillfully. This is a very old word, in Old English: "sangstre."

The interesting thing is that a thousand years ago, this word referred *only* to female singers. It wasn't until the 1300s that "songster" began to designate male singers as well.

Then, in the early 1700s, it was decided (by patriarchal men?) that "songsters" should apply *only* to male singers. Henceforth, a female singer should be called a "songstress." How's that for a linguistic gender switch?

Of course, the -ess suffix started to become common back in the 12th century with words borrowed from the French Normans: (for example, countess, hostess, princess, mistress). And later -ess was added to English words (priestess, authoress, poetess, etc.) However, in the late 20th century, in the interest of gender equity, -ess has been removed from words.

Most females in acting professions prefer to be caller "actors" rather than "actresses." Other words have been changed completely. Airlines used the word "stewardess" since 1931, but in the late 1970s it was replace with "flight attendant." Likewise, a "waitress" is now a "server."

bumper a cup or glass (of wine, beer, etc.) filled to the brim, especially when drunk as a toast. It brings to mind the phrase "bumper crop," used at harvest time when a field is filled up with a good yield. (The term might come from the word "bump," a swelling.)

tried (archaic) settling a matter or quarrel by a test or contest; fought out. Web NW gives the example: "The knights tried the dispute in a joust." (from the Late Latin "tritare," to *grind out*)

Cuckoo Why was this bird chosen as the villain? Well, for one thing, the European cuckoo (like the American cowbird) does not build its own nest, but lays its eggs in the nests of other birds. Moreover, to add insult to injury, the young cuckoos hatch first and push the eggs of the host bird out of the nest. In addition, unlike the robin and the wren, the cuckoo shies away from humans. It usually stays hidden and is rarely seen. This fact gave rise to the superstition that if you see a cuckoo, you will die within the same year. (Paysan, *Birds of the World*, 6, 80)

rout uproar, noisy disturbance. (Now, usually a *disorderly flight*.)

Time for a sigh of relief; the next Wren/Robin poem has only *four* verses:

> Little Jenny Wren
> Fell sick **upon a time**.
> In came Robin Redbreast,
> And brought her cake and wine.
>
> "**Eat of** my cake, Jenny,
> Drink of my wine."
> "Thank you, Robin, kindly,
> You shall be mine."

> Jenny, she got well,
> And stood upon her **feet**.
> And told Robin plainly
> She loved him not a **bit**.
>
> Robin he was angry,
> And hopped upon a twig.
> Saying, "**Out upon** you! **Fie** upon you!
> **Bold-faced jig!**"

upon a time once upon a time; but not just shortened here for the sake of meter. "Upon a time" was (once upon a time) a phrase in itself. For example, in the 1534 edition of the *Coverdale Bible*, in Job 1.6: "Now vpon a tyme..." [Printers in the 1500s used **v** for **u**]

eat of This use for "of" after a verb is now archaic—if not obsolete. (see "eating of" on page 108 above)

feet ... bit It's possible that there was a vowel rhyme with "feet" and "bit." The **i** in "bit" has had the same sound as in "sit" since Old English times; so apparently in this poem "feet" was pronounced like "fit." In his book *English Pronunciation* 1500-1700, the author says that this change in the vowel sound was rare before a single consonant, but that "feet" occasionally sounded like "fit." In fact, a 1673 homophone list paired "fit" and "feet." (Dobson, I, 408; II, 503-04). Similarly, the vowel sound of "creek" changed in Early Modern English from "crick" to "creek." But even today, in many parts of the United States, the word "creek" is still pronounced like "crick."

out upon (archaic and dialectal) an exclamation expressing reproach or abhorrence. Actually, the word "out" was also used by itself in the same way, as in Shakespeare: "Out, out, Lucetta. That will be ill-favored" (*The Two Gentlemen of Verona*, 2.7.54)

Apparently, "out" came to be used alongside "shame," which eventually acquired a similar meaning and was used as a substitute for "out," as in the phrase "shame upon you."

fie an expression of disgust or disapproval, another way of saying "shame upon you." Taken from an Old French word, it has been used in English since the 1300s.

bold-faced impudent, saucy (first used in the late 16th century). In the late 19th century, the term "boldface" came to be used in a different way by printers: to refer to the heavy-faced **bold** type print.

jig an accusatory term used by Robin against Jenny for being a thankless lover. This word was hard to find, but as near as I can determine, it's a variant of the obsolete "gig," a wanton, silly girl; a flighty person. Robin would appreciate the OED's example (from the late 16th century): "Thou selfewill gig that dost detest my faithful loue . . ." The CD tells us that "gig," used in this sense, was properly pronounced like "jig."

"Gig" could have been a short form of the Elizabethan word "giglet" or "giglot," meaning a *lewd, wanton woman*. "Gig" was probably taken from the Old French "gigolette," a *public dancer*, a *prostitute*, which later was used to form the English word "gigolo."

The next nursery rhyme was another poem based on an old traditional song. It had 13 verses with two lines in each verse, but a refrain was sung before and after the second line:

	A frog, he would a wooing go,
(Refrain):	Heigho! says Rowley,
	Whether his mother would let him or **no**.
(Refrain):	With a **rowley, powley, gammon** and spinach.
	Heigho! says **Anthony Rowley**.
	So off he set with his **opera hat**,
(Refrain):	Heigho! says Rowley
	And on the way he met with a rat.
(Refrain):	With a rowlley, powley, gammon and spinach.
	Heigho! says Anthony Rowley.
	"Now pray, Mr. Rat, won't you come with me
	Kind **Mrs**. Mousy for to see?"

And when they came to Mousy's hall,
They gave a knock and they gave a call.

"Pray, Mrs. Mouse, are you within?"
"Yes, kind sirs, I'm sitting to spin."

"Pray, Mr. Frog, will you give us a song?
But let it be something that's not very long."

"Indeed, Mrs. Mouse, I shall have to say no.
A cold has made me as hoarse as a crow."

"Since you have caught cold, Mr. Frog," Mousy **said**,
"I'll sing you a song that I have just made."

But while they were all **a-merrymaking**,
A cat and her kittens came tumbling in.

The cat she seized the rat by the **crown**.
And the kittens pulled the little mouse down.

This put Mr. Frog in a terrible fright.
He put on his hat and wished them good-night.

As Froggy was crossing over a brook,
A lily-white duck came and gobbled him up.

So here is an end of one, two, three—
The Rat, and the Mouse and little Frog-gee.

The lines of this poem's *refrain* are not found anywhere before the 19th century, but there are a number of older versions of the song's *story* dating back as far as the 16th century. (Opie, 179)

no not. In the Scots dialect, "no" is commonly used for "not," but in other dialects this use of the word is preserved in the phrase "whether or no" (as in this rhyme).

Love and/or Marriage

rowley, powley (the **ow** sounds like "oh") an obsolete or dialectal variant of "roly-poly," and was originally one word: "rowley-powley."

It's not a very old term, since it did not appear in writing until 1820, and it referred to anything or anyone that was short and pudgy. By 1836 in Britain, it began to designate a sweet pastry dough that was filled with fruit or jam, formed into a roll, and baked or steamed. It's also called "roly-poly pudding."

So, although some parts of this nursery rhyme may be very old, this particular refrain must be from the early 1800s.

gammon a ham or side of bacon, salted and smoked or dried. It also could mean the bottom piece of a side (flitch) of bacon, including the hind leg (from an old word in Normandy, France: "gambon," from "gambe," leg. This is also the source of *gams*, which is the slang word for a woman's legs.) I suppose one could make a hearty meal from roly-poly, gammon, and spinach.

Anthony Rowley This name seems to have been made up to go with "rowley-powley." I was unable to find out who (if anyone) Anthony Rowley was. "Rowley" itself is a common name for several places in England. It literally meant "rough meadow" (from Old English "ruh," *rough* + "leah," *lea* or *meadow*.)

opera hat The opera hat that's been in style since about 1800 is the cylindrical top hat (like Abe Lincoln wore). Prior to that time, the term "opera hat" referred to a flat, three-cornered hat (like Napoleon wore) that came into fashion about 1770. It was known as a "chapeau-bras," literally: 'arm-hat,' apparently because two corners poked out like small arms to the left and right.

So, Mr. Frog could have worn either hat, depending on the time when the second verse was written. I'd go with the top hat.

Mrs. This was the abbreviation of "Mistress," a title once conferred on married *and* unmarried women alike. The term was so used in Shakespeare's *The Merry Wives of Windsor*. A dictionary published in 1740 said that the title "sometimes signified the chief or principal person of a house or family of the female kind, whether single or married; sometimes a sweet-heart, or one that a man is courting for a wife." (Dyche & Pardon, *A New General English Dictionary*)

Of course, the title "Mr." (for 'Mister') still can refer to a married or an unmarried man. So it's an interesting thought that if the double meaning of "Mrs." had not changed, then the modern term "Ms." need never have been invented!

said The vowel sound in this word used to be the same as in "laid," so the word "said" rhymed with "made" in the next line. In fact, "said" was commonly spelled "sayed" from the 15th through the 17th century. And Lady Gardiner, in a letter written in 1642, used "sade" (as recorded by Davies, *English Pronunciation*, 121).

a-merrymaking another example of **ng** sounding like **n** at the end of words, giving the next line the same end-rhyme. (For **a-** + verb, see page 96.)

crown the top part of the head.

This next story of the courtship of a frog and a mouse is still a popular song—both in its traditional form and in more recent versions. Here are two renditions which I found in the 1961 book *Folksongs for Fun*, (22–23), edited by Oscar Brand. In his preface, Brand says: "Recomposition is a lot healthier than decomposition. These songs live and breathe because they are always on the go, ever changing, always being sung." (3)

>Mister Frog would a-wooing ride, ah hah!
>Mister Frog would a-wooing ride,
>A sword and pistol by his side, ah hah!
>
>He rode up to Miss Mousie's house, (repeat first line)
>"Will you agree to be my spouse?"
>
>"You must get Uncle Rat's consent,
>But he's a very fussy gent."
>
>Uncle Rat he then came home,
>Saying, "Who's been here since I been gone?"
>
>"There has been a handsome gent,
>To marry me he wants your consent."

Gentleman Rat, he rode to town
To buy Miss Mousie's wedding gown.

Where will the **infare** supper be?
Down in the swamp in the **holler** tree.

What will the wedding supper be?
Three green beans and a **black-eyed pea**.

First to come was Mister Moth
Dressed to spread the table cloth.

Next to come was the bumble-bee,
With his **banjo** on his knee.

Next to come was Mister Flea,
Out to have a merry spree.

Then crept in old Mister Cat,
And all the company went **SCAT**!

infare a feast given on entering a new home, especially the reception of the bride in her new home. This custom began in the 1300s and was still very common in the 1800s. (The noun "infare" literally means an *in-going*. It was used in Scotland, north England, and U.S. dialects.)

holler Appalachian dialect word for "hollow," usually a small valley or a lowland between mountains. (See also "fellow," and "feller," above on page 63.)

black-eyed pea This was a staple food of African Americans since the 1600s when the slaves were first brought over from West Africa. By the mid-1700s, slave-owners, including Thomas Jefferson, were growing and eating these peas as well. They are still a popular food, especially in the American South, and eating them is considered to be good luck—especially on important occasions, such as the birth of a new child, New Year's Day, homecomings, and weddings.

banjo a very popular instrument in America since the 17th century, especially for festive or informal occasions.

SCAT If spoken loudly, it's a good way to end the story and to make the little kids jump, scream, and giggle. "Scat" is not a very old English word, not recorded until 1838. It was originally used to drive away a cat.

This next version is an updated one. In the U.S. it became popular in the early 1960s. I learned it from Oscar Brand's *Folksongs for Fun*, (22–23) and love to play it with my baritone uke.

Frogg went a-courtin' and he did go, uh huh.
Frogg went a-courtin' and he did go, uh huh.
Frogg went a-courtin' and he did go
To the Coconut Grove for the midnight show,
Uh huh, uh huh, uh huh.

Molly Mouse was a hat check girl—woo woo
(He knew it all the time)
Molly Mouse was a hat check girl—woo woo
Molly Mouse was a hat check girl.
He thought he'd give this chick a whirl,
Woo woo, woo woo, woo woo.

He sauntered up to Molly Mouse's side, uh huh.
(The direct approach)
He sauntered up to Molly Mouse's side, uh huh
When he got up to Molly Mouse's side,
He whispered, "Molly, will you be my bride?"
Uh huh, uh huh, uh huh.

Not without Uncle Rat's consent, uh uh.
(Her uncle wrestled on TV)
Not without Uncle Rat's consent, uh uh
Not without Uncle Rat's consent
I wouldn't marry the president.
Uh uh, uh uh, uh uh.

Uncle Rat said, "Clyde, better hit the road. Farewell.
Uncle Rat said, "Clyde, better hit the road. Goodbye.
Uncle Rat said, "Clyde, better hit the road.
You ain't no frog. You're a horny toad.
Farewell, goodbye, adios."

    This last story about Frog and Miss Mouse was carefully crafted with metrical lines (iambic tetrameter). It also has a happy ending.

A Frog among some rushes dwelt.
A bachelor was he.
No frog was ever so **polite**,
Or such a beau could be.

In passing near a cottage once,
He chanced to look above,
And there beheld a pretty Mouse,
With whom he fell in love.

Her eyes and whiskers he admired,
Her coat of softest fur,
And wished to make her feel for him
The love he felt for her.

So he put on his scarf of red,
His opera hat he wore.
And, hopping to the house,
He gave a rat-tat at the door.

Mousey, as bashful as a **miss**.
Retired from Froggy's view,
But peeped at him from out her hole,
As Froggy nearer drew.

Froggy approached and doffed his hat.
Then bending on one knee,
Said, "Fairest Mouse, pray listen
To my tale of love for thee.

In me, the wretchedest of Frogs.
You see a love-sick **swain**.
Oh, say you'll **Mistress** Froggy be
And make me well **again**.

A tiny house I have, **hard by**
'Tis built among the rushes.
You shall have **dainties** every day,
With **hips** from wild-rose bushes."

Miss Mousey **simpered** and looked prim,
Then, modestly she said,
"I do admire your **yellow dress**
And handsome **scarf of red**.

Oh, how can I resist that tongue,
Those **eyes of golden red**.
Your offer I accept at once,
And will no other wed.

polite This word meant not just well-mannered, but also "fine, well-bred, or accomplished with all manner of genteel arts, or useful learning." (as defined in Dyche & Pardon's 1740 dictionary)

miss This word was "sometimes a term of gentility for a young girl of the better sort."
(quoting again from Dyche & Parton)

swain (archaic and poetic) a country lover, wooer, or sweetheart, especially in pastoral poetry.

Mistress Here, the title of "Mistress" is used for a soon-to-be *married* woman, as opposed to "Miss Mouse" (two verses later) which refers to an *unmarried* woman.
  So, this poem if probably more recent than the one on page 177, "A frog, he would. a-wooing go." The mouse in that poem had the title of "Mrs." which, in the 18th century, could be used for an unmarried female (unless

the mouse were widowed—or divorced), but in this poem notice that the unmarried mouse had the title of "Miss," denoting a later time of origin

again In British English, the vowel sound is the same as in "gain," and in this verse, "again" rhymes with "swain."

hard by near-by, very close (Old English "hearde," *firmly*)

dainties rich delicacies, pleasing in appearance, aroma, and taste.

hips the fruits of the rose flower, which appear after the petals fade away. The seed pod is usually red, about the size of a small marble, and oval or round in shape. The outside cover is smooth and firm. A pleasant tasting tea can be made from rose hips (and they're very high in vitamin C).

simpered smiled in a silly, self-conscious way.

yellow dress yellow clothing; dressed in yellow. Does England have yellow frogs? There is a frog with a yellowish light brown skin, and throughout the British Isles and northern Europe it is quite common. It's called—believe it or not—the Common Frog (*Rana temporaria*).

scarf of red There is a thin dark red stripe under each side of the Common Frog's jaw.

eyes of golden red The iris of the Common Frog's eyes is gold in color.

CHAPTER 17

Rhymes of Scotland and Northern England

The nursery rhymes in this chapter all contain words that have been used in the northern dialects of Great Britain, particularly in Scotland and the northern counties of England.

> "Shake a leg, wag a leg,
> When will you **gang**?"
>
> "At midsummer, Mother,
> When the days are **lang**."

The second verse was probably sarcasm, much as "I'm coming, Mother." "Yes. So is Christmas."

gang go, leave, depart (archaic and poetic). It was often used by Robert Burns 200 years ago). Old English had two words for "go"—*gan* and *gangan*; "gan" later replaced "gangan" and became "go," except in the North. But "gangan" survives in our words "gangway," and "gangplank" and is the base of "gang," a group of individuals who *go* places together.

lang long. (*lang* and *gang* both rhyme with *sang*). In Old English there were two words for "long"—*lang* and *long*. The word *lang* came to be used only in the North, and *long* in the South. This was due to a general phonetic development in southern England's Middle English, in which the vowel sounds changed before nasal consonants /n/, /ng/, and /m/.

Therefore, the OE nouns "stan" and "sang" remained as "stane" (sounds like "steen") and "sang" in the North, but these OE words became "stone" and "song" in the South.

So, how long are the *midsummer* days in northern Britain? Well, at the end of July, Glasgow, in the southern part of Scotland, has almost 16 hours of daylight (not counting the one or two hours of extended twilight); the town of Thurso, up on the northern coast of the Scottish Highlands, has 17.5 hours of daylight with sunset around 10 p.m. By comparison, the town of Canton, in northern New York state, has about 14.5 hours of daylight at midsummer, with sunset at about 8:30. (Summer begins, as you know, on the *longest* day, June 20 or 21.)

> **Bobbie Shaftoe** has a cow,
> Black and white about the **mow**.
> Open the gate and let her **through**,
> Bobbie Shaftoe's **ain** cow.
>
> Bobbie Shaftoe had a hen,
> **Cockle button**, cockle **ben**,
> She lays eggs for **gentlemen**,
> But none for Bobbie Shaftoe.

Another version of this rhyme, in *The Oxford Dictionary of Nursery Rhymes*, begins: "Charlie Warley had a cow." According to Opie (117), this poem may be part of an old Scots song about a certain Katherine Bairdie which dates back to the early 17th century.

A similar poem, found in Montgomerie's *A Book of Scottish Nursery Rhymes*, (79), has four verses. The first two are:

> Katie Beardie had a cow
> Black and white about the mom
> Wasna that a dainty [fine, nice] cow?
> Dance Katie Beardie!
>
> Katie Beardie had a hen
> Cackled but and cackled ben
> Wasna that a dainty hen?
> Dance Katie Beardie!

Bobbie Shaftoe The identity of Bobbie Shaftoe is unclear, although he was the subject of a number of nursery rhymes. In 1849 Halliwell (in his book *Popular Rhymes and Nursery Tales*, 201) said that most ancient verses of this old song seem to be:

> Bobby Shaftoe's gone to sea,
> Silver buckles on his knee.
> He'll come back and marry me,
> Bonny Bobby Shaftoe.
>
> Bobby Shafto's bright and fair,
> Combing down his yellow hair.
> He's my ain for evermair,
> Bonny Bobby Shaftoe.

An apocryphal (more recent?) verse goes:

> Bobby Shafto's getten a bairn,
> For to dangle on his arm —
> On his arm and on his knee.
> Bonny Bobby Shaftoe.

Halliwell went on to say that "Miss Bellasyse, the heiress of Brancepeth, died for love of Robert Shafto, of Whitworth [located in Lancashire, north of Manchester] whose portrait at Whitworth represents him as very young and handsome, with *yellow* hair. He was the favourite candidate in the election of 1791, when he was popularly called Bonny Bobby Shafto; and the old song of the older Bobby, who, it seems, was also 'bright and fair, combing down his *yellow* hair,' was revived . . ." (210) And this verse was added:

> Bobby Shafto's looking out,
> All his ribbons flew about,
> All the ladies gave a shout—
> Hey, for Bobby Shafto!

According to Baring-Gould, "the original Bobby Shafto is said to have lived in Hollybrook, County Wicklow [in southern Ireland] and died in 1737." (117). Is this Bobby Shafto the one who went to sea with "silver buckles at his knee," that is, the "older" Bobbly referred to by Halliwell? Perhaps. But this Bobby died in 1737, and knee-band buckles did not come into fashion until after 1735. (Cunnington, *English Costume in the 18th Century*, 66)

As you can see, it's very difficult to give a specific date to any poem if it had different verses composed at different times.

mow (also spelled "mou") a Scots variant of "mouth." This word rhymes with "cow."

through This word also rhymes with "cow." The Scots also used the spelling "throw" (pronounced the same way) from the 14th to the 19th century. (This word also rhymes with the British pronunciation of "slough")

ain Scots for "own." The word can also mean *one* or *only*.
(from Old English "an" for *one*)

cockle to cluck like a hen. (From Middle English "cakelen," which was also the origin of "cackle.")

button (in the) outer room of a two-room house, out in the kitchen. (This is a variant of the Old English and Middle English "buton," *outside of*.)

ben (in the) parlor, the inner room of a cottage. (From Old English "bin," *in, within*.) Thus, the Scots phrase "but and ben" means *all through the house*, literally: *without and within*.

gentlemen To quote again from Dyche and Pardon's 18th century dictionary: ". . . in the present common acceptation of the word, any person that does not follow a mean or mechanical business is called a *gentleman*, as lawyers, physicians, &c." So, it had very little to do with politeness or good manner, but much to do with class distinction.

If you got your hands dirty baking bread, fixing wagons, or laying bricks, you were definitely in the lower working class. Only upper-class men were "gentlemen."

> **Bessy** Bell and Mary Gray,
> They were two **bonny** lasses.
> They built their house upon the **lea**
> And covered it with **rushes**.
>
> Bessy **kept** the garden gate,
> And Mary kept the pantry.
> Bessy always had to **wait**,
> While Mary lived in **plenty**.

Bessy A nickname for "Elizabeth" and was commonly used (you guessed it) during Elizabethan times. According to Merriam-Webster, "Bessy" was "a stock character in English folk dances and plays, played by a man dressed as a woman."

The name "Elizabeth" (or "Elisabeth") has been in use for thousands of years. It comes from the Hebrew phrase "consecrated to God." In the New Testament it was the name of the mother of John the Baptist. Throughout history it has been changed into *many* different forms, including these 21 names: Bess, Bessy, Bessie, Bet, Bett, Bette, Betty, Betsy, Babette, Beth, Bettina, Ellie, Elsa, Elsbeth, Elise, Eliza, Liza, Lisa, Lizzie, Liz, and Lisbeth.

bonny pretty, good-looking, or nice, excellent. In the 18th century it also could have meant *genteel, well-accomplished*, or simply *happy*. This was once a common English word, but now it's found only in Scotland, the North and Midland dialects of England, or—rarely—in some parts of North Ireland.

lea (archaic or poetic) a meadow or pasture; a tract of open ground. It can be pronounced like /lee/ or /lay/. Here it rhymes with "Gray." After the 17th century, "lea" often rhymes with "sea." Today either pronunciation is acceptable. The word originally meant "a light, open place in the middle of a woods, a glade." It's related to the English word *light* and Latin word "lux," (light, especially daylight).

If you like doing crossword puzzles, you'll often use the word "lea."

rushes Rushes are wild plants that grow in wetlands. Because they have long strong leaves, with cylindrical or hollow stems, for hundreds of years they often have been used, like straw or reeds, for thatching roofs. Up to the 17th century, they were also used for covering the stone or dirt floors of castles, churches, and homes. They were plentiful, inexpensive, easily replaced, and gave insulation against the cold. They were often sprinkled with sweet-smelling herbs, which also discouraged mold and bugs.

The word "rushes" is pronounced and spelled "rashes" in the Scots dialect, as in Robert Burns' "Green Grow the Rashes, O" (For the full text of Burns' poem, see Appendix 1.)

This was no doubt the way the word was pronounced in the original version of this nursery rhyme because in the first verse, "rashes" would have rhymed with "lasses."

kept kept watch over, was in charge of.

wait to wait on people, to serve them.

plenty in plentiful, comfortable conditions (with lots of food in the pantry!)

> **Hush-a-ba**, birdie, **croon**, croon,
> Hush-a-ba, birdie, croon.
> > The sheep are **gane**
> > To the **silver wood**,
> And the cows are gane to the **broom**, broom.
>
> And it's **braw** milking the **kye**, kye,
> It's braw milking the kye.
> > The birds are singing,
> > The bells are ringing,
> And the wild **deer** come galloping by.
>
> And hush-a-ba, birdie, croon, croon,
> Hush-a-ba, birdie, croon.
> > The **gaits** are gone
> > To the mountains **hie**,
> And they'll **no** be **hame** till noon, noon.

hush-a-ba the Scots form of "hushaby" See "Bye Baby Bunting," above (127–28). Lullaby words, especially when sung, are used to bring calm and quiet peace.

croon to sing in a low, murmuring tone. (a northern dialect word in Middle English; now chiefly Scots). This word became popular in the U.S. during the Big Band era of the 1930s and 40s. It meant "to sing popular songs in a soft, sentimental manner." My mother called Bing Crosby her favorite "crooner." Others were Tony Bennet, Perry Como, and Nat "King" Cole.

gane the Scots word for "gone" (from "gae," go). It rhymes with "lane."

silver wood This probably refers to the *silver birch*, one of the oldest native tree species in Scotland, being one of the first to emerge after the retreat of the last Ice Age. It's recognized by its whitish bark and its gracefully *drooping* branches (hence its scientific Latin name: *Petula pendular*. Other English words from the same Latin root are *pendulum* and *pendant*.)

broom a shrub with large, handsome, yellow, butterfly-shaped flowers. It is abundant on sandy banks, pastures, and heaths in Britain and western Europe. Brooms for sweeping have been made from this and similar plants. (See "green broom" above, 130.)

braw This is the Scots form of "brave" and it means *fine, nice, good, enjoyable*. In northern dialects, the **v** is often dropped at the end of words, for example *hae* or *ha'* for *have*, and *gie* for *give*. Compare this with the American slang: "gimme" for "give me."

kye (archaic and dialectal) This was a word for "cattle" or "cows" (from Old English "cy," the plural of OE "cu," cow) This word has the same vowel sound as "sky" and rhymes with "by" at the end of the verse

Today the word "coos," the plural of "coo," is more common. In Scotland, late-comers who often show up at the end of a line are said to be "aye [always] at the coo's tail."

deer Since they're "galloping by," we can assume these are probably roe deer or red deer, both native to Scotland.

However, the term "deer" was once used to apply to any four-legged animals. For example, in 1605, Shakespeare wrote: "But mice and rats, and such small deer, / Have been Tom's food for seven long year." (*King Lear* 3.4.144–45).

Red deer are very large, thriving in the northern Highlands and islands of Scotland. An adult male could weigh up to 440 pounds (compared to 150 pounds of America's white-tailed deer). The red deer are sometimes farmed for their meat, hides, and huge antlers.

The roe deer are much smaller, with the males weighing no more than about 77 pounds. Roe deer are increasing in numbers in southern Scotland and can now be sighted in and around towns and cities.

gaits goats (from OE "gat")

hie high. Since Middle English times, this word was used in northern dialects of England and in Scotland. It was pronounced like "hay" and, if so, would have a vowel rhyme with "gane" in the middle of the same verse.

no A common form of "not" in Scots and northern dialects.

hame home. Rhymes with "tame." (from the OE word "ham," [rhymed with "Tom"] which meant *home* or *village*, so it also gave us our word "hamlet.")

> **Thumbikin**, Thumbikin broke the barn.
> **Pinnikin**, Pinnikin stole the **corn**
> **Long-back Gray**
> Carried it away.
> Old **mid-man** sat and saw,
> But **Peesy-Weesy** paid for **a'**.

This nursery rhyme is a finger game played with young children. The adult would touch or squeeze each finger in sequence, from the thumb to the little finger. The rhyme itself will probably remind you of the toe game "This little Piggy went to market."

Thumbikin a small thumb. The "-kin" is a Middle English suffix meaning "little," as in *lambkin* or *catkin*.

(The word "thumbikin" was also a Scotch word for "thumbscrew," a torture device brought to Britain from Moscow around 1684. However, that use of the term would not fit here.)

Pinnikin the index finger. I couldn't locate this word itself, but it's probably a diminutive of "pin" a Scotch word meaning to *steal, pilfer, pinch.*

The 19th century word "pannikin" refers to a small metal pan or cup for drinking. But "pinnikin" may have just been a nonsense word invented by the author to rhyme with "Thumbikin."

corn The Scots word for "oats." It rhymes with "barn." (See "corn," page 136.)

Long-back Gray the long middle finger. "Gray" is the common name for any gray horse. My dad used to sing a song from the early 1900s: "The Old Gray Mare, She Ain't What She Used to Be." (For other verses, Google it.) Which is it "gray" or "grey?" (See above, page 16.)

"Long-back" is an equestrian adjective for any horse whose back is longer than average. The ideal length of a horse's back is 1/3 of its total body length, measured from the withers (the top ridge between the shoulders) to its hips. Having a long back makes it easier for the horse to turn or jump, and some people think long-backs look more elegant. But its back may weaken over time if the horse has to carry or pull heavy loads. So as a long-back horse gets older, its back may dip into a "swayback." Any horse with a back *less* than 1/3 its length is called a "short-back." Many short-backs are very good work horses because they can handle heavy loads more easily. But if their backs are too short, it's hard to fit a saddle onto them.

mid-man This is an obsolete term for a mediator, an uninvolved "man in the middle." Here it refers to the ring finger, which is in the middle between the long finger and the little finger.

Peesy-weesy Apparently, this is a variant of the Scots word "peerie-weerie," the little finger or the little toe. Both words were probably formed from "pee-wee" (the origin of which is unknown). However, it may be a *reduplication* of "wee," like "teeny-weeny" or "itsy-bitsy." (Of course, "wee" is a common Scots word for *tiny* or *small.*)

In Middle English, "we" (or "wei") was a *noun* for "quantity, amount." So "a little we," was a small amount or a little thing. After a while, the word became an *adjective*, a synonym for "little." It's still used as a noun in Scotland, for example "bide a wee" means "wait a minute." (In Old English "weigh" also used to be a noun for *weight*.)

a' the Scots form for "all." According to the OED, **a'** is "the current spelling in modern literary Scotch." It rhymes with "saw." In 1794 Robert Burns used it in his famous poem "For a' That and a' That."

> Clap, clap handies,
> Mammy's wee, wee **ain**.
> Clap, clap handies,
> Daddie's comin' hame,
> Hame **till** his bonny
> Wee **bit laddie**.
> Clap, clap handies,
> My wee, wee ain.

ain one (or) own. Rhymes with "rain" and here with "hame."

till to. In Old English, "till" was probably a noun and meant "a fixed point" (in time or place). So, our word "until" originally meant "up to a certain *time*" and the word "unto" meant "up to a certain *place*." In fact, in the 1600s the *King James Bible*, "unto" was used in the same sense as "to." For example: "they came unto the sepulcher" (Mark 16.2) and "his disciples came unto him" (Matt 5.1).

bit tiny, very small. (As in a "bit" part in a play.) Also, the nursery term "itty-bitty" comes from the phrase "little bit."

laddie a lad. This, of course, is the well-known Scots word for a boy or young man. The original sense of the word was something like "young sprout." (There is an Old English suffix "-led" which still survives in some place-names, such as "Sumerled, literally, 'summer sprout.'")

> Love your **own**, kiss your own,
> Love your own mother, **hinny**;
> For if she was dead and gone,
> You'd never get such another, hinny.

own a term used to refer to blood relatives; here: the child's "own" mother, as opposed to a step-mother. It has long been a popular belief that no bonds could be stronger than those with "your own flesh and blood."

The words "own" and "gone" in this poem may originally have been an end-rhyme using the words "ain" and "gane."

hinny a Scots variant of "honey"

> Cripple Dick upon a **stick**
> And **Sandy** on a **sow**,
> Riding away to **Galloway**
> To buy a pound **o' woo**.

In the *Oxford Dictionary of Nursery Rhymes*, Opie remarked that "This is considered an excellent jingle while astride a hobby horse." (363)

stick a walking stick, such as a crutch or a cane.

Sandy In the U.S. "Sandy" is a common nickname for "Sandra," both of which are short for "Alexandra." However, the "Sandy" in this poem is a man. "Sandy" is the usual Scots abbreviation for "Alexander."

Eventually, *Sandy* became the nickname for any Scotsman, just as *Paddy*, *Pierre*, or *Hans* are all nicknames for a man in Ireland, France, or Germany.

sow an adult female pig. Here "sow" sounds just like "sue" and has a vowel rhyme with "woo" at the end of the last line. The alternate northern dialectal spelling is "soo," and the Scots spelling is "sou," each of which is found in "soo-wee" or "sou-wee," a hog-call, which is still used in America.

Galloway a district in southwestern Scotland. It includes the counties of Dumfries, Kirkcudbright, and Wigtown. For many years, this area has been famous for it wool.

o' sounds like /uh/ and is a very common pronunciation for "of," especially in spoken or informal English of Britain or America.

For example, "Do you want a piece **o'** cheese?"

woo Scottish and dialectal for "wool" and rhymes with "too."

> I'll buy you a **tartan** bonnet,
> And some feathers to put on it,
> Tartan **trews** and a **philibeg**,
> Because you are so like your daddy.

tartan plaid. A kind of woolen cloth woven in various colored stripes, criss-crossing at right angles to form a regular pattern; worn especially in the Highlands, each clan having its own pattern.

The word's origin is uncertain, but it probably comes from "tiretaine" (or "tiretanni"), a fine woolen cloth much used for ladies' dresses in the 13th century and generally of scarlet color. "Scarlet" was used by early writers to refer to just about any mixture of red and blue. So "tiretaine" probably got its name from "teint" (meaning *tint* or *color*) from the name of *Tyre*, an ancient Mediterranean town on the coast of Lebanon and the original source of the famous Tyrian purple, a crimson or purple dye used by the ancient Romans and Greeks. It was made from certain mollusks.

bonnet a flat, brimless, woolen cap, traditionally worn by men and boys in Scotland. The type most people think of as the quintessential tartan bonnet is the Balmoral bonnet, in use since the 1500s. It has a small "toorie" (pom-pom) on top and is sometimes finished off with a plume. It's worn off to one side of the head, sort of like a beret.

trews close-fitting tartan *trousers*.

philibeg a variant spelling of "filibeg," a kilt. This word comes from the Gaelic "feileadh beag;" "feileadh" meant *wrap* or *fold* and "beag" meant *little* (as opposed to "feileadh-mor," the large ancient kilt).

The last Scots rhyme in this chapter needs some introduction. There is a popular English nursery rhyme that's been around for a long time (1802) that goes:

> Pussy cat, pussy cat, where have been?
> I've been to London to visit the queen.
> Pussy cat, pussy cat, what did you there?
> I frightened a little mouse under her chair.

Well, in 1950, Paul Gallico (who was the author of many humorous stories, including *Mrs. 'Arris Goes to Paris*) wrote a wonderful book about cats, called *The Abandoned*, and right before the title page, Gallico put in an old traditional Scottish version of this rhyme (from 1842):

Poussie, poussie, **baudrons**,	Pussy, pussy, cat
Whaur hae ye been?	Where have you been?
I've been **tae** London	I've been to London
Tae see the queen.	To see the queen.
Poussie, poussie, baudrons,	Pussy, pussy, cat
Whit gat ye there?	What got you there?
I gat a **gut** fat **mousikie**,	I got a good fat mousey
Rinnin' up a **stair**!	Running up a stair.
Poussie, poussie, baudrons,	Pussy, pussy, cat
Whit did ye **wi'it**?	What did you with it?
I **pit** it in **me meal-poke**	I put in in my lunch-bag
Tae eat **tae ma breid**.	To eat with my bread.

baudrons a Scots affectionate name for a cat (like "Reynard" is used for a fox). It's pronounced "bawdruns."

The origin is unknown, but the OED speculates that it may come from the Gaelic word "beaurach," a frolicsome, playful girl.

However, I think it seems to be closer to the Gaelic word "bodhran" (pronounced "bah-drawn"), a small one-sided drum, whose surface looks like a large tambourine, and is played with a two-headed drumstick. Sometimes the sound of its drumroll could be similar to the purring of a cat.

whaur This Scots word for "where" is pronounced "whawr." Some descendants of the Scotch-Irish in Appalachia say it the same way: "Whar y'all goin' now?"

hae have. Pronounced like "hay." The "v" sound is sometimes dropped after a vowel in Scots and northern dialects. So "brave" became "braw" (which can also mean "fine" or "good'), and "give" became "gie" (pronounced like the "gee" in "geek"). In fact, the "v" in "give" is also silent in informal English: "Gimme your hand."

ye A well-known Old English word for "you." Originally used *only* in the plural and as the subject of a sentence. For example, "Ye are gods; and all of you are children of the most High." (*King James Version* of Ps 82.6)

tae The Scots word for "to." Pronounced like "tay." (It can also mean "too" or "toe.") At the end of the last verse of this poem, it also means "with" or "to the side of."

whit what. (as in "Whit's he up tae?")

gat got. It's the archaic past tense of "get." The word "gat" goes back to the 13th century. Pronounced like "git" and rhymes with "pit."

rinnin' runnin' or running. The words "rin" and "ryn" are alternate Scots forms of "run."

stair a common Scots variant of "stairs."

wi'it with it. This contraction sounds like "weet." Rhymes with *eat*.

pit Scots for "put."

meal-poke probably a lunch-bag. I could not find this term in any of my sources, but "poke" is an old Scots word for 'bag.' It's still used in the U.S. by the Scotch-Irish mountain folk of the South, as in the proverb: "Don't buy a pig in a poke," an old saying warning us not to purchase anything sight unseen.

tae ma breid When speaking of food, "tae" means "to go with." (pronounced like "tay") For example: "Would ye like a biscuit tae your tea?"

ma a common Scots word for "my."

breid the Scot word for "bread." It's pronounced "breed" and has a vowel rhyme with "wi'it" at the end of the second line in this last verse.

CHAPTER 18

Gray Goose and Gander

> **Gray goose** and gander,
> Waft your wings together
> And carry the good king's daughter
> Over the **one-strand** river.

It's not certain how old this poem is, but there is some evidence to indicate it might date back to Old English times, over a thousand years ago.

Gray goose This is probably the graylag goose (or greylag goose) of Europe. What is this bird's scientific name? The answer is Anser anser (literally Goose goose). They're commonly found in parks, farms, and nursery rhymes.

The term "graylag goose" was originally three separate words, and sometimes is still written that way. The OED says that the "lag" in its name stems from the fact that these geese *lag* behind many of the other birds who begin their migration earlier.

However, another possibility is that the word may come from an obsolete word for water: "lag" (from Old English "lagu," meaning *water* or *sea*, and—not unimportantly—"lagu" was also the name of a runic letter. (Information on the shape and a description of this rune is available online; look up "the luguz rune.")

Runic alphabets were used by the people of northern Europe from 100 to 1100 A.D. Each letter had its own name. A rune standing by itself stood for its name and was often used for magic. Thus, "lagu" could have been inscribed on ships, for example, for good luck on sea voyages. This rune was used in the 9th century by the Anglo-Saxon poet Cynewulf in signing his name in the Old English poem "Elene."

(See Anderson, *The Literature of the Anglo-Saxons*, 129–30, 149.)

The wild graylag goose is the only goose indigenous to the British Isles and is the ancestor of the domestic gray goose (often with white feathers). Today its breeding grounds extend from Iceland to eastern Asia. In former days it bred abundantly in the English fen country. A powerful flyer with a five-foot wingspan, it sometimes migrates to mainland Europe, the fens of Flanders being a favorite hibernal haunt.

(Roger Tory Peterson, *A Field Guide to the Birds of Britain and Europe*, 36. See also: Witherby, *The Handbook of British Birds, III*, 179–86. Google "graylag" for great pictures.)

strand (archaic) a shore of a sea, lake, or (obsolete) of a river.

A **one-strand** river, therefore, could be a metaphor for the sea and is reminiscent of early Anglo-Saxon imagery. (Opie, 190)

Indeed, it is much like the *kennings* used in Old English poetry. These were usually two-word phrases, such as "whale-path" for the sea, "wave-traveler" for a boat, or (my favorite) "sky-candle" for the sun. In fact, kennings were so common that it makes us wonder if this nursery rhyme actually originated in Anglo-Saxon times.

Next, we need to answer FOUR questions:

ONE: How far back can this present version of the poem be traced? Opie (190) said that the lines were printed in 1844 by Halliwell, "but where [he] obtained them is unknown."

In 1897 Francis Morris wrote *A History of British Birds*, a large but interesting work, chatty and informal, containing several stories (fact and fiction) about birds. In it, Morris speaks of the graylag goose: ". . . whose gray wing has so long been celebrated in the old poem . . ." (Vol. V, 76). He may be alluding to the poem "Gray goose and gander," but we have no way of knowing how long "so long" was, nor how old "the old poem" was.

TWO: Is the poem related to, or is it a fragment of, an old story or legend? Is there anything in our folklore about a princess being transported over a body of water by geese? I could find no direct parallels to such a theme. The closest thing to it that's listed in Thompson's *Motif-Index of Folk Literature* is an oral tale from India about a goose that brings a sleeping princess to its master. But this story may have come to England long ago and since been lost. Several European folk tales are thought to have originated in India. (Thompson, *The Folktale*, 16)

Mother Goose herself is often pictured riding through the air on a goose. This characterization of her probably stems from the chapbook story of the adventures of Mother Goose and her son Jack

It was published about 1815, and it begins with:

> Old Mother Goose,
> When she wanted to wander,
> Would ride through the air
> On a very fine gander.

And this old chapbook story ends with:

> Jack's mother came in,
> And caught the goose soon,
> And mounting its back,
> Flew up to the moon.

(For the complete story, see: singbookwithemily.wordpress.com and scroll down to: "Full Original Mother Goose Nursery Rhyme.")

In France, Mother Goose was known as a story-teller, at least by the 17th century, and perhaps as far back as the 11th century. But to English-speaking children, she was not well known until the 1800s.

It's interesting to note that the goose is an important figure in folklore and in many of the world's religions. It plays a prominent role in the creation stories of Egypt and India. Also, because the goose mates for life, it is a symbol in many countries for conjugal happiness and faithfulness. (Jobes, *Dictionary of Mythology*, 676.)

THREE: Is there any historical basis for the poem? That is, was there a "good king" in Old English times that had a daughter who made a trip across the sea? Actually, there was. Alfred the Great, still referred to in England as Good King Alfred, had a daughter named Ælfthryth (born about 877) who, sometime between 893 and 899, married Baldwin II, Count of Flanders (a coastal area between France and the Netherlands, now the northern part of Belgium).

To become his wife, of course, she would've had to cross the English Channel—the "one-strand river." Although only 20 miles across the Dover Strait, this was often a dangerous voyage for ships, but comparatively easy for strong-winged birds. Thus, in Old English poetry, "swan-road" was a common kenning for the sea.

Couldn't Baldwin have traveled to England for the wedding? Probably not. He was very busy at home, trying to defend Flanders from Viking raids, building forts, and extending his southern border.

Most likely Baldwin married King Alfred's daughter to strengthen his own power by having a strong ally across the English Channel. For thousands of years, one of the best ways to connect with a powerful ruler was to marry into the family.

So this poem may have been a bon voyage wish (perhaps even a magical charm or incantation) that the journey of the king's daughter be as safe and successful as that of the gray goose and gander. The marriage may have taken place in the autumn, when the geese were migrating to Flanders and points south. (We remember the old poem "In Flanders Fields.")

The poem's use of a goose and gander may have been a metaphor representing two of the princess's close traveling companions, perhaps a lady-in-waiting and a thane as a bodyguard. Or if King Alfred sent her on one ship with a second ship as an escort, for safety and for a show of power, then these two vessels could be the "goose and gander" taking the king's daughter across the channel.

Was her trip important enough to warrant special attention? The answer again is yes. Hodgkins tells us that her marriage was historically significant. For one thing, "hitherto the kingly families of the English, with very few exceptions, had found their wives and husbands within the island [of Britain]." For another thing, "it shows that Alfred realized the need for solidarity among the Christian rulers who bordered the English Channel; it was the beginning of a new policy . . . The choice of young Baldwin is also interesting owing to the fact that he was the son of Judith, Alfred's own step-mother..." (*A History of the Anglo-Saxons, II*, 634)

FOUR: Could this poem be a modern version of an Old English poem? To answer this, we can try changing the words back into Old English. The first step is to become familiar with some of the Old English letters that are no longer used in Modern English:

Notes on Old English letters: their names and their pronunciation:

- þ thorn   (from the Anglo-Saxon rune)
- ð eth   (formed by crossing the **d** of the Roman alphabet)

The *thorn* and *eth* can be voiced or unvoiced and are pronounced like **th** in "this" or "thin."

- æ   ash (ash tree) (in OE: æsc)
- Æ   the capital letter of ash

The sound of /æ/ is like the **a** in "apple" or "hat."

The next step is to translate the poem into Old English, line by line and word by word, as literally as possible.

So "Gray goose and gander" would be: "**græg gos and gandra.**"
(Even today, in most Germanic languages—such as Dutch, Swedish, and German—the graylag goose is called simply "gray goose.")

The second line is "Waft your wings together." "Waft" dates back only to 1500, but "glide" comes from Old English, and the OE word for "wings" was feþra (the singular, "feðer" meant *feather*). So, the second line in Old English is "**glidaþ eowere feþra togædere.**" (OE eowere = your.)

The third line, "And carry the good king's daughter" becomes:
"**And feriath thaes godes cyninges dohtor.**" (OE "ferian," to carry, is the source of our modern English *ferry* boat.)

The last line, "Over the one-strand river," in OE would be:
"**Ofer thone an-strand stream.**" The word "river" is early Middle English (from Old French "riviere"). OE "stream" was used for a *stream* or a *river*.

The next task of putting this poem into Old English was to make the lines conform to the alliterative and metrical scheme used in the poetry of the 9th century West Saxon dialect. (For more on the importance of OE alliteration, see Appendix 3.)

In Old English poetry (such as *Beowulf*) each line contains four stressed syllables along with a number of unstressed syllables. Each line of the poem is split into two half-lines, with a definite pause between them. The lines do not *rhyme*, but there is a strong use of *alliteration* with consonants, and sometimes with vowels. Alliteration connects the two half-lines, using the following scheme:

> The first half-line has *stressed syllables* (SS) 1 and 2.
> The second half-line has SS 3 and 4.
> > SS 1 always alliterates with SS 3.
> > SS 1 sometimes alliterates with SS 2.
> > SS 1 almost never alliterates with SS 4.

This scheme of alliteration is evident in the opening lines of *Beowuld.*
(The words that begin with stressed syllables are underlined. Letters that alliterate are in **bold** print.]

> Hwæt! We **G**ar-**D**ena   in **g**ear **d**agum,
> **þ**eod-cyninga   **þ**rym **g**efrunon,
> hu ða **æ**þelingas   **e**llen **f**remedon.
> Oft **Sc**yld **Sc**efing   **sc**eaþena þreatum,
> **m**onegum **m**ægþum,   **m**eodo-setla ofteah

Here is the literal translation of those five lines:

> What! We of the Spear-Danes   in days-of-yore
> of the people-kings   glory heard,
> how the noblemen   valor did.
> Often Scyld son-of-Sceaf   from enemies' troops
> from many tribes   mead-benches took away

(Ouch! What could be crueler than stealing their beer tables?)

In order for me to write lines that were in keeping with these poetic devices, it was necessary to re-arrange some of the words. But I felt no compunction in doing so because, as George Anderson says, "freedom of word-order" and "a considerable license in syntax" were "earmarks of Germanic verse in general and of Anglo-Saxon verse in particular." *(The Literature of the Anglo-Saxons,* 49)

For the purpose of alliteration, "king's" (OE "cyninges") has to become "Ælfredes" (King Alfred's). In Old English, "stream" was pronounced like /stray-ahm/). In this reconstructed Old English version of "Gray goose and gander," the words in parentheses can be left out. Also, conjunctions (like "and" or "but") and articles (like "a" or "the") were frequently omitted in Old English.

Again, the stressed words are underlined, and the alliterative letters are in bold print:

Græg gos and **g**andra,   **gl**idaþ to**g**ædra
feðra eowera   (and) feriaþ dohtor
Ælfredes godes   ofer (ðone) **an**-strand stream.

In Modern English:

Gray goose and gander   glide together
your wings   and carry (the) daughter
(of the) good (King) Alfred over the one-strand river.

Does this prove that such a poem existed in Old English? No. But it does show that it *could* have. Even if it did, it may not have been written down until much later. There are many poems, tales, charms, proverbs, and nursery rhymes that have been preserved for centuries through oral tradition. At any rate, "Gray goose and gander" just might be one of the oldest nursery rhymes in the English language.

AFTERWORD

Our Changing American Language

Many people don't realize it, but just since the 1970s there has been a remarkable change in American English. One of its linguistic sounds has been fading out of use, and in many places is seldom heard anymore. For example, the words "cot" and "caught" used to have different vowel sounds, but now—for many Americans—they sound exactly the same. How come?

To better understand vowels, we need to realize that although there are six different vowel *letters* in our English alphabet (a e i o u y), there are also about eleven different vowel *sounds* called phonemes. Humans can produce different vowel sounds in the vocal tract by moving the tongue up, down, forward towards the teeth, or back towards the throat (as with *all*, *hall*, and *call*).

The International Phonetic Alphabet (IPA) uses a special symbol for each English sound, as shown in this chart:

	FRONT	CENTRAL	BACK
HIGH	/i/ (feet)		/u/ (food)
	/I/ (fit)		/U/ (full)
MID	/e/ (bay)		/o/ (most)
	/ə/ (bet)	/ʌ/ (cut)	
LOW	/æ/ (sat)	/a/ (pot)	/ɔ/ (talk)

Afterword: Our Changing American Language

All of these phonetic sounds have been used in the English language for over a thousand years. However, in America the low back vowel /ɔ/ has been gradually moving forward and for many speakers it sounds like the low central vowel /a/. So "talk" (which usually had an "aw" sound, and still does in British English) now often sounds like "tock." Similarly, "law" often sounds more like "la" and "paw" may sound like "pa" for many speakers in the U.S.

There are several nursery rhymes that have this low back vowel sound /ɔ/. For example, just to name a few:

- In "Thumbikin" (p. 193) the last two end-rhymes: *saw* and *'a*.
- In "We're all in the dumps" (p. 3) at the end of line 3 and line 6: *St. Pauls* and *walls*.
- In "There was an old woman of Glouster" (p. 21) the first 2 end-lines: *Glouster* and *cost her*.
- In "Good people all, of every sort" (p. 56) at the end of line 2 and 4: *song* and *long*.

This vowel sound may never be noticed by most American talkers, except by old talkers such as I am (or should that be "tockers?")

It's important to realize that languages all over the world are always changing in vocabulary and pronunciation from one generation to the next and from one region to the next.

I have an elderly neighbor who immigrated from Germany in the 1950s. She now tells me that she has a good bit of trouble understanding today's German.

The sounds of English, for example, had a big change during the Great Vowel Shift that occurred from about 1450 to 1500. The writer Albert Baugh tells us that there was "a greater elevation of the tongue and closing of the mouth" (*A History of the English Language*, 287–89).

For instance, the word *feet* used to sound like *fit*, *boot* sounded like *boat*, *cat* sounded like *cot*, and *root* sounded like *rote*.

(I find it interesting that linguists—with a lot of hard work—can explain the *what*, *when*, *where*, and *how* of language changes, but often have trouble determining the *why*. Some parts of life may always be mysteries.)

APPENDIX 1

"Green Grow the Rashes"

Full text of Robert Burns' poem "Green Grow the Rashes" [Google this title for a beautiful short video.]

    Green grow the rashes , O;
    Green grow the rashes , O;
    The sweetest hours that e'er I spend,
    Are spent amang the lasses, O.

    There's nought but care on ev'ry han',
    In ev'ry hour that passes, O;
    What signifies the life o' man,
    An' 'twere na for the lasses, O.

    The *war'ly* race may riches chase,   (*worldly*)
    An' riches still may fly them, O;
    An' tho' at last they catch them fast,
    Their hearts can ne'er enjoy them,

    But *gie me a cannie* hour at e'en ,   (*give me a nice*)
    My arms about my dearie, O;
    An' war'ly cares, an' war'ly men,
    May *a' gae tapsalteerie* , O!   (*all go topsy-turvy*)

Appendix 1: "Green Grow the Rashes"

For you *sae douce*, ye sneer at this: (so quiet)
Ye're nought but senseless asses, O;
The wisest man the warl' e'er saw,
He dearly lov'd the lasses, O.

Auld Nature swears, the lovely dears
Her noblest work she *classes,* O;   (*classifies*)
Her prentice han' she try'd on man,
An› then she made the lasses, O.

Green grow the *rashes* , O;   (*rushes*) (1st verse of a folksong).
Green grow the rashes , O;
The sweetest hours that e'er I spend,
Are spent amang the lasses, O.

APPENDIX 2

The Power of Poetry

The power of poetry in nursery rhymes is very strong. How is an ancient set of oral literature kept alive? Without knowing a written language, how could people remember all 35 verses of a nursery rhyme about Jenny Wren? The English nursery rhymes were created to be spoken, and they were passed along this way from one generation to the next. For many of these rhymes, it was hundreds of years before they were ever written down. Until books became more affordable, after the invention of the the printing press in 1440, nursery rhymes, folktales, news reports, historical facts, etc. were commonly transmitted by word of mouth.

All languages of the world began as oral languages, and there are still thousands of languages that still do not yet have a written form, but the people have had a deep well of factual and fictional information—stories, poems, and songs—that have been passed down for hundreds of years. To help them remember the spoken lines, the composers of folklore used the repetition of some words and phrases. In addition, to remember the sounds of their words, they used alliteration, rhyme, and rhythm.

For example, every line in the Old English tale of Beowulf has alliteration ("with weapons of war and weeds of battle"). The composers of nursery rhymes often used alliteration too (*Bye Baby Bunting, Simple Simon, Peas Porridge Hot, Sing a Song of Sixpence, Georgy Porgy Pudding and Pie*).

Of course rhymes were used in almost all nursery rhymes. Words that rhyme not only sound good, but—like alliteration—they're easier to remember. They're very enjoyable to listen to, especially by the very young who can't read well yet. Their literature is oral, spoken to them by family, friends, and caregivers. Every generation of children likes rhymes. That's one reason why Dr. Seuss is still so popular.

Not only do the lines rhyme, but they usually have a pleasant rhythm as well: a steady progression of metrical sounds with a bouncy beat that children can clap hands to, or get bounced on a knee, or skip a rope. Nursery rhymes can involve the whole child: physically, mentally, and emotionally.

As they get older, young people can begin to enjoy adult poetry. I remember when I was about eight years old, I found a small leather-bound book on my uncle's dresser. It was a poem by Edgar Allen Poe called The Raven. I sat down on the floor and read it aloud to myself. I didn't know what all the words meant, but it didn't matter. I was fascinated by the sounds of the words. A lot of them rhymed or started with the same letter, and all of them had a very regular bouncy beat. I loved it. As soon as I was done, I read it again three or four times. Some poetry, like nursery rhymes, should really be read aloud.

APPENDIX 3

Oral Literature

Oral literature is very strong and enduring. In fact, many ancient languages of the world, such as Tuvan in south central Russia, having only oral literature, have used alliteration to help them remember their traditional stories (Harrison, *The Last Speakers*, 191).

Our ancient oral literature is disappearing, not only old nursery rhymes, but thousands of world languages which have never had a written form. They have so much to teach us.

> "We need to hear [them]. Let's listen while we still can."
> (Harrison, *The Last Speakers*, 274)

Bibliography

Abbott, E. A. *A Shakespearian Grammar*. London: Macmillan, 1870.
American Heritage Dictionary. New York: American Heritage Publ. Co. and Houghton Mifflin, 1969.
Anderson, George K. *The Literature of the Anglo-Saxons*. Rev. ed. Princeton, NJ: Princeton University Press, 1966.
An English-Reader's Dictionary. A. S. Hornby and E. C. Parnwell, eds. 2nd edition. Oxford University Press, 1980.
Arbuthnot, May Hill. *Children and Books*, 3rd ed. Chicago: Scott, Foresman & Co., 1964.
Bain, Robert. *The Clans and Tartans of Scotland*. Enlarged and re-edited by Margaret o. MacDougall. London: Collins, 1968.
Baldwin, Ruth. One Hundred Nineteenth-century Rhyming Alphabets. Carbondale, IL: Southern Illinois University Press, 1972.
Bane, W. N., as quoted by Samuel Eliot Morison and Henry Steele Commager in *The Growth of the American Republic*, 4th ed., rev. (vol. I, p. 499). New York: Oxford University Press, 1958.
Baring-Gould, William and Ceil Baring-Gould. *The Annotated Mother Goose*. New York: Clarkson Potter, 1962.
Baugh, Albert C. *A History of the English Language*, 2nd ed. New York: Appleton, 1963.
Berne, Eric. *Games People Play*. New York: Grove, 1964.
Berry, Lester V. and Melvin Van den Bark. *The American Thesaurus of Slang*, 2nd ed. New York: Crowell, 1953.
Bett, Henry, *Nursery Rhymes and Tales*. London: Methuen, 1924,
Birds in Our Lives. Alfred Stefferud, ed. Washington: U.S. Gov Printing Office, 1966.
Blakeborough, Richard. *Wit, Character, Folklore & Customs of the North Riding of Yorkshire*. 1898, rpt. Wakefield, Yorkshire: EP Publishing Ltd., 1973.
Book of Nursery and Mother Goose Rhymes. Marguerite de Angeli, ed. Garden City, NY: Doubleday & Co., 1953
Bosworth, Joseph. *An Anglo-Saxon Dictionary*. Ed. and enlarged by T. Northcote Toller. Oxford: Clarendon, 1882–98.
Brand, Oscar. *Folksongs for Fun*. New York: Berkley, 1961.
Bright's Old English Grammar & Reader, 3rd ed. Frederic G. Cassidy and Richard Ringles, eds. New York: Holt, Reinhart & Winston, 1971.
British Literature. Hazelton Spencer, ed. Boston: D. C. Heath, 1951.
Bulfinch, Thomas. *Bulfinch's Mythology*, 1863: rpt. New York: Crowell, 1970.
Burns, Robert. "Green Grow the Rashes, O." *scottish-country-dancing-dictionary.com*.

Bibliography

Century Dictionary and Cyclopedia. William D. Whitney, ed. New York: Century Co., 1914.

Collins Pocket Scots Dictionary. Glasgow: Harper Collins Publishers, 1996.

Collier's Encyclopedia. New York: Crowell-Collier Corp., 1970.

Complete Works of Shakespeare, George Lyman Kittredge, ed. 1936; rpt. New York: Grolier, 1958,

Cunnington, C. Willett and Phillis. *Handbook of Costume in the Eighteenth Century*. Bostons Plays, 1972.

Dana, Richard Henry. *Two Years Before the Mast*. 1840; annotated version by Roy Scher. Lanham, MD: Sheridan House, 2013.

Davies, Constance. *English Pronunciation from the Fifteenth to the Eighteenth Century*. London: J. M. Dent, 1934.

Dictionary of American English, Sir William Craigie, J. R. Hulbert, et al., eds. Chicago: University of Chicago Press, 1940.

Dictionary of National Biography. Leslie Stephan and Sidney Lee, eds. 1917; rpt. London: Oxford University Press, 1960.

Dictionary of the Scots Language. Online: @dsl.ac.uk.

Dobson, Eric J. *English Pronunciation 1500–1700*. 2nd ed. Oxford: Clarendon, 1968.

Dyche, Thomas and Pardon, William. *A New General English Dictionary*. 1740; rpt. New York: Georg Olms Verlag, 1972.

Eckenstein, Lina. *Comparative Studies in Nursery Rhymes*. London: Duckworth, 1906.

Ekwall, Eilert. *The Oxford Dictionary of English Place-Names*, 4th ed. Oxford: Clarendon, 1960.

Encyclopaedia Britannica. London: William Benton, 1973.

Encyclopaedia of the Social Sciences, Edwin Seligman, ed. New York: Macmillan, 1967.

Encyclopedia Americana. International edition. New York: American Corp., 1970.

Encyclopedia International. New York: Groller, 1969.

English Dialect Dictionary. Joseph Wright, ed. New York: Putnam, 1898.

etymology.org. [This site is based on information in the OED]

Farmer, John S. and W. E. Henley. *A Dictionary of Slang and Colloquial English*. Abridged from *Slang and Its Analogues*. London: Routledge, 1912.

Farmer, John S. and W. E. Henley. *Slang and Its Analogues*. London: Routledge & Kegan Paul Ltd., 1890.

Farmer, John S. *Vocabula Amatoria*. New Hyde Park: New York University Books, 1966. (This was written as vol. VIII of *Slang and Its Analogues*, but has been published separately.)

Folksongs for Fun. Oscar Brand, ed. New York: Berkley Publishing Corp., 1961.

Fowler, Henry W. *A Dictionary of Modern English Usage*. 2nd ed., rev. by Sir Ernest Gowers. Oxford: Clarendon, 1965.

Franklyn, Julian. *A Dictionary of Nicknames*. London: Hamish Hamilton, 1962.

Funk & Wagnalls *New Standard Dictionary*. New York: Funk & Wagnalls Co., 1963.

Gallico, Paul. *The Abandoned*, 1950. rpt. New York: The New York Review of Books, 1971.

grammarphobia.com. [Grammar, etymology, usage, etc.] Patricia T. O'Conner and Stewart Kellerman, eds.

Halliwell-Phillipps, James Orchard. *Dictionary of Archaic and Provincial Words*. London: Smith, 1878.

———. *Popular Rhymes and Nursery Tales*. 1849; rpt. Detroit, MI: Singing Tree Press, 1968.

Bibliography

Hardy, Thomas. *The Return of the Native*, 1878, rpt. New York: Lancer, 1968.

Harrison, K. David. *The Last Speakers*: The Quest to Save the World's Most Endangered Languages. Washington, D.C.: National Geographic, 2010.

Hazlitt, W. C. *Faiths and Folklore of the British Isles*. 1905; rpt. New York: Benjamin Blom, 1965.

Henderson, Yorke, et al. *Christmas Holiday Book*. New York: Parents' Magazine Press, 1972.

Herriot, James. *All Creatures Great and Small*. 1972, rpt. New York: Bantam, 1974.

Hodgkin, Robert H. *A History of the Anglo-Saxons*. 3rd ed. London: Oxford University Press, 1952.

Jameison, John. *An Etymological Dictionary of the Scottish Language*, rev. by John Longmuir and David Donaldson. Paisley, Scotland: Alexander Gardner, 1879.

Jameison's Scottish Dictionary. New York: AS Press, 1966.

Jobes, Gertrude. *Dictionary of Mythology Folklore, and Symbols*. New York: Scarecrow, 1961.

Johnson's Dictionary, A Modern Selection. E. L. Madam, Jr. and George Milne, eds. New York: Pantheon, 1963.

Kammlade, William G., Sr. and William G. Kammlade, Jr. *Sheep Science*. Chicago: Lippincott, 1955.

Kannick, Preben. *Military Uniforms in Color*. New York: Macmillan, 1968.

Kurath, Hans. *Word Geography of the Eastern United States*. New York: University of Michigan Press, 1949.

Kurath, Hans and S. M. Kuhn, eds. *Middle English Dictionary*. Ann Arbor: University of Michigan Press, 1956.

Laing, Alexander. *American Ships*. New York: American Heritage, 1971.

Lear, Edward. *Nonsense Books*. Boston: Little, Brown, and Co., 1888.

Leisy, James F. *Hootenanny Tonight!* Greenwich, CT: Fawcett, 1964.

Life in Shakespeare's England. John Dover Wilson, ed. 1911; rpt. Harmondsworth, Middlesex: Penguin Books, 1959.

Lindheim, Leon. *Facts and Fictions about Coins*. Cleveland: World, 1967.

Lindsay, Philip and Reg Groves. *The Peasants' Revolt 1381*. London: Hutchinson & Co. Ltd. (no date).

Lloyd, Richard. *Northern English*. Leipzig: Teubner, 1908.

Logan, William H. *A Pedlar's Pack of Ballads and Songs*. Edinburgh: William Patterson, 1869.

Lutes, Della T. *Modern Priscilla Cook Book: One Thousand Recipes Tested and Proved at the Priscilla Proving Plant*. Boston: Priscilla Publishing Co., 1924, 1928.

Mackay, Charles. *A Dictionary of Lowland Scotch*. 1888; rpt. Detroit, MI: Gale Research Co., 1968.

Margetson, Stella. *Regency London*. New York: Praeger, 1971.

McCrum, Robert, with William Cran and Robert MacNeil. *The Story of English*. New York: Viking Penguin Inc., 1986

Merriam Webster's Collegiate Dictionary, 10th ed. Springfield, MA: 1999.

Mercer, Blaine. *The Study of Society*. New York: Harcourt, Brace, & Company, 1958.

Montgomerie, Norah and William. *A Book of Scottish Nursery Rhymes*. London: Oxford University Press, 1965.

Moore, Samuel and Thomas A. Knott. *The Elements of Old English*. 10th ed., Ann Arbor, MI: Wahr, 1969.

Bibliography

———. *Historical Outlines of English Sounds and Inflections.* Rev. by Albert H. Marckwardt. Ann Arbor, MI: Wahr, 1957.

Morison, Samuel Eliot and Henry Steele Commager. *The Growth of the American Republic.* 4th ed., rev. New York: Oxford University Press, 1958,

Morris, Francis o. *A History of British Birds.* London: John C. Nimmo, 1897.

Mother Goose. Singbookwithemly.wordpress.com

Mother Goose: The Complete Book of Nursery Rhymes. Dorthea J. Snow, comp. Racine, WI: Whitman, 1941.

Motif-Index of Folk Literature. Stith Thompson, ed. Revised and enlarged. Bloomington, IN: Indiana University Press, 1955.

Nares, Robert. *A Glossary: A Collection of Words, Phrases, Names, and Allusions in the Works of English Authors, Particularly Shakespeare and His Contemporaries.* 1822; rev. ed. by James O. Halliwell and Thomas Wright, 1876; rpt. Detroit, MI: Gale Research Company, 1966.

New American Encyclopedia. Lewis Adams, ed. rev. ed. New York: Books, Inc.,1957.

Northall, G. F. *English Folk-Rhymes.* 1892; rpt. Detroit, MI: Singing Tree Press, 1968.

Oaks, Alma and Margot Hamilton Hill. *Rural Costume.* London: B. T. Batsford, 1970.

Onions, Charles I. *Shakespeare Glossary*, 2nd ed., rev., 1911; rpt. Oxford: Clarendon, 1969.

Opie, Iona and Peter Opie. *The Oxford Dictionary of Nursery Rhymes.* 1951; rpt. Oxford: Clarendon, 1962.

Oxford Book of Sixteenth Century Verse. E. K. Chambers, ed. Oxford: Clarendon, 1961.

Oxford Dictionary of English Proverbs. W. G. Smith, comp. 3rd ed., rev. by F. P. Wilson. Oxford: Clarendon, 1970.

Oxford English Dictionary. James A. H. Murray, et al. eds. 1933: rpt. Oxford: Clarendon, 1961.

Partridge, Eric, ed. *Dictionary of Slang and Unconventional English.* 7th ed. New York: Macmillan, 1970.

Payne, Blanche. *History of Costume.* New York: Harper & Row, 1965.

Paysan, Klaus. *Birds of the World.* Minneapolis, MN: Lerner, 1970.

Percy, Thomas. *Reliques of Ancient English Poetry.* 1765; rpt. London: John Nichols & Son, 1812.

Peters, Robert. *A Linguistic History of English.* Boston: Houghton Mifflin, 1968.

Peterson, Roger Tory. *The Birds.* New York: Time-Life, 1969.

Peterson, Roger Tory, ed. *A Field Guide to the Birds of Britain and Europe.* Boston: Houghton Mifflin, 1966.

Picturesque Word Origins. Springfield, MA: Merriam, 1933.

Piggot, Stuart. *Ancient Europe.* Chicago: Aldine, 1965.

Random House Dictionary. New York: Random House, 1966.

Road Atlas Britain. Edinburgh: John Bartholomew & Sons, 1989.

Reaney, P. H., ed. *A Dictionary of British Surnames.* 1958; rpt. London: Routledge and Kegan Paul, 1970.

Schmidt, Alexander. *Shakespeare Lexicon.* 3rd ed., revised and enlarged by Gregor Sarrazin. New York: Benjamin Blom, 1968.

Schur, Norman W. *British Self-taught with Comments in American.* New York: Macmillan, 1973.

Scots Dictionary. Alexander Warrack. University of Alabama Press, 1965.

Shipley, J. *Dictionary of Word Origins.* New York: Philosophical Library, 1945.

BIBLIOGRAPHY

Skeat, Walter W. *Etymological Dictionary of the English Language*. Oxford: Clarendon, 1893.

Skelton, John. *The Complete Poems of John Skelton*. Philip Henderson, ed. London: J. M. Dent & Sons, 1959.

Smith, Elsdon C. New Dictionary of American Family Names. New York: Harper and Row, 1973.

Smith, Lacey Baldwin. *Henry VIII*. Boston: Houghton Mifflin, 1971.

The American Heritage Dictionary. Boston: Houghton Mifflin, 1991.

The Real Mother Goose. Chicago: Rand McNally & Co., 1916. 55th printing, 1971.

The Riverside Anthology of Children's Literature, 6th ed. Boston: Houghton Mifflin, 1985.

The Story of English. Robert McCrum, William Cran, & Robert MacNeil, eds. New York: Viking, 1986.

Thomas, Charles Kenneth. *An Introduction to the Phonetics of American English*, 2nd ed. New York: Ronald Press, 1958.

Thompson, Stith. *Motif-Index of Folk Literature*. Bloomington: Indiana University Press, 2nd edition, 1966.

The Folktale. New York: Holt Rinehart, and Winston, 1946.

Trench, Richard, ed. *Dictionary of Obsolete English*. New York: Philosophical Library, 1958.

Universal World Reference Encyclopedia. Chicago: Consolidated, 1966.

Visser, Frederic I. *An Historical Syntax of the English Language*. Leiden: Brill, 1963.

Volume Library. New York: Educators' Association, 1928.

Webster's New Collegiate Dictionary. Springfield, MA: Merriam, 1959.

Webster's New World Dictionary. New York: World, 1960.

Webster's Seventh New Collegiate Dictionary. Springfield, MA: Merriam, 1971.

Webster's Third New International Dictionary. Springfield, MA: Merriam, 1963.

Wentworth, Harold, ed. *American Dialect Dictionary*. New York: Crowell, 1944.

Whiting, Barlett Jere. *Proverbs, Sentences, and Proverbial Phrases*. Cambridge, Mass. Belknap, 1968.

Witherby, Harry F., ed. The Handbook of British Birds. London: Witherby, 1948.

Withycombe, E. G. *The Oxford Dictionary of English Christian Names*, 2nd ed. Oxford: Clarendon, 1963.

World Book Encyclopedia. Chicago: Field, 1971.

Wright, Joseph and Elizabeth Mary. *An Elementary Middle English Grammar*, 2nd ed. London: Oxford University Press, 1928.

Wright, Thomas. *Dictionary of Obsolete and Provincial English*. London: Bohn, 1857.

Index of First Lines

A cow and a calf, 134
A curious discourse about an Apple-pie, 87
A dog and a cock, 99
A frog among some rushes dwelt, 183
A frog, he would a-wooing go, 177
A gentleman of good account, 26
A little bit of powdered beef, 150
A little cockerel, pert and vain, 79
A moony old cat, 141
A pye sat on a pear tree, 43
As high as a castle, 36
As I was going up Primrose Hill, 77
As I was going up the hill, 46
As I went over the water, 40
As Tittymouse sat in the witty to spin, 103

Baby and I, 9
Bad news is come to town, 90
Barnaby Bright he was a sharp cur, 98
Bessy Bell and Mary Gray, 190
Bobbie Shaftoe has a cow, 187
Bobbie Shaftie's gone to sea, 188
Bossy-cow, bossy-cow, where do you lie?, 2
Bounce buckram, velvet's dear, 91
Brave news is come to town, 89
Bye, Baby Bunting, 127

Calls for the robin redbreast and the wren, 31
Charley wag, 53
Clap, clap handies, 195
Cock-a-doodle-do, Daddy;s gone to ploo, 113

Cock-a-doodlle-do! My dame has lost her shoe, 114
Come dance a jig, 47
Come let's to bed, 82
Come take up your hats and away let us haste, 32
Come when you're called, 78
Cripple Dick upon a stick, 196
Cross Patch, 81
Cushy cow, bonny, let down thy milk, 118

Dame, what makes your ducks to die?, 116
Dibbity, dibbity, 151
Did you see my wife, did you see, did you see, 153
Diddle diddle dumpling, my son John, 43
Doctor Sacheveral, 53

Elsie Marley is grown so fine, 83

Fa fe fi fo fum!, 143
Father Short came down the lane, 120
"Fire! Fire!" said the town crier, 88
Four-and-twenty tailors went to kill a snail, 60
Froggy went a-courtin' and he did go, uh huh, 182

Good people all, of every sort, 56
Gray goose and gander, 200

Hark! Hark! The dogs do bark, 86
Have you seen the old woman of Banbury Cross, 73

Index of First Lines

Hector Protector was dressed all in green, 55
Here goes my lord, 7
Hey ding a ding, what shall I sing?, 57
Hickle them, pickle them, 78
Hickory, dickory, dock!, 104
Ho ho ho! Ha ha ha!, 117
How do you do, neighbor?, 66
Hush-a-ba, birdie, croon, croon, 191

I do not like thee, Doctor Fell, 54
I had a little doll, 15
I had a little hobby horse, 14
I sat next to the Duchess at tea, 22
I saw a ship a-sailing, 124
If I had as much money, 128
If many men knew what many men know, 58
I'll buy you a tartan bonnet, 197
I'll tell my own daddy, when he comes home, 51
In a cottage in Fife, 25
Is John Smith within?, 122
It was on a merry time, 165
It's once I courted as pretty a lass, 164, 276
Jack Jingle went prentice, 123
Jack Sprat could eat no fat; his wife could eat no lean, 156
Jack's Mother came in, 202
Johnny's clocked stockings, 75

Katie Beardie had a cow, 187
Kitten, kitten, in my lap, 81

Little Bo-peep has lost her sheep, 114
Little Bob Snooks was fond of his books, 76
Little Jenny Wren, 175
Little lad, little lad, where wast thou born?, 142
Little Miss Muffet, 107
Little Poll Parrot, 106
Little Tom Dogget, 132
Little Tom Tucker, 38
Love your own, kiss your own, 195

Maid Marian is Queen of May, 96

Margaret wrote a letter, 162
Margery Mutton-pie and Johnny Bo-peep, 8
Merry are the bells, and merry would they ring, 42
Millery, millery, dustipole, 61
Mister Frog would a-wooing ride, ah hah, 180
Muley cow, muley cow, why do you low, 135
My dear, do you know, 31
My father he died, 48

Oh, rare Harry Parry, 154
Old Mother Goose, 202
Old Mother Niddity Nod, 161
Old Toby Sizer is such a miser, 80
Old woman, old woman, shall we go a-shearing?, 153
On Christmas Eve I turned the spit, 91
On Saturday night, 163

Peas porridge hot, 11
Pit, pat, well-a-day, 5
Ply the spade, 112
Polly put the kettle on, 149
Poussie, poussie, baudron, 198
Pretty John Watts, 106
Pussy cat, pussy cat, where have you been?, 197
Pussy-cat sits by the fire, 39
Pussy-cat, wussy-cat, with a white foot, 101

Railroad crossing! Look out for the cars, 37
Ride a cock-horse to Banbury Cross, 6
Rise up, fair maids, fie, for shame, 95
Robert Barnes, my fellow fine, 121
Robin and Richard were two pretty men, 83
Robin Hood, Robin Hood, 145
Rub-a-dub-dub, 64

Says A, Give me A good large slice, 70
St. Swithin's Day, if thou dost rain, 97
Shake a leg, wag a leg, 186
Simple Simon met a pieman, 147
Sing, sing, what shall I sing?, 47

Index of First Lines

Some up and some down, 87

Teeter, teeter, little Peter, 53
Tell-tale Tit, 52
The daughter of the farrier, 162
The late Madam Fry, 59
The mice with satin slippers on, 102
The miller he grinds his corn, his corn, 136
The sow came in with the saddle, 92
There was a little guinea pig, 23
There was a little nobby colt, 13
There was a little woman, 129
There was an old man, and he lived in a wood, 112
There was an old man in a velvet coat, 18
There was an old man of Tobago, 22
There was an old man who lived in a wood, 118
There was an old woman, as I've heard tell, 19
There was an old woman of Gloucester, 21
There was an old woman who lived by the sea, 17
There was an old woman who lived in a hat, 18
This crow says, 10
Thumbikin, Thumbikin broke the barn, 193
This is the death of little Jenny Wren, 62
Thomas A 'Tattamus took two T's, 37
To make your candles last for aye, 38
Tom, Tom, the piper's son, 45
Tommy Tonsey's come from France, 88
Tomorrow the fox will come to town, 126
Trip and go, heave and ho!, 95
Two little dickey-birds sat upon a hill, 10
Two monkeys came from native wood, 67

Upstairs, downstairs, upon my lady's window, 151
Under the furze, 85
Under the marble lies the dust, 54

We're all in the dumps, 3
What is the rhyme for porringer?, 37
What! We of the Spear-Danes, 205
What's the news of the day, 89
When I was a little girl, 109
When the sand doth feed the clay, 113
Where was a jewel and pretty?, 1
Who liveth so merry in all this land, 113
With a tingle, tangle, titmouse, 68

You shall have an apple, 3

Index of Words and Phrases

a', 195
abroad, 1, 160
a fine lady, 6
a-fleeting, 115
again, 43, 67, 185
agog, 88
ah! 16
ain, 189, 195
all, 20, 146
allow, 120
a-maying, 96
a-merrymaking, 180
ampersand, 73
and there is that, 116
Angle-land, 113
Anthony Rowley, 179
arise, 107
army blue, 103
as, 170
as . . . as
as I am certified, 24
a-shearing, 154
A 'Tattamus, 45
away, 131
aye, 38

bade, 173
bag, 53
baker, 66
balsam, 64
Banbury Cross, 6, 90
band, 171
banging, 116
banjo, 182
barley, 84

Barnaby, 99
Barnes, 121
baudrons, 198
be, 69, 79
be patient, 10
bear away the bell, 174
before, 83, 92
Beggars, 86
behind, 92
bell, 75
bellows, 74
bells on her toes, 7
ben, 189
beneath . . . death, 100
Be patient, 10
besides, 88
Bessy, 190
between the decks, 125
bid, 78
bidding, 155
bill, 130
billy-horse, 2
bit (adjectiv), 195
bit (verb), 4
black birds, 40
black-eyed pea, 181
bled, 63
blow up, 142
blowsey boys bubble, 49
Bob, 172
Bobbie Shaftoe, 188
bold-faced, 177
bonnet, 197
bonnie, 6
bonny, 118, 190

225

Index of Words and Phrases

Bo-peep, 8, 115
bossy, 2
bottle and bag, 83
bough, 149
bounce, 91
brave, 90, 160
braw, 192
breid, 199
brook (noun), 159
brook (verb), 80
broom, 49, 85, 192
buckram, 91
bullfinch, 111, 174
bumper, 175
bunting, 128
burnt, 62
button, 189
bye, 127

called, 41
candlestick-maker, 66
canter, 7
care, 163
carol, 17
carried, 90
carrion, 135
carry, 46
carry a mustard pot, 15
carter, 137
'cause, 72
chains about their necks, 125
chancing, 124
charge, 30
chid, 78
chimney, 50
chop-nose, 9
clerk, 99, 110, 173
clocked stockings, 76
clogs, 85
clouted cream, 137
cock, 124
cock-a-doodle-do, 113
cockerel, 80
cock-horse, 6
cockle, 189
codlins, 129
collar, 76

Colly, 134
comfits, 125
common meter, 53
companies, 88
constable, 93
contrive, 25
convey, 81
convincins, 72
cooks, 88
corn, 136, 194
cousin, 66
cow . . . low, 136
cowly, 135
cow's feet, 166
cradle, 93
croon, 192
crosspatch, 81
crowdy, 48
crown, 180
crumpets, 59
Cuckoo, 175
cunning, 63
cur, 99
curds, 108
curl, 163
curly tail, 159
currant wine, 171
cushy, 118
cut it, 39

dainties, 185
dam, 162
dame, 121
damsels, 138
Darlington, 110
dear, 91
dearly, 154
death, 123
decay, 139
declare, 173
deer, 192
desire, 127
devise, 29
dibbity, 152
dickey-birds, 11, 149
dimity, 153
dinner horn, 118

Index of Words and Phrases

ditter, 152
Doctor Sachevera, 54
doe, 152
dogs do bark, 86
dollar, 93
Dolly, 137
dome, 173
dormouse, 34
doth, 88
doublet, 104, 158
doubt, 140
down, 122
drake, 159
draw, 81
dropped me a courtesy, 78
dry, sir, 81
dub, 64
duck, 199
durst, 60
dustipole, 61
duty, 67

earnt, 51
eat, 24, 25, 30
eat of, 176
eating o', 116
eating of, 108
e'en, 61
e'er, 39
ell, 34, 73
Elsie Marley, 84
emmet, 34
estate, 28
evening, 35
eyes of golden red, 185

fa, 143
fain, 50
fair, 49
Fair, 161
fairly, 24
fall to, 131
fan, 172
fare, 49
farrier, 163
Father, 121, 202
fe, 143

feed, 113
feet, 25, 30
feet . . . bid, 176
fell, 100
fell at, 30
fell fast asleep, 115
fellow, 63
fetched, 135
fi, 143
fie, 177
Fife, 25
fine, 84, 172
fire, (noun) 49
fire, (verb) 131
fo, 143
foot, 102
footman, 8
for to, 20
fortune, 174
four and twenty, 117
four in the morning, 121
fritter, (noun) 152
From the town to the grove, 95
full, 46
full sorely, 35
full sore, 30, 146
fum, 143
furmety, 41
furze, 85

gainsaying, 96
gaits, 193
Gad-fly, 33
galloped, 75
Galloway, 196
gammon, 179
gane, 192
gang, 186
garrett, 107
gat, 199
gay, 43
gazers, 35
gentlemen, 189
German glees, 103
glass, 80
Gloucester, 21
glow-worm, 35

Index of Words and Phrases

go, 19
gobble, 79
godly race, 58
Goldfinch, 172
good account, 28
good e'en, 104
good . . . food, 142
good lack, 67
Goody, 89
Gracechurch Street, 9
Grahamites, 102
Gray, 16, 243
Gray goose, 200 a`
greasy, 158
great, 109
great A, 70
greedy, 82
green brooms, 130
grinding, 74
groat, 18, 52, 158
Grom-skin, 18
gruel, 23
grunter, 159
gude, 104
guineas, 21
gut, 248

had got, 158
hadn't got, 109
hae, 198
half-a-crown, 78
hall, 127
hallo, 127
hame, 193
hang, 61
hard by, 115, 185
Harry Parry, 155
hartshorn, 63
haunts, 67
he, 120
Hector, 67
heels an ell high, 59
heigh ho, 44, 116
her, 38
Hey, Jenny, 15
hie, 193
hickle, 79

hickory, dickory, dock, 105
high . . . ho, 120
hinny, 196
hips, 185
hobble, 79
hogtub, 164
holler, 181
hollow, 42
home, 136
hoops, 102
hop, step, and a jump, 137
horn, 134
horns, 60
horse, 6, 74
hose, 43
hound, 117
how d'ye do, 40
husbandman, 140
hush-a-ba, 191

I can't tell you, 49
I'll, 88
I'm come, 159
in a thrice, 70, 100
in a tricey, 1
In the dumps, 3
in the spring, 135
in time, 17
in tune, 18
infare, 181
is come, 90
is gone, 89, 145
is grown, 84
Islington, 58
it, 58
It will serve, 159
It's once, 164
ivory mill, 74

jackass, 46
Jack Nag, 83
Jack Sprat, 158
jackdaw, 160
Jacky Dawbin, 54
jags, 87
Jemmy, 90
Jenny, 15

Index of Words and Phrases

Jenny Wren, 170
jig, 177
Joan Cole, 158
jockety-hitch, 7
John Boldero, 38
John Watts, 106
jug, 173

K...confessed, 72
keep, 127
ken, 84
kept, 191
king's highway, 20
kirk, 110
kitten, 82
knaves, 66
kye, 192
Kyloe, 61

lack-a-mercy on me, 21
laddie, 195
Lancashire, 143
lancet, 63
lang, 186
late, 122
lay by, 34
lea, 190
left their tails behind them, 115
licks the dish, 73
light, 78
like to, 29
Linnet, 173
little drum, 74
little lad, 179
lived on the dew, 142
Long-back Gray, 194
look to, 29

ma, 199
Madam Fry, 59
made free, 100
made . . . to, 20
maid, 18
maids, 131
make away, 29
makes much of, 29
making the hay, 138

mammy, 51, 114
-man, 144
mark (noun), 200
mark (verb), 174
Margery, 8
marry (interjection), 122
marry (verb), 39
master, 7
me, 144, 248
meal-poke, 199
men, 67
mickle, 145
mid-man, 194
millery, 61
mind, 172
minikin, 91
minuet, 35
mischance, 16
miss, 184
Mistress, 184
moileth, 140
mood, 29
moony, 141
morn, 10
Mother, 161
Mother Hubbard's books, 173
mousikie, 248
move, 126
mow, 189
Mrs., 179
muffet, 108
mutton, 23
muley, 135
my own, 100

na mair, 97
Nan, 82
native wood, 67
ne'er, 24
Negro songs, 103
net, 151
Nidditty Nod, 161
nigh, 2
nightingale, 137, 173
no, 178, 193
no love . . . was lost, 29
nobby, 13

Index of Words and Phrases

noddle, 43
none, 18
none of, 23
noon . . . done, 139
Norfolk, 28
notable, 160

o', 196
obliged, 121
odsplut, 93
oft, 164
'oman, 104
one-strand, 201
opera hat, 179
organ and flute, 74
out upon, 176
over the hills and far away, 45
own (noun), 122, 195
own (verb), 96

packet, 125
pantry, 106
pap, 82
parcel, 64
parson, 99
passion, 131
past all relief, 30
patch, 196
pate, 43
pay, 9
peas, 11
peck, 61
Peesy-Weesy, 194
pelf, 161
petticoats, 20
philibeg, 190
pickle, 79
Pinnikin, 194
pipe, 46
pique, 58
pit, 199
pitch, 158
plaster, 76
players, 87
Please to give, 152
Pleiades, 142
plenty, 191

ploo, 113
plough, 140
ply, 112
polite, 184
Poll Parrot, 107
Polly, 150
polly-wogs, 116
poor, 134
porridge, 11, 151
porringer, 38
porter, 100
potato, 65
pouce straw, 14
pound, 117
powder my locks, 163
powdered, 151
prate, 30
prattle, 30
pray, 47, 89, 159
pretty, 30, 83, 106, 159, 210, 174
pretty babes, 29
pretty speech, 35
Primrose, 77
Primrose Hill, 78
private ends, 71
prod, 122
pudding(s), 53, 160
pudding-bag, 161
pudding-poke, 114
pudding-stick, 93
pudding-string, 47
pumpkin, 179
ppumps, 88
pye, 44

quacks, 64
Queen . . . again, 56
Queen of May, 96
quince, 72
quoth, 124

race, 151
rail, 124
rare, 154, 160
rattle-basket, 3
rawdy, rowdy, dowdy, 47–48
red coral, 2

Index of Words and Phrases

repair, 34
revels, 33
ring, 164
rinnin,' 199
Robin, 64, 70
Robin and Richard, 83
Robin Redbreast, 170
Robin . . . with leaves, 30
Rook, 173
roundelay, 172
rout, 175
rowley, powley, 179
run, 105
running leather, 88
rushes, 190
russet, 172

_'s to, 102
sack, 151
sago, 23
said, 72, 75, 180
St. Paul's, 4
St. Swithin's Day, 97
salt / To put upon his tail, 149
sand, 139
Sandy, 196
sate, 100
save, 18
scarce, 25
scarf of red, 185
SCAT, 182
sealed it with her finger, 162
see't, 89
selleth, 139
serve me so, 19
serving-man, 140
shaven, 34
shoe, 122
should, 60
siller, 162
silver wood, 192
simpered, 185
Simple Simon, 149
sing saddle, 49
skimmer, 47
slough, 149
sly, 34

small mirror, 74
smart, 196
Smith, 122
snail, 60
snooze, 130
So fine and, so neat, 166
sober, 160
songster, 174
sore, 29, 149, 131, 182
sow, 93, 196
speech, 32
spicey, 1
spin, 81
stair, 199
stare, 160
stead, 120
steam engine, 75
stick, 41, 196
still, 115
Stoken Church, 161
stone, 110
stopped, 158
stump, 130
sucking, 59
Sukey, 150
sup, 82
swain, 184
sway, 97

tae 199
tailors, 60
tallow, 134
tallow-chandler, 134
tartan, 197
tattoo, 74
tea, 107, 150
tee, 118
tell, 128
telling his beads, 146
tell-tale, 52
teeth, 41
The cock sparrow . . . table, 92
The houses . . . without walls, 4
The moon's in a fit, 4
The naked . . . he clad, 58
thick, 154
This is none of I, 20

Index of Words and Phrases

thorn, 143
three times a day, 135
through, 189
Thumbikin, 193
tick, tack, too, 123
tickle, 79
tidy cow, 120
till, 17, 195
tingle, tangle, 69
tipple, 8
tit, 52
titmouse, 69
tittymouse, 103
to call, 16
to my Granny's pig, 47
Tobago, 23
Toby, 81
Tom, 45
Tom Dogget, 134
Tom Tucker, 39
tom-tit, 63, 217
Tonsey, 88
too, 122
took, 124
took a whim, 24
top-knot, 46
to't, 102
trews, 197
tried, 175
tried at, 124
trio, 116
trip, 95
tripe-woman, 135
tripping, 137
trumps, 3
trundle bed, 82
T's, 37
tub, 65
tuffet, 108
tups, 37
turn out, 66
twain, 29
two, 122
two-penny, 7

unto, 29
up and down, 30, 74, 87, 95

up to the life, 72
upon a time, 176
usher, 76

vastly, 21
velvet coat, 18
velvet gowns, 106
vex, 1
viands, 35
victuals, 18, 70
vi'lent, 24
vowed, 63

wag, 64
waist, 97
wait, 191
ware, 184
warning, 55
wast thou, 143
wasted, 124
wastle, 36
watched it vanish, 72
water-dock, 35
wee, 53
weeds, 146
well-a-day, 5, 113
went prentice, 124
what, 174
what the pize, 116
what think you, 10
whaur, 198
whelp, 58
When apples . . . are ripe, 155
whey, 134
whilst, 70
wi'it, 199
whit, 199
white bread, 39
whoop, 127
wife, 84
wind, 46
winding, 136
wing, wang, waddle, 49
witty, 103
wonder, 21
wonderful, 9, 74
wondering, 58

232

Index of Words and Phrases

wondrous, 58
woo, 196
wood, 145
Woodstock, 15
work, 16
worried, 100
wot, 87
wasted, 124
wretch, 30

X ... "cooks," 72

Y ... "I'll," 72
ye, 199
yellow dress, 185
you, 35

Z ... "as," 73

www.ingramcontent.com/pod-product-compliance
Lightning Source LLC
Chambersburg PA
CBHW062014220426
43662CB00010B/1329